# Salesforce®

for
# dummies®
A Wiley Brand

# Salesforce®

7th Edition

## by Liz Kao and Jon Paz

## Salesforce® For Dummies®, 7th Edition

Published by: **John Wiley & Sons, Inc.,** 111 River Street, Hoboken, NJ 07030-5774, www.wiley.com

Copyright © 2020 by John Wiley & Sons, Inc., Hoboken, New Jersey

Published simultaneously in Canada

For general information on our other products and services, please contact our Customer Care Department within the U.S. at 877-762-2974, outside the U.S. at 317-572-3993, or fax 317-572-4002. For technical support, please visit https://hub.wiley.com/community/support/dummies.

Wiley publishes in a variety of print and electronic formats and by print-on-demand. Some material included with standard print versions of this book may not be included in e-books or in print-on-demand. If this book refers to media such as a CD or DVD that is not included in the version you purchased, you may download this material at http://booksupport.wiley.com. For more information about Wiley products, visit www.wiley.com.

Library of Congress Control Number: 2019953291

ISBN 978-1-119-57632-7 (pbk); ISBN 978-1-119-57633-4 (ebk); ISBN 978-1-119-57631-0 (ebk)

Manufactured in the United States of America

V10015277_110419

# Contents at a Glance

# Table of Contents

# Introduction

Salesforce.com For Dummies, 7th Edition, is for users of Salesforce, including those users who have the Unlimited, Enterprise, or Professional Edition. It's for Salesforce users who want to quickly know how to use this web-based application in its new user interface, the Lightning Experience. As a web-based application, Salesforce runs "in the cloud" — also known as software-as-a-service (SaaS) — for sales, marketing, and customer service.

## About This Book

Don't use this book to find out how Salesforce works. Use this book to find out how you can manage your customers and your teams and close more business transactions by using Salesforce:

>> **If you're a sales rep,** this book shows you how to navigate Salesforce to manage your leads, accounts, contacts, and opportunities. Spend less time doing administrative work and more time focused on making money.

>> **If you're a sales manager,** this book shows you how to use Salesforce to track team activities and pipeline, shorten the ramp-up time on new hires, and pinpoint key deals that require your involvement.

>> **If you're in marketing,** this book shows you how to use Salesforce to make an immediate and measurable impact on your sales organization. We cover how to manage campaigns and track leads to fill your funnel.

>> **If you're in customer service,** this book shows you how to manage customer issues, from creation to resolution. Support managers will see how to improve agent productivity and customer self-sufficiency.

>> **If you sit on the executive team,** this book shows you how to use Salesforce for internal collaboration and to measure your overall business with reports and dashboards.

>> **If you're an administrator or involved in your company's customer relationship management (CRM) initiative,** this book gives you practical knowledge for customizing, configuring, maintaining, and successfully implementing your solution.

We show you everything you need to know to manage the life cycle of your customer relationships in Salesforce, from qualifying leads to closing opportunities to handling service agent inquiries. Along the way, we share a laugh or two. And this book can expose you to useful features and functionality that you might not have even known existed!

*Note:* Not all portions of this book necessarily apply to your edition of Salesforce. Different editions have varying degrees of features and functionality. We make sure to point out the differences where relevant.

This book has been revised to reflect the latest Salesforce.com product and feature offerings as of the Summer 2019 release. Also, as of this edition, we provide configuration guidance for the Lightning Experience UI, which applies to new customers and is the eventual direction for customers who are still using the Classic UI. Salesforce is an Internet-based service where new releases occur simultaneously for all customers, about three times a year, without your having to lift a finger (okay, except to just log in). Because of this model, Salesforce.com can release new versions of its product faster than many traditional software vendors — and faster than we can write! We did our best to update this book to the current version of the product, but please bear in mind that new versions of Salesforce are always in the works.

Keep in mind that references to the product and company use the word *Salesforce.* That's a tiny detail, but we didn't want you to think our eagle eyes had glossed over it!

Finally, within this book, you may note that some web addresses break across two lines of text. If you're reading this book in print and want to visit one of these web pages, simply key in the web address exactly as it's noted in the text, pretending as though the line break doesn't exist. If you're reading this as an e-book, you've got it easy — just click the web address to be taken directly to the web page.

# Foolish Assumptions

Please forgive us, but we make one or two foolish assumptions about you, the reader. We assume the following:

>> You have a Salesforce account and some interest in knowing how to use it, beyond the mere curiosity of reading our riveting prose.

>> Your company's Salesforce instance is using or transitioning to the Lightning Experience UI.

>> You have some business experience — at least enough to understand that winning deals is good, and losing deals is bad.

>> You have at least a vague idea of what a database is, including basic concepts such as fields, records, files, and folders. (Imagine an organized filing cabinet and all its contents.)

# Icons Used in This Book

To help you get the most out of this book, we place icons here and there that highlight important points. Here's what the icons mean:

**TIP**

Next to the Tip icon, you can find shortcuts, tricks, and best practices to use Salesforce more effectively or productively.

**WARNING**

Pay extra attention when you see a Warning icon. It means that you might be about to do something that you'll regret later.

**REMEMBER**

When we explain a juicy little fact that bears remembering, we mark it with a Remember icon. When you see this icon, prick up your ears. You can pick up something that could be of wide or frequent use as you work with Salesforce.

**TECHNICAL STUFF**

When we're forced to describe something geeky, a Technical Stuff icon appears in the margin. You don't have to read what's beside this icon if you don't want to, although some readers might find the technical detail helpful.

# Beyond the Book

In addition to what you're reading right now, this product also comes with a free access-anywhere Cheat Sheet that tells you how to perform your day-to-day functions in Salesforce. To get this Cheat Sheet, simply go to www.dummies.com and type **Salesforce.com For Dummies Cheat Sheet** in the Search box.

# Where to Go from Here

If you're just getting started with Salesforce, you may want to turn the page and start reading. If you're an administrator and have a deadline, you may want to jump to Part 6. If you're a manager, try reading about reports and dashboards in Part 7. Sales reps and service reps should start in on Parts 8 and 4, respectively. Regardless of what you choose, we're sure that you'll find what you're looking for!

# 1

# Introducing Salesforce

**IN THIS PART . . .**

Understand more about customer relationship management and the life cycle of a customer.

See how Salesforce can improve various parts of your sales process.

Get the highlights of Salesforce's primary product lines.

# Chapter 1

# Customer Relationship Management at a Glance

You may not realize it yet, but every time you log in to Salesforce, you're accessing an extremely powerful lever of change for you, your group, and your company.

Sounds like a tall order, but consider this: What value do you put on your customer relationships? Your partner relationships? If you're a sales rep, it's your livelihood. And if you're in management, you have fewer assets more valuable than your existing partner and customer base. What if you had a tool that could truly help you manage your partners and customers?

That's where customer relationship management software comes in. *Customer relationship management* (CRM) is an umbrella term for the parts of your business that are "front office," also known as those that have direct interactions with your customers and prospective customers. The CRM life cycle encompasses business processes and associated applications that help businesses better track their leads, manage customers, track opportunities, resolve cases, and more.

The more you and your team adopt a CRM system into your work, and you determine how you want your business process to be reflected within the technology, the more information you'll have at your fingertips to deepen customer relationships and improve your overall business.

In this chapter, we establish a common understanding of the CRM life cycle. Then we describe areas where a CRM can improve your business.

# Introducing the Customer Relationship Management life cycle

Under the umbrella of CRM additional processes exist that focus on specific areas of the customer life cycle. For example, you might hear the phrases *marketing automation, sales force automation,* and *service and support.* These are front-office areas of your business that vendors (like Salesforce.com!) work on to make your front-office teams more efficient and productive.

## Understanding your customer's customer

How can you sell to and retain customers if you don't understand their needs, key contacts, and what account activities and transactions have taken place? A CRM system allows you to track all your important customer interactions and data so that you can develop solutions that deliver real value to your customers, which in turn should mean higher customer satisfaction with *their* customers. Whether people are in marketing, sales, or customer support, they should all have the ability to access the same source of truth about your customer. After all, how can your company serve its customers well if you're not familiar with how your products and services help improve your customers' customers' (no, that's not a typo) experience?

## Centralizing customer information under one roof

How much time have you wasted tracking down a customer contact or an address that you know exists within the walls of your company? What about trying to find out which sales rep owns the relationship with a subsidiary of a global customer? A good CRM system lets you quickly centralize and organize your accounts and contacts so that you can capitalize on that information when you need to.

# Looking to Customer Relationship Management to Solve Critical Business Challenges

We could write another book telling you all the great things you can do with Salesforce, but you can get the big picture about CRM systems' benefits from this chapter. We focus here on the most common business challenges that we hear from sales, marketing, and support executives — and how a CRM system can overcome them.

## Expanding the funnel

Inputs and outputs, right? The more leads you generate and pursue, the greater the chance that your revenue will grow. So, the big question is, "How do I make the machine work?" A CRM application helps you plan, manage, measure, and improve lead generation, qualification, and conversion. You can see how much business you or your team generates, the sources of that business, and who in your team is making it happen.

## Consolidating your pipeline

Pipeline reports give companies insight into future sales, yet we've worked with companies in which generating the weekly pipeline could take more than a day of cat herding and guesswork. Reps waste time updating spreadsheets. Managers waste time chasing reps and scrubbing data. Bosses waste time tearing their hair out because the information is old by the time they get it. The prevalence of cloud computing makes this traditional method of siloed data collection obsolete (or pretty darn inefficient). A good CRM system helps you shorten or eliminate all that pulling and pasting of data across multiple sources. As long as reps use the system to manage all their opportunities in one place, managers can generate updated pipeline reports with the click of a button.

## Collaborating effectively with your colleagues

Remember when you were the new person at the company, and you had to find the veteran who knew everything in order to get more info on a particular customer, process, or product? Even at smaller companies, it takes time to discover who holds that extra bit of historical knowledge that could help you close that important deal or resolve a support issue. Other times, you may be so busy that you're out of the loop on certain key company updates, even when departments try to keep you informed. What if you could harness the insights from others within the company, yet not be overwhelmed by information overload? A CRM system should provide a means for employee communication that decreases email, and increases internal awareness on the business issues that matter the most to you, so you're always up to date and never caught unawares.

## Working as a team

How many times have you thought that your own co-workers got in the way of selling? Oftentimes, the challenge isn't the people, or even the technology, but standardizing processes and clarifying roles and responsibilities. A CRM system will let you define teams and processes for sales, marketing, and customer service so that the left hand knows what the right hand is doing. It should also be flexible enough to change all those team members the next time a reorg happens. Although a CRM system doesn't solve corporate alignment issues, the tool should drive and manage better team collaboration.

## Extending your sales force with partners

In many industries, selling directly is a thing of the past. To gain leverage and cover more territory, many companies work through partners. CRM systems should let your channel team track and associate partners' deals and get better insight about who their top partners are. Partners now can strengthen their relationships with their vendors by collaborating more easily on joint sales and marketing efforts.

## Beating the competition

How much money have you lost to competitors? How many times did you lose a deal only to discover, after the fact, that it went to your archenemy? If you know who you're up against, you can probably better position yourself to win the opportunity. CRM systems let you and your teams track competition on deals, collect competitive intelligence, and develop action plans to wear down your foes.

## Improving the customer experience

As a salesperson, have you ever walked into a customer's office expecting a bed of roses only to be hit with a landmine because of an unresolved customer issue? And if you work in customer support, how much time do you waste on trying to identify the customers and reviewing the context of previous support interactions? A CRM system should let you efficiently capture, manage, and resolve a high volume of customer issues that come in from a variety of communication channels. The customer relationship doesn't end once they've bought your product — that's just the beginning. A CRM system should allow sales reps to have visibility into the health of their accounts, and service can stay well informed of sales and account activity.

## Measuring the business

How can you improve what you can't measure? Simple, huh? If you use your CRM system correctly and regularly to manage customers, you have data to make informed decisions. That benefits everyone. If you're a rep, you know what you need to do to get the rewards you want. If you're a manager, you can pinpoint where to get involved to drive your numbers. A CRM system's reporting and dashboards should provide easy-to-use tools to measure and analyze your business.

# Selecting Salesforce as Your Customer Relationship Management System

Salesforce wasn't the first CRM system to hit the market, but it's dramatically different from the other CRM systems you may have used (spreadsheets and sticky notes count as a system, too!). Unlike traditional CRM software, Salesforce is the first successful business application offered as an Internet service. You sign up and log in through a browser, and it's immediately available. We currently call this *cloud computing*, where the customers access "the cloud" (that is, the Internet) for their business needs, and are not required to install any traditional software on, presumably, Earth. As long as you have an Internet connection, you can be anywhere in the world and have access to the clouds.

You may already be at a company that uses cloud-based applications, as Salesforce. com's success has spawned a whole new marketplace full of business applications done "in the cloud." Or you may just be entering the workforce, but you're very familiar with the use of Internet-applications in your personal life (think Twitter, Instagram, or Facebook). If this is your first foray into cloud computing, you may be taking a first step by yourself or with the rest of your company. Don't worry — your company made the right choice by picking Salesforce.

Salesforce customers typically say that it's unique for three major reasons:

- **»** **It's fast.** When you sign on the dotted line, you want your CRM system up and running yesterday. Traditional CRM software can take more than a year to deploy; compare that to months or even weeks with Salesforce.

- **»** **It's easy.** End user adoption is critical to any application, and Salesforce wins the ease-of-use category hands down. You can spend more time putting it to use and less time figuring it out.

- **»** **It's effective.** Because it's easy to use and can be customized quickly to meet business needs, customers have proven that it has improved their bottom lines.

Salesforce's success has empowered a whole new generation of managers and administrators to become business operations gurus. Cloud computing's generally lower licensing costs, its ability to allow system configuration to happen with no prior programming experience, and its ability to make modifications quickly to the system mean that newer businesses can compete with slower, older, bigger competitors, but at a fraction of the cost.

In the next chapter, we cover more specifics about Salesforce.com's products.

# Chapter **2**

# Discovering Salesforce. com's Products

N ow that you have a general idea about what Salesforce is, let's delve into the various products that Salesforce.com offers. Generally speaking, the products we cover here fall into the three major categories or departments traditionally used to understand customer relationship management (CRM): sales, marketing, and service.

You may not have thought about it yet, but if you think about the basic structure of CRM, it follows the customer journey from pre-sales to sales and finally post-sales. In other words, marketing departments market the business to spark interest in a customer base and attract potential leads for your sales teams. When those leads are good and qualified, the lead is handed off to sales to close a deal. After the sale, the customer interacts with customer support for service, questions, or feedback about the product sold.

When you step back and look at the big picture, this entire life cycle centers around the customer. As you can see, we're trying to sufficiently hammer home the fact that Salesforce.com and its products are all about enhancing the relationship between your business and your customer. Although it's important to see this big picture, Salesforce.com also recognizes that the devil is in the details, especially from your customers' perspective. Salesforce.com encourages its users to capture customer details and use them to improve this customer relationship.

In this chapter, we discuss three of Salesforce.com's products and show you how they can transform a relationship between an organization and its customer base. First, we show you how you can improve your selling with Sales Cloud. Then we talk about Marketing Cloud — how it improves lead quality and automates important marketing tasks. Then we look at customer support and the features of Service Cloud that streamline it. Finally, we wrap up the chapter by helping you decide which Salesforce edition is right for you.

# Using Sales Cloud to Win More Deals

Sales Cloud helps companies increase their sales success in a number of ways that we describe in the next few pages. But first, it's important to note that any system you use is only as good as the data entered in it. This is an important point that cannot be emphasized enough throughout this book. If your data is stale and outdated or just plain incorrect, the entire infrastructure built around it is essentially worthless. And that's why user adoption is so important. With Salesforce, it's easy to put in place a number of guardrails to ensure that the integrity of your data isn't compromised. Assuming that data is up to date and accurate, Salesforce is a powerful sales machine that gives organizations all around the world insight into their businesses.

## Making sales groups more effective

So, how does Salesforce do it? Let's look at a few ways Sales Cloud makes sales teams more efficient at their jobs.

Account management and contact management are the focal point of sales teams and the foundation of Salesforce.com's products. What would a CRM tool be if you couldn't use it to track your customers and the organizations they're a part of? Accounts are those organizations or businesses. Contacts are the individuals that belong to those Accounts. Salesforce lets you establish and differentiate between your customers, partners, competitors, and distributors effortlessly. It also shows you valuable information about these people and organizations in one place (again, assuming someone is inputting that data).

This allows any company using Salesforce to view customer details quickly and easily. It is also built with the user in mind, providing an attractive and intuitive user interface so that inputting this crucial information isn't too cumbersome. The user interface has gotten a facelift recently, and has come with some fundamental changes under the covers. It's called the Lightning Experience (LEX or Lightning, for short), but we'll get much more into that later. Of course, regardless of how simple the interface is, a system can't read your mind and data entry is ultimately necessary. Entering this data can get laborious over time if you aren't careful. But Salesforce gives administrators what they need to make entering or updating accounts and contacts easy.

Another way Salesforce boosts sales efficiency is by minimizing time spent trying to communicate across and within teams. Salesforce provides multiple tools for on-demand work collaboration, as well as quick communication. Many companies see a dramatic decline in emails after using Chatter. Tasks and events that are automatically created and synced to the digital calendars of sales teams also increase efficiency, forecasting, and opportunity management.

## Improving sales productivity

Sales Cloud can be used to dramatically increase sales productivity for many organizations. Sales Cloud can increase forecasting accuracy which has many obvious benefits. Tracking and managing leads, following up with them, and converting them with a single click of a button can help sales teams focus more on selling and less on entering data into a cumbersome Excel spreadsheet. Organizing massive amounts of data and presenting these results in a way that makes sense to users in real time is one of the most powerful weapons of Sales Cloud.

In essence, there really is no secret formula to how Salesforce boosts productivity and efficiency for sales teams. You can manage and view all customer information in one place, while updating contacts or following up with them (again, from the same single place), and track all this using powerful reporting to see trends over time and act accordingly. You can organize your tasks by priority, forecast more accurately, and respond to customers more quickly, thereby helping your business become a "customer company."

# Generating Better Leads with Marketing Cloud

We could write a separate book about Salesforce Marketing Cloud and do a deep dive into the various features it offers, but you can get the big picture from this section. Marketing Cloud is really a suite of multiple product offerings, but in this section we focus on email campaigns, marketing automation, and lead management, and how Marketing Cloud can improve your organization's ability to execute on all of them.

## Managing email campaigns with Marketing Cloud

How can you drive online commerce, as well as sell to and build customer relationships, without email? Email is the engine behind these forces. Marketing Cloud gives companies the tools to quickly create and automate attention-grabbing emails to customers throughout the customer life cycle. It's essentially a user interface for managing communications and content to a wide customer base. The platform maintains mailing lists and schedules and can modify email messages based on what recipients read, click, and forward. You can easily filter your subscriber base so that you're sending specific, targeted emails based on criteria or events of your choosing. You don't want certain customers to be bothered by email campaigns? No problem. All of this can be set up and monitored as you desire.

TIP

ExactTarget is the name Marketing Cloud used to go by, so if you see ExactTarget in documentation somewhere, don't get confused.

## Improving marketing automation

How much time have you wasted tracking down customer activity, emailing potential buyers that weren't even interested, or trying to understand who clicked your links? *Marketing automation* is a general term for platforms that enable the automation of repetitive tasks, as they relate to marketing on multiple online channels. In other words, automating marketing communication. So, via multiple channels, a company that uses marketing automation is able to manage and automate the targeting, timing, and content of outbound messages. What's more, it can do this intelligently, using cues from prospective actions and behaviors on the customer side.

Think of this like responding to body language. In today's world, consumers do their homework and visit the websites of multiple competitors before deciding which product they want to buy. Email blasts are no longer acceptable means of capturing a large piece of the consumer pie. More personalized and sensitive communications must be sent out, based on various criteria such as the buyer's role in his or her organization or the buyer's purchase readiness. It's more important than ever to send the right message at the right time.

Marketing Cloud includes a host of features that assist in automating these marketing processes. Even better, Marketing Cloud is already part of the Salesforce network, meaning that you can leverage all the information in one database, instead of worrying about complex integration of various systems feeding into one another. Now it's easier than ever to manage these interactions and deploy online campaigns from a central platform.

## Identifying qualified leads with Pardot

Leads are the lifeblood of your business. The more leads you generate and pursue, the greater the chance that your revenue will grow. We already know that with Salesforce, you can plan, manage, measure, and improve lead generation, qualification, and conversion. You can see how much business you or your team generates, the sources of that business, and who in your team is making it happen. What about the step preceding that, though? There's no use in filling your pipeline with leads that won't actually follow through. So, how do you make sure your leads are qualified?

Pardot, Salesforce's marketing automation tool, ensures that you fill your pipeline with the highest-quality leads. You can use the tool to create custom landing pages, lead capture forms, and targeted personalized emails. This helps your business shorten the sales cycle and close deals faster. You can set up personalized lead scoring based on criteria that you decide, to evaluate how qualified prospective buyers are. You can control which marketing content and messaging goes out to those leads based on that score criteria. Finally, you can add those leads that aren't quite ready to buy to your nurture campaigns, so that you can spend more time "nurturing" them into high-scoring leads that will more likely purchase your product. This, in turn, accelerates your pipeline and ensures that team effort is being spent where it will pay off most, all from a central place.

# Providing Excellent Customer Service with Service Cloud

When the sale is closed, good companies don't say sayonara. An organization should still keep tabs on customers, or have relevant purchase history ready on the off chance that the customer will reach out with questions or issues. This is the foundation of customer support. Salesforce Service Cloud is a tool that helps call centers and customer service agents track customer interactions after point of sale.

This section provides an overview of what you can do with Service Cloud. For a lot more information, see *Salesforce Service Cloud For Dummies*, by Jon Paz and TJ Kelley (Wiley).

## Managing customer interactions with cases

Remember when you used to call a toll-free number about a broken product that you bought? Maybe you emailed a support email address or filled out a web form. Whichever method you chose, chances are, you weren't at your happiest at that moment. And who can blame you? It's critical that customers receive world-class customer service from companies. Today, customers demand satisfaction more than ever before. If they aren't satisfied, they can easily turn to competitors, or even worse, create smear campaigns against a company with bad customer service on social media networks.

Have you ever heard a customer service representative say, "One second while I pull up your record"? Those records are what we call *cases* in Service Cloud. Cases are related to contact records, so when a customer calls in, an agent can quickly pull up her record and see not only her purchase history, but also a record of every issue and interaction that customer has had with your organization. Cases, and the ability to clearly see what's going on with customers, make both your customer service reps, as well as your customers themselves, much happier. Nobody wants to be transferred to another agent, only to have to repeat the issue for the third time.

Service Cloud uses case management to expedite and streamline customer service, creating a much more efficient experience for everyone involved and bringing your service organization into the 21st century.

## Interacting with the customer across multiple channels

Service Cloud has an added benefit: the ability to interact with customers across multiple channels. Or perhaps it's better said differently: Service Cloud gives your customers the choice of how they want to connect with your company.

Not only can customers choose to contact you anytime, anywhere, and from any device, but they can also choose the medium through which they do so. Some customers are old-fashioned and prefer calling a toll-free number. Other customers dread long hold times and would rather chat with an agent online. Giving your customers the choice to contact you the way they see fit will do wonders for their perception of your company. Service Cloud gives you many different ways to do this, and it will pay off in terms of satisfaction, as well as reduced operational cost.

# Deciding Which Salesforce Edition Is Best for You

If you already use Salesforce, this topic may be a moot point. At the very least, you know which version of Salesforce you have.

**TIP**

If you're not sure which edition you have, look at the top of your browser after you've logged into Salesforce.

All versions have the same consistent look and feel, but each varies by feature, functionality, and pricing. If you're considering using Salesforce, consult with an account executive for more details about edition differences, pricing, and upgrade paths. The licensing and pricing can get complicated depending on the specific type of product or functionality you are looking for. Additionally, editions and edition names can change frequently. For the purposes of this book, we will introduce you to Sales and Service Cloud editions (by far the most common). As of this writing, there are four versions of Salesforce.com's service:

» **Salesforce Essentials:** This edition is a basic, out-of-the-box CRM system that offers basic account and contact management for sales and case management for service, for up to ten users. This edition is great for small businesses and others who want to start small.

» **Lightning Professional:** A thorough CRM system for any size organization that's starting to nail down processes. Again, you can track the full sales life cycle from a new lead to a closed opportunity. Chatter allows greater collaboration across the organization. Dashboards allow managers to track key metrics at a glance. Some features for businesses with more detailed process needs (such as managing multiple record types per object, profiles, page layouts, and security permissions) come in a capped or pared-down capacity relative to the editions below.

» **Lightning Enterprise:** More sales and service functionality for more complex organizations. This includes the ability to integrate with other systems within your company, the ability to create custom solutions with code, and gives you access to unlimited workflow and process automation, reducing the amount of custom code your company actually has to write. Additionally, this is the minimum baseline edition for customers who want to purchase specific (mostly AI-centric) add-on features. If you absolutely need your business processes to look and act a specific way, this edition provides more ways to make that happen for you.

>> **Lightning Unlimited:** Even more customization capabilities for extending Salesforce to other business uses, such as Live Agent Chat for Service Cloud. This edition also gives you access to Salesforce support or sandboxes and testing resources that typically come at an additional cost with other editions. You need a dedicated (and usually technical) administrator to take advantage of all the options that this edition delivers.

**TECHNICAL STUFF**

Salesforce.com also provides another edition, Developer Edition, which is a free instance of Salesforce with which developers can test and build third-party solutions. It has full functionality but a very limited license count and storage space.

Whichever edition you choose, the good news is that every edition of Salesforce is rich with features that can help companies of every size address their business challenges. You can choose a more basic edition today and upgrade later, as needed. Upgrades happen in the background and are easy, so you can focus on the business processes that drive the need for new functionality. And when Salesforce.com rolls out new releases of its service, it provides product enhancements for the different editions wherever relevant.

## PROFESSIONAL OR ENTERPRISE EDITION?

Most companies tend to make a decision between using Professional or Enterprise Edition. Budget may be an issue, but the decision usually boils down to core business needs. Consider these questions:

- Does your company have different groups with distinct sales processes, customers, and products?
- Does your company plan to integrate Salesforce with other applications?
- Does your company require complex data migration into Salesforce?
- Does your company need greater control over users, what they see, and what they can do?
- Does your company sell in defined teams with specific roles?
- Does your company require consistent, specific workflow or approval steps to further automate processes?

If the answer to any of these questions is a definitive "Yes," your company should probably at least evaluate Enterprise Edition, and possibly Unlimited Edition.

# 2

# Understanding Salesforce Features

**IN THIS PART . . .**

Learn basic Salesforce terms so you're able to talk the talk.

Navigate the Lightning Experience landscape of Salesforce to know where to go for what.

See how you can make Salesforce your own with personalization tips, including the Salesforce mobile app.

Get acquainted with collaborating in Salesforce and see how your sales, marketing, and customer service organizations can benefit from it.

# Chapter **3**

# Navigating Salesforce

I f an application isn't easy to use, you won't use it. Period. Salesforce succeeds not only because it offers a universe of integrated tools but also because users can pick it up within minutes. You navigate Salesforce much the same way you do other websites: by clicking links and buttons. And for those of you who could navigate Salesforce's "Classic" interface with your eyes closed, this chapter helps familiarize you with their new Lightning Experience (LEX) interface.

Whether you're in LEX or Classic, you have so many ways to navigate Salesforce that it makes sense to lay down the obvious (and not-so-obvious) best practices for getting around the application.

TIP

Even if you're familiar with Salesforce, you may want to scan this chapter because we cover terms that we use repeatedly throughout this book.

In this chapter, you can find out how to log in to Salesforce, then understand what the Lightning Experience is all about. Then we review how you can use the Lightning home page to manage your activities, create records, and jump to other tabs. We briefly review the major functional areas and describe how to use the internal home pages.

# Getting Familiar with Basic Salesforce Terms

Before we delve into the mechanics of navigating Salesforce, familiarize yourself with these basic terms:

» **Salesforce:** The secure website that your users log in to that contains your customer information. Salesforce, Inc., offers a family of products used by hundreds of thousands of customers, but each company's secure website is separate from the other websites and may look different in order to suit that company's unique needs. When we use the terms *Sales Cloud, Marketing Cloud* or *Service Cloud,* those are parts of Salesforce specifically meant for use by sales and marketing or by a support organization.

» **Home page:** Also known as the Lightning Experience home page. The main page that appears when you log in to Salesforce or click the Home tab.

» **Tabs:** Clickable words appear in a row (also known as the *navigation bar*) across the top of any Salesforce page. When selected, a word is highlighted and looks like a tab. Each tab represents a major module in which your company needs to know some information. By clicking a tab, you go to a tab-specific home page. For example, if you click the Accounts tab, the Accounts home page appears. Tabs in LEX also now come with their own drop-down menu that provide a quicker way to access recent records and list views (more on that later).

» **Tab home pages:** These are the pages where you go to find, organize, and manage specific information related to a particular tab. For example, to access your Opportunity records, you could go to the Opportunities home page.

» **Object:** Often used interchangeably with the name of a tab. Generally used by administrators when talking about creating custom apps. For example, you may tell a user to "click the Account tab," or you may hear your system administrator refer to the "Account object."

» **Apps:** Tabs that have been grouped together and given a name, providing you with the convenience of seeing only those tabs most relevant to you.

» **Record:** A record is a page in Salesforce made up of a bunch of subtabs and fields that hold information to describe a specific object. For example, a Contact record typically contains fields pertinent to a person, including name, title, phone number, and email address. A record is displayed on a detail page.

» **Detail page:** A web page that shows both the saved record's details and a set of related lists pertinent to the record. With LEX, to reduce scrolling down a long screen, Salesforce organized various sections into subtabs and sidebars so users could access what they needed with minimal vertical scrolling.

>> **Chatter feed:** If you have Chatter enabled (see Chapter 6), you'll see the right sidebar of a record with a chronological list of updates made by you or other co-workers, under a subtab named Chatter. This feed is a critical way for Salesforce users within your organization to communicate with each other.

>> **Search bar:** In the top-middle portion of your Salesforce page, a search field resides as another way you can quickly find companies or contacts. Search results returned can be fine-tuned to return only results from a certain type of record.

**REMEMBER**

We often use the terms *record* and *detail page* interchangeably. From a detail page, you can perform and track a variety of tasks related to the specific record. For example, if you have and are looking at an Account detail page for Twitter, you see fields about the company and lists of other records related to Twitter.

>> **Related lists:** Lists that comprise other records linked to the record that you're looking at. For example, the Account record page for Acme may display a Related subtab with sections of contacts and opportunities.

>> **Sidebar:** Located at the right margin of a Salesforce page, the sidebar displays activities and Chatter posts.

# Accessing Salesforce

You need to log in to your account to access your company's instance of Salesforce because every company's Salesforce website is separate, and the company goes to great lengths to protect your company's information.

## Setting up a password

The first time you log in to the Salesforce service, you'll do so from an email you receive containing your Salesforce login information. To set your password, follow these steps:

1. **Open the email and click the link provided.**

   A page appears, prompting you to set a new password and security question.

2. **Complete the fields.**

   Be sure to select a question and provide an answer that can verify your identity if you forget your password. Use this password from now on unless your administrator resets the password.

3. **When you're done, click Change Password.**

   Your Salesforce home page appears.

# Logging in

You log in to Salesforce just as you would any other secure website.

To log in, open a browser and follow these steps:

**1.** **In your browser's address bar, type** `https://login.salesforce.com` **and then press Enter.**

The Salesforce.com login page, shown in Figure 3-1, appears.

**TIP**

To save yourself steps when logging in, bookmark the login page in your favorite web browser.

**2.** **Enter your username and password, and then click the Log In button.**

Your username is typically your corporate email address. Click the Remember Me check box if you want your computer to remember it. After you click Log In, you may be asked to register your mobile phone. This is an additional, optional security step. After this step, your main home page appears.

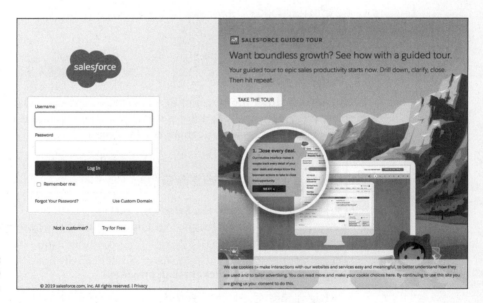

**FIGURE 3-1:**
Logging in to
Salesforce.

**TECHNICAL
STUFF**

For security purposes, Salesforce notices when you're trying to log in to the website from a different computer or a different browser than the one you first used. If this happens, make sure that you have access to your email or mobile phone (remember when Salesforce asked you to register your mobile phone number?) because Salesforce emails or text messages you a confirmation code to confirm that you are who you say you are.

# Explaining the Lightning Experience

Late in 2015, Salesforce.com debuted a revamped user experience in Salesforce, called the Lightning Experience (LEX). It was based on extensive user research and provided a look and feel that would be more consistent across both desktop browsers as well as a mobile interface. LEX also updated how users interacted with records in Salesforce, which, in the Classic experience, was often taking up lots of time vertically scrolling longer and longer record pages.

In this section, we discuss LEX fundamentals, and other chapters discuss details assuming LEX since new customers are defaulting to this user interface, and existing customers are eventually migrating to it, too. As more Salesforce features and enhancements are being offered only in LEX, companies are finding more and more compelling reasons to go out with the old (Classic interface) and in with the new. Our screenshots are taken in LEX, unless otherwise noted.

Existing customers can choose to enable and switch to the Lightning Experience when they're comfortable and ready. Even then, Salesforce.com allows a user to switch back and forth between the Salesforce Classic and Lightning Experience UIs. Make sure you read Chapter 25, "Ten Keys to a Successful Migration to Lightning" to ensure a smooth transition.

**TIP**

Make sure you read the fine print in the Salesforce release notes (http://docs. releasenotes.salesforce.com) to thoroughly understand what features are and are not yet supported in the Lightning Experience. With three releases a year, the list of enhancements continues to evolve. Also make sure you understand Lightning Experience's impact on your users by testing business processes out in a sandbox environment before turning this on.

## Navigating the Lightning Home Page

Every time you log in to Salesforce, you begin at your home page. The look and feel of the elements on your home page are similar to other users' home pages, but the tasks and events that appear in the body of the page are specific to you.

Use the home page to manage your calendar and tasks, jump to other areas by clicking tabs on the Navigation Bar, or access recent items by using the drop-down menu next to the relevant tab.

The home page in the Lightning Experience has been re-envisioned to empower a salesperson to more efficiently manage her day in Salesforce.

You may see some different sections on your home page, depending on whether your administrator has already customized it. Starting from the top of the page, make sure to familiarize yourself with the following home page concepts, as shown in Figure 3-2:

**FIGURE 3-2:**
Presenting the home page in the Lightning Experience.

**FIGURE 3-2:**
Presenting the home page in the Lightning Experience.

>> **Search Bar:** Located in the top middle portion of every page is a global search bar. You'll learn later about how to narrow down your search results to quickly get to what you're looking for.

>> **App Launcher:** Instead of going to a drop-down in the upper-right corner of the screen to switch between clusters of tabs as you did in Salesforce Classic, click the icon on the top left of the page, that looks like a 3 x 3 grid of little squares, as shown in Figure 3-3. Hovering over that icon changes it from boring gray squares to colored ones. Clicking the icon results in the App Launcher page showing. If you click a tile, you're taken to that app's Home page (with a specific set of tabs in the Navigation Bar).

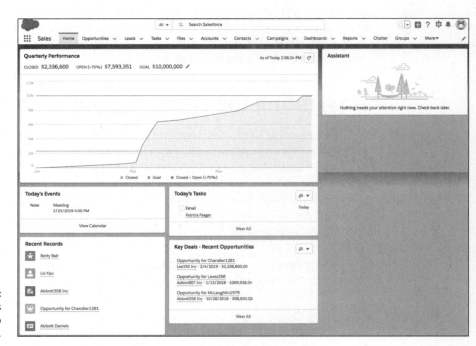

**FIGURE 3-3:**
Accessing apps using the App Launcher.

>> **Navigation Bar:** This is the top area with words across it (where the words used to represent Tabs and some people still refer to it that way). Notice that each word has a little 'V-like image to its right. That's a tab's related drilldown menu. Hover and click over a drilldown image and you'll be able to create a new record, see recent records, and recently viewed lists, all for that object.

>> **The gear icon:** The Setup link from the Classic UI has been replaced by the gear icon with a lightning bolt in it. System administrators need to click the gear (shown in Figure 3-4), to get to their familiar Setup area, which is now called Setup Home.

**FIGURE 3-4:**
Getting to the
Setup Home.

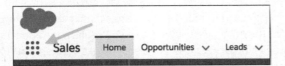

>> **Quarterly Performance chart:** Designed for people using Opportunities to track their sales performance, this chart appears prominently on the home page. A rep can add her goal for the quarter and quickly see how close she is to hitting this quarter's target. Opportunities with close dates this quarter that are already closed or with probability of greater than 70 percent will show up here.

The chart is also interactive. Hovering over it can reveal specific Opportunities with close dates in this quarter. Clicking the corresponding blue dot opens a pop-up window with some additional Opportunity details, so a sales rep can quickly prioritize her work.

>> **Assistant:** The right-hand column of your screen now displays a combination of overdue and open tasks with some details, as well as Leads assigned to you and activities related to Opportunities that should matter to you.

>> **Today's Events:** Below the Quarterly Performance chart is an area that displays your calendar events for today, which you can get by syncing your work calendar with Salesforce.

>> **Today's Tasks:** Next to Today's Events is an area that displays your Tasks for today, based on the Task's due date. You can modify this view to get the best to-do list for your organizational style.

>> **Recent Records:** This section shows a list of records that you most recently viewed. In Salesforce Classic, this used to be on the left sidebar.

>> **Key Deals – Recent Opportunities:** This section shows a default view of your most recently-visited Opportunity records. You can modify this view to get the best one that displays the Opportunities most important to you.

# Finding records with Search

At the top of every Salesforce page, you'll find the Global Search bar. You can find a majority of the information that you want by using Search. To search for information, follow these steps:

1. **At the top of Salesforce, enter keywords into the Search.**

   When you first put your cursor in the Search box, a list of Recent Items will appear. This is meant to save you time in quickly accessing a record without having to search for it. As you type in the search box, you'll see some additional records show up in a list, as Salesforce tries to help you get to your record faster by making an educated guess on what you're searching for as you type. If none of those recommended records are a match, finish typing in the search box and click the magnifying glass. A Search Results page appears, as shown in Figure 3-5. Salesforce organizes the search results in lists according to top results based on the records it thinks are most relevant to you, and then the major types of records, including Accounts, Contacts, Leads, and Opportunities. If you anticipate too many results, filter your results to a single type of object by clicking on the All drop-down menu just to the left of the search box.

2. **Scroll down the page. If you find a record that you want to look at, click a link in the Name column for the row that represents that record.**

   The detail page appears, allowing you to review the record and its related lists.

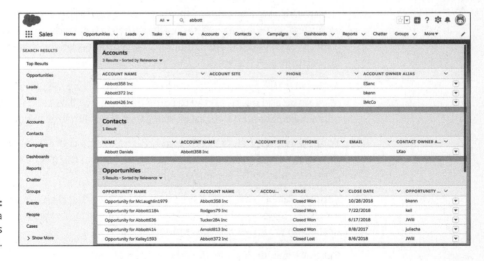

**FIGURE 3-5:**
Looking at a Search Results page.

**3.** **If you see too many results, you can limit them a single type of record from the list in the sidebar.**

If you can't find what you're looking for, try adding the asterisk (*) wildcard before, after, or in the middle of your keywords to expand your search to words that start with, end with, or are similar to your keywords.

If you're focusing on a page (such as a list of search results or a report) and want to open one of the results in a new browser tab, instead of clicking the link, right-click that link and choose Open Link in New Tab from the contextual menu that appears.

TIP

# Defining Apps

Salesforce allows you to organize tabs into groups. These groups, also known as *apps*, help reduce screen clutter and give you quicker access to the tabs that you use the most. For example, a marketing manager may rarely use the Cases or Opportunities tabs but spend most of her time looking at Campaigns and Leads.

Salesforce empowers your company to create custom apps for more specific uses within customer relationship management (CRM) — or for anything else, for that matter. Sales reps can use an expense reporting app, and product managers can use a product release app to manage their product requirements. The mind-blowing part of all of this is that apps can be composed of standard tabs or *custom ones that you create.* Anyone in your company can benefit from sharing one set of data. And don't worry if you're not the most creative type. Salesforce has a bunch of prebuilt apps available (for free or for an additional charge), which we discuss in more detail in Chapter 19.

# Uncovering the App Launcher

From the app menu, selecting the App Launcher option takes you to the App Launcher page where all your apps are now displayed as clickable tiles, as shown in Figure 3-6. Depending on what other systems your company has integrated with Salesforce, you may also see installed app icons for other applications used at your company, like Gmail or Concur.

# Managing your calendar

The My Events section of the home page shows your events for the day. Your scheduled events are based on events with specific start times and durations, that you assigned to yourself or that other users have assigned to you. From there you can click View All to be taken to the Calendar view for the week.

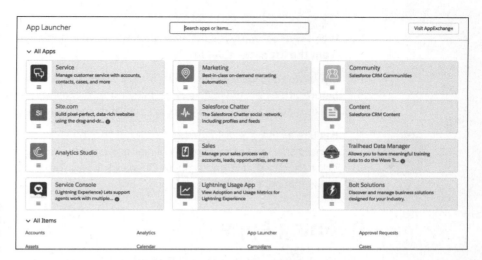

**FIGURE 3-6:**
Viewing apps
in the App
Launcher.

If your company's corporate calendar tool is Microsoft Outlook or Google Calendar, Salesforce allows you to selectively sync relevant contacts and appointments between your work calendar and Salesforce. This allows a record of your relevant customer interactions to be captured in Salesforce without you having to spend extraneous mouseclicks to re-create the event in a second tool.

The details of syncing your events between your corporate and Salesforce calendar are too extensive for this book. We recommend you talk to your Salesforce Account Executive about Lightning Sync for (Google or Microsoft Exchange), to see if it's a fit for your needs.

## Tracking your tasks

On the home page, you see a section entitled Today's Tasks, which displays tasks that you created for yourself or that have been assigned to you.

A *Task* is an activity that you need to do, and it can have a due date. Unlike an Event, however, a Task doesn't have a specific time and duration. For example, if you want to remind yourself to send a proposal, you typically create a Task instead of scheduling an Event. (See Chapter 5 for additional tips on managing Tasks.)

From the Today's Tasks section (shown in Figure 3-7), you can do the following:

>> **Change Task view.** Use the drop-down list at the top right of the Today's Tasks section to select from a list of common Task views. For example, select All Overdue to see your open Tasks that are past their respective due dates. The name of the section will change accordingly.

>> **Review a Task.** Click the Subject of the Task to review a Task. A Task record appears with details.

>> **Go to associated records.** Click other links in the Task (like the person, Account, or Opportunity the Task is associated with).

>> **Complete the Task and enter any details before saving.** Click the check box next to the Task to complete it and have a line appear across the Task just as if you were crossing it off an old paper listYou can also uncheck the check box to update a Task. A pop-up window will appear and Salesforce will ask that you select an updated Status field before you save it.

>> **See more Tasks.** If you have several Tasks in your list, the View All link appears at the bottom of the Today's Tasks section on the home page. Click it to go to the Tasks home page. The Recently Viewed list appears, along with Tasks due today, your open Tasks, and ones completed in the last seven days.

**FIGURE 3-7:**
Reviewing the My
Tasks section on
the home page.

# Navigating the tabs

In this section, we describe the major tabs that appear in apps across the navigation bar and show you how to use the tab home pages to quickly access, manage, or organize information.

Each tab within Salesforce represents a major module or data element in an interconnected database. That's as technical as we get.

In the following list, we briefly describe each of the standard tabs (as shown in Figure 3-8). We devote a chapter to each of the tabs mentioned here:

>> **Campaigns (see Chapter 15):** Specific marketing efforts that you manage to generate leads, and stimulate demand for your products and services.

>> **Leads (see Chapter 7):** Prospective people and companies with whom you want to do business. But don't start grilling your lead about where she was on the morning of July 23, because the only clue you'll gather is the sound of a dial tone.

>> **Accounts (see Chapter 8):** Companies with whom you hope to do, currently do or previously did business. You can track all types of accounts, including customers, prospects, former customers, partners, and competitors.

>> **Contacts (see Chapter 9):** Individuals associated with your Accounts.

>> **Opportunities (see Chapter 10):** The deals that you pursue to track transactions or drive revenue for your company. Your open Opportunities constitute your pipeline, and Opportunities can contribute to your forecast.

>> **Cases (see Chapter 13):** Customer inquiries that your support teams work on to manage and resolve.

>> **Files (see Chapter 16):** Files that you store in Salesforce, that are ultimately intended to be shared with other coworkers or groups, for collaborative purposes.

>> **Reports (see Chapter 22):** Data analyses for you and your entire organization. Salesforce provides a variety of best practices reports, and you can build custom reports on the fly to better measure your business.

>> **Dashboards (see Chapter 23):** Graphs, charts, and tables based on your custom reports. You can use dashboards to visually measure and analyze key elements of your business.

>> **Chatter (see Chapter 6):** Manage all aspects of your collaboration efforts here. From the Chatter home page, you can view all updates to your feed. If you don't see this tab, you may not have Chatter enabled in your organization.

**FIGURE 3-8:**
Navigating
through the tabs
along the
navigation bar.

## Accessing shorcuts from the navigation bar drop-down menus

Each tab in the navigation bar comes with a drop-down menu. Use the drop-down menu to create new records, quickly go back to pages you recently accessed, and visit recent list views.

### Creating new records

Use the appropriate drill-down menu to access the "+ New [Object]" option for that object to quickly create any new record.

### Getting to recent records

The Recent Records portion of the drill-down menu displays up to three records of that object that you most recently clicked. Use the list to quickly get back to records that you've been working on, even if you logged out and logged back in. To visit the detail record of a recent item, simply click a listed link.

### Revisiting recent lists

The Recent Lists portion of the drill-down menu displays up to three recent lists of that object. Use a list view to quickly see a pre-filtered set of records for that tab. To visit a recent list view, simply click the link with the same name.

## Discovering a tab home page

When you click a tab, the tab's default list view appears. For example, if you click the Accounts tab, the Recently Viewed list of Accounts appears, along with buttons in the upper right to allow for specific actions to be performed, and edits to be made to the list of Accounts currently displayed. The tab's home page is where you can view, organize, track, edit, and maintain all the records within that tab.

Do this right now: Click every tab visible to you.

The look and feel of the interior home pages never change, regardless of which tab you click (except for the Home, Reports, and Dashboards tabs). On the top-left of the page, you have the current name of the view, below the object's name. Click the drop-down list to see other list views to select. The pushpin icon next to the view name allows you to see that same view the next time you return to this home page. On the upper-right, you have a New button to create a new record of that particular object (see Figure 3-9).

**FIGURE 3-9:** Deconstructing the tab home page.

## Reviewing tab-specific buttons

In the upper right portion of a tab's home page, Salesforce provides unique buttons associated with a particular tab. Depending on which tab you're viewing, use
these buttons to help you perform certain actions within that tab. For example, on
the Accounts home page, you can click the Import button to import more Accounts.
See the related chapters later in this book for details on using specific buttons.

## Using the View drop-down list

Strategy and execution are all about focus. With custom list views, you can see and
use lists to better focus on your business. A *list view* is a segment of the tab's
records based on defined criteria. When you select a list view, a list of records
appears based on your criteria.

On each tab, Salesforce provides a selection of popular default views to get you
started. To try a list view (using Accounts as the example), follow these steps
(which apply to all tabs):

1. **Click the Accounts tab.**

   The Accounts home page appears (refer to Figure 3-8).

2. **Select My Accounts from the View drop-down list.**

   A list page appears that displays a set of columns representing certain
   standard Account fields and a list of your Account records. If no Account
   records appear, you don't own any in Salesforce.

3. **From the list page, you can perform a variety of functions:**

   - *Re-sort the list.* Click a column header. For example, if you click the Account
     Name header, the list sorts alphabetically, as shown in Figure 3-10.

   - *Search this list.* For longer list results, use the Search box in the tab home
     page to further filter down your list view. Usually people search by the
     account name, in this example.

   - *View a specific record.* Click the link for that record in the Account Name
     column. The Account detail page appears, displaying the record and its
     related lists.

   - *Update a specific field.* Hover over a cell in a row. If you see a little pencil
     icon appear, that means you can double click that field and make an edit
     right then and there.

   - *Edit a specific record.* Each row has a drop-down menu in its far right
     column. Click that drop-down menu and the Edit option appears. When
     you choose that option, the account record appears in Edit mode.

- *Delete a record.* From the drop-down menu, select the Delete option. A pop-up window appears, prompting you to click OK to accept the deletion. If you click OK, the list page reappears, minus the account that you just wiped out. Don't worry — in Chapter 5, we show you how to bring recently deleted records back to life.

**FIGURE 3-10:**
Re-sorting a list.

## Building a custom list view

If you have a particular way that you like to look at records, you can build a custom list view. If you have the right permissions, you can share this view with other groups or your entire organization. (Or maybe you should just keep your views to yourself.)

To create a custom list view (using Accounts as the example), follow these steps (which apply to all tabs):

**1.** **Click the Accounts tab.**

The Accounts home page appears.

**2.** **To the right of the search box, click the gear button to access List View Controls.**

Several List View Control options appear in a drop-down list. See that you can edit the current view's filters, clone it, create a new view from scratch, modify what columns are displayed in the current view, and other options. Select New.

**3.** **Name the view by typing a title in List Name field.**

For example, if you want to create a list of your accouns that are your most strategic Accounts, use a title like My Strategic Accounts.

**4.** **Decide whether you want others to see your custom view.**

Administrators and certain users have this permission. Your decision is made simple if the step doesn't appear. Otherwise, select one of the three options. (Basically, the three radio buttons translate to none, all, or selective.) If you choose the third option, use the drop-down list to select a group and then click the arrows to move that group into the Shared To column. Click Save.

**5.** **Select your list view's filter criteria.**

After saving, your new list appears with the Filter button toggled. Decide if you want to search for just My Accounts or click that filter selection to All Accounts.

6. **(Optional) Add additional filter criteria as needed.**

   A basic criteria query is made up of three elements:

   - *Field:* The first box is a drop-down list of all the fields on the account record. In this example, choose Account Name.

   - *Operator:* The middle box is a drop-down list of operators for your search. That sounds complicated, but it's easier than you think. For this example, select the Contains option.

   - *Value:* In the lower box, type the value that you want in the search. In this example, you might type **abbott**.

7. **Click Save.**

   A new list view appears based on your custom criteria. If you don't get all the results that you anticipate, double-check and refine the filter criteria. For example, if your list should include global accounts but doesn't, click the List View Controls button and select the Edit List Filters option to update the view.

   As long as you save your custom list view, you can use it later from the Views menu. To reduce list view clutter, be considerate and lean toward saving list views that are visible only to yourself. Otherwise, you risk flooding your public list view with several similar-but-slightly-different views that aren't culled over time.

**REMEMBER**

8. **(Optional) Select the columns that you want to have displayed by selecting the corresponding option from the List View Controls drop-down list (that's the button with the gear icon on it.)**

   Although Salesforce's preset views have common fields, such as Phone and Email, you can select any of up to 15 fields to display on your custom view page. Remember to click Save once the desired column name fields have been selected.

# Navigating a record in the Lightning Experience

When you're looking at a record, realize that LEX is meant to reduce the vertical scrolling that is predominant in the Salesforce Classic UI. The elements of the old UI still exist; they've just moved around.

Here are some common properties on a LEX record page, as shown in Figure 3-11:

>> **Standard fields are highlighted at the top of the page.** The top part of a record displays a subset of fields in what's called the Highlights panel. When scrolling down, the record name is anchored so you never forget which record you're seeing details about.

>> **Key buttons are on the right.** Edit and Delete buttons still exist. They're just off to the right. If you can't see one of your buttons listed, click the little triangle to the right of existing buttons to see a list of additional ones.

>> **Related lists appear as cards.** For some objects, this appears below the highlights panel. For other objects, related lists appear on the right-hand side. They all take the form of cards, where a few fields are exposed to give users some context around that record.

>> **Former Activity buttons are now subtabs in the Activity subsection.** For some objects, the Activity subsection appears in the main part of the record, below the highlights panel. For other objects, the Activity area is in the right-hand sidebar. Subtabs allow you to log a call, or create a new task, event, or email.

>> **Record details are located in the Details tab.** This is meant to both reduce the amount of vertical scrolling, while also allowing you to quickly get to additional fields on your record. The Details tab appears below the highlights panel.

>> **Chatter resides as a subsection next to the Activity subsection.** You'll see all the posts from your Chatter feed here, related to whatever record you're on. You'll be able to post a comment, share a link, or create a poll, under respective subtabs. Again, this helps reduce the vertical scrolling on a record.

**FIGURE 3-11:**
Dissecting the Account record.

IN THIS CHAPTER

» Updating your profile

» Learning about the Settings menu

» Changing your personal settings

» Setting up Salesforce for your mobile device

» Adding your contacts to Salesforce

» Working with Salesforce on the go

# Chapter **4**

# Personalizing Salesforce

S alesforce was built by salespeople for salespeople. The tool had to be simple to use, relevant to the business of selling, and customizable so that you could use it to do your job (the way *you* do it) more effectively.

In the previous chapter, we introduced the Lightning Experience (LEX or Lightning). Personalizing Salesforce has somewhat changed from the previous Classic interface. If your organization is still using Salesforce Classic, you can find more information about personalizing your experience in Chapter 4 of the 6th Edition of this book.

Your profile page captures information that you want your colleagues to see about yourself, to improve collaboration across your company. Think of it as a directory listing for everyone who works in Salesforce.

From the Settings page (formerly known as My Settings or the Personal Setup page), you can personalize details of your application to better suit the way you look at and manage your daily tasks. And if you capitalize on the tools available in Salesforce, you can give yourself an edge against the competition and your peers.

In this chapter, we describe how to update your personal information in your profile, modify your settings, change your display, and access Salesforce anytime, anywhere.

# Completing Your Profile Page

Your profile page acts like a cross between a corporate intranet page about your-self and a news feed about your collaborations within the company. Later, we talk more about Chatter and how the concept of feeds appears in many places in Salesforce. For now, think of feeds as proactive status updates across your com-pany so that people interested in the same things (like an Account, Contact, or Opportunity) can follow each other and stay up to date on the latest news.

To locate and update your profile page, follow these steps:

1.  **After logging in to Salesforce, click the (avatar) photo in the upper-right corner of the Salesforce page, and then click your name or the (avatar) photo to the left of your name.**

    Your profile page appears. The top header displays the most relevant at-a-glance information: your photo, your name, your title, and About Me. Beneath this header are the basic contact fields where this information comes from. Under that is the feed that shows your most recent activities (similar to a feed on a social network). The folks you follow, the ones who follow you, and what Chatter groups you belong to, are all visible in the related list cards on the right-hand panel of the page (see Figure 4-1).

2.  **To upload a photo, click the camera icon under the circle profile picture at the top-left of the page, click Update Photo.**

    The Upload Photo box appears.

3.  **Click the Upload Image button to upload a small circular photo of yourself.**

    A file selection window opens so that you can browse and select a photo from your computer.

**REMEMBER**

Though you may prefer to submit a cartoon (as we did) or the back of your head, don't forget that this is for work collaboration. Help your fellow employ-ees out (especially the newer ones) by posting a clear photo of yourself.

4.  **After you've clicked your photo file, click Choose.**

5.  **Click Save on the Upload Photo screen.**

    *Voilà!* Your photo appears. A smaller version of your photo will now appear to the left of your name within any Chatter feeds so that you can be quickly identified.

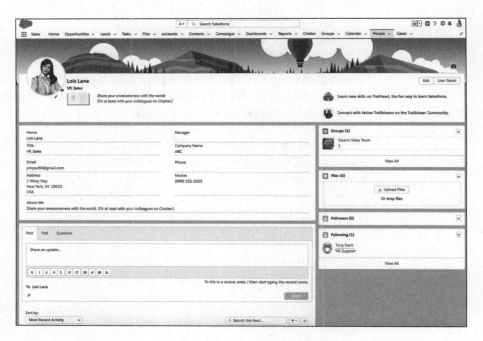

FIGURE 4-1:
Reviewing the
profile page.

Now, to update your contact information so that people know a little more about you, follow these steps:

1. **To the right of the Contact heading, click the edit button.**

   The Edit Profile page appears. The email associated with your Salesforce account appears, along with other contact information taken from the details provided upon registration. Complete what you feel is necessary for co-workers who need to reach you.

   The only field you cannot update in this section is the Manager field, which is editable by an administrator.

   **TIP**

2. **Click Save All when done.**

   The updates are now reflected on the Profile page.

This profile page is especially helpful for companies with users who aren't all in the same location.

# Using the Settings Menu

The Settings menu, which you access by clicking your photo or avatar and then clicking Settings, is the enhanced user interface for what used to be called My Settings in Salesforce Classic.

The Settings menu is where you customize Salesforce according to your individual preferences. You can decide to show only certain information on pages, synchronize your Salesforce data with your email program, set how often you want to get Chatter updates, and work with Salesforce while you're not connected to the Internet.

Salesforce makes it easy for you to better personalize your system by providing all your setup tools in one area.

To locate and navigate you're the Settings area, follow these steps:

1. **Click your photo or avatar in the upper-right corner of any page, and select the Settings link.**

   The Personal Information page opens with your user information on the page and the Settings menu appears in the left-hand sidebar, as shown in Figure 4-2.

   The Settings menu lists each of its main headings in the expandable sidebar. You can also use the Quick Find search bar above the menu headings to find what you're looking for quickly, but we like to use the sidebar so that we don't get lost.

2. **Click each of the section headings to expand them and see the full range of options (see Figure 4-3).**

   Subsections appear. The body of the page doesn't change if you simply expand the section within the sidebar.

3. **Click any subsection.**

   The page for that subsection appears.

4. **Click any other section heading to open that heading's page.**

   You've mastered basic navigation in the Settings menu.

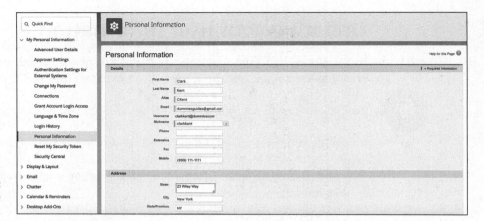

**FIGURE 4-2:**
Looking over the
Settings menu.

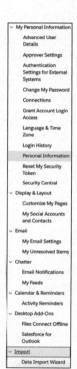

**FIGURE 4-3:**
Expanding the
sections.

# Modifying Your Personal Information

Under the My Personal Information heading, you can keep your user record current, grant your administrator login access (to login as you and troubleshoot a problem), and even change your password.

# Updating your user information

In Salesforce, you have a user record that corresponds to you. You can use that record to keep other users up to date on your contact information.

**TIP**

To find out how to navigate to the Settings area, see the preceding section.

To modify your user record, follow these steps:

1. **Click the My Personal Information heading on the sidebar (refer to Figure 4-2).**

   A series of options appears below the heading.

2. **Click the Advanced User Details subheading and click Edit.**

   Details of your user record appears in edit mode. Review the accuracy of your personal information and update it.

**REMEMBER**

   Especially if you travel frequently, make sure that you update your time zone both in Salesforce and on your laptop, reflecting your current location. This is particularly important if you're managing your schedule and synchronizing with offline tools, such as Outlook.

3. **When you're done, click Save.**

   Your user record appears again with the updated information.

# Customizing pages

You can personalize your display by changing the layout on a record page. Doing so enables you to see the most relevant sections first. For example, if you work in a call center, you may want to see cases at the top of your related lists on an account page.

To customize the display of a page, follow these steps:

1. **Click the Display & Layout heading on the Settings sidebar (refer to Figure 4-3).**

   The Display & Layout section expands on the sidebar.

2. **Go to the Customize My Pages subsection and select a specific tab that you want to modify (the Accounts tab, for example). Then click the Customize Page button.**

   The default Selected List shows the related lists (and their order) that display on the page you selected. Salesforce pregroups its standard related lists on pages based on various common business processes. Depending on your business, having these related lists visible may be perfect, or you may want to see more or fewer of them.

3. **Use the Add or Remove arrow buttons to highlight a tab and then add it to or remove it from your display, respectively, as shown in Figure 4-4.**

   For example, if you sell directly to customers, you may want to remove the Partners related list from the Account's Selected List column.

4. **Use the up and down arrows to change the order of how the items will appear on your page layout.**

5. **When you're done, click Save.**

   The Change My Display page reappears, and your pages reflect the changes.

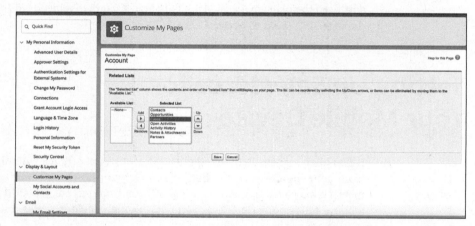

**FIGURE 4-4:** Modifying your related lists.

## Granting login access

When you need help from your administrator, Salesforce.com customer support, or customer support from a third-party AppExchange package that was installed in your environment, you can grant any of these folks temporary login access to your account. By gaining access to your account, the person helping you can provide better assistance from your perspective, because she can view your pages as you do.

To grant login access, follow these steps:

1. **Click the Grant Account Login Access subheading from the My Personal Information section of the Settings sidebar (refer to Figure 4-3).**

   The Grant Account Login Access page appears.

2. **Grant support and/or administrator access for a duration of up to one year by selecting the appropriate time frame from the Access Duration picklist.**

   Your administrator, Salesforce.com support, or the AppExchange vendor's support contact will be able to log in as you through the expiration date.

3. **When you're done, click the Save button.**

   The page reloads and your changes are saved.

TIP

If you're an administrator and a user has granted you access, you can log in to the user's account as follows: Click the gear icon located in the top-right of any page, and click Setup to open the Setup menu in Lightning. In the Setup sidebar, under the Administration section, click the Users heading and then select Users. From the list of users displayed, click the Login link to the left of the user's name. If you don't see the user, make sure the list view of users displayed (in the picklist above the user list) is set to Active Users.

# Setting Up Salesforce for Your Mobile Device

It feels like a given that any application you frequently use will also be accessible from your mobile device. Whether you're flying to Hong Kong for an important meeting and need to update critical information on your tablet, or you're in a cab looking up a contact's address on your phone, Salesforce was built with the user in mind to accomplish these tasks.

## Downloading and installing Salesforce on your mobile device

In today's world of tablets and mobile devices, you can be anywhere and access Salesforce. To best experience Salesforce from your mobile device, find the Salesforce app in the iTunes App Store (if you're an iPhone user) or the Google Play marketplace (if you're on the Android operating system). They're free to download and you get instant access to your most-viewed Accounts, Contacts, Opportunities, Cases, Leads, and any other custom tabs specific to your company.

REMEMBER

The downloadable Salesforce app is supported on Android 5.0 operating system or later and iOS 11.3 or later.

To download and install Salesforce on iOS via the App Store, follow these steps:

1. **From the home screen of your iPhone or iPad, select the App Store icon.**

   The App Store home page appears.

2. **In the Search field, type Salesforce.**

   A list of search results appears.

3. **Select the Salesforce app in the list of search results.**

   The Salesforce app page appears.

4. **Tap Get to install the app.**

   You may have to enter your iTunes account/Apple ID and password for the download to begin.

   The download begins and finishes, and the app appears on your home screen.

5. **Select the Salesforce icon on your home screen and click I Agree.**

   You're prompted to enter your Salesforce account's username and password.

6. **Select Login once you're done to enter Salesforce and get started.**

Now that you've installed Salesforce on your device, let's talk about the configuration options you have to make it your own.

## Configuring the Salesforce mobile app for your needs

Much of the Salesforce mobile app at this point is just enabling it for your users and organization. However, there are a few things you can customize and tweak to make it easy and efficient to work in the field. You can define the users who can access Salesforce app, customize how data appears in it, create actions to add new records, and tweak it to make it match the look and feel of your company's branding. Let's look at how to find and accomplish some of these configurations.

Salesforce makes this customization simple by giving administrators the Salesforce Mobile Quick Start wizard, which guides users with step-by-step customization options (from the full site, on your computer) to make sure admins don't overlook any features.

To start configuring the Salesforce app, click the gear icon located at the top-right of your page, and click Setup to open the Setup menu in Lightning. In the Setup sidebar, under the Platform Tools section, click the Apps heading, select Mobile Apps, then Salesforce, and then follow these steps:

1. **Click Salesforce Mobile Quick Start from the Setup left-hand sidebar (see Figure 4-5).**

   The Salesforce Mobile Quick Start page appears.

2. **Click the Launch Quick Start Wizard button.**

   The Quick Start Wizard home page appears.

3. **Click Let's Get Started.**

   In the first step, you can set up the left-hand navigation menu for your users in the Salesforce mobile app. You can reorder or remove items using a drag-and-drop interface.

4. **Click Save and Next to move onto arranging your Global Actions.**

   Global Actions allow users to create new records quickly and easily, but these records aren't tied to any other records in Salesforce. For example, an Opportunity record won't be automatically tied to an Account record. For more information about global actions and how to create them, see Chapter 17.

5. **Click Save and Next and then Create Compact Layout to move onto creating a compact layout.**

   The compact layout used by Salesforce determines which key fields will be displayed at the top of the record detail display on the app. For example, you can choose to display a Contact's name, email, and phone number at the top of your contact records in the Salesforce mobile app for quick viewing.

6. **When you're finished, click Save and Next to preview your basic configuration thus far.**

   Here you can look at different aspects of your configuration and see a simulation of the mobile app.

7. **After previewing what Salesforce will look like, click Next to invite some pilot users to take a test drive and give you feedback.**

   This page allows you to email those users directly. Start typing their names in the To field and, if they exist in Salesforce, they'll be suggested as you type (see Figure 4-6).

8. **Click Send, Next, and then Finish when you're done.**

   Congratulations! The basic setup of Salesforce is complete and you're taken back to the Salesforce Mobile Quick Start. Now you can configure some other aspects of the app, such as in-app or push notifications, the appearance and branding of the app, or user access to it.

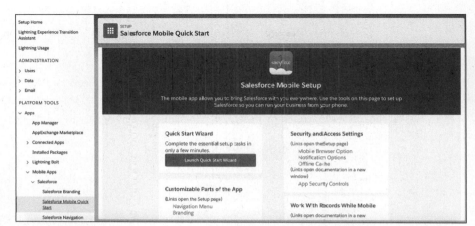

**FIGURE 4-5:**
Using the Salesforce Mobile Quick Start menu.

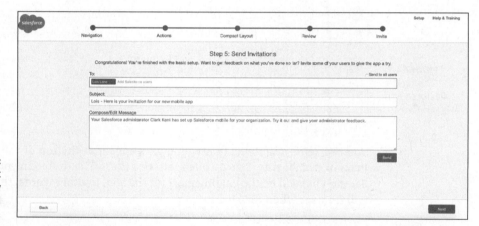

**FIGURE 4-6:**
Inviting pilot users to try Salesforce and provide feedback.

## Navigating in the Salesforce mobile app

The Salesforce application is very easy to navigate and was designed in a way that is similar to many other apps you probably use. Let's look at a few navigation tips and tools to get you well on your way to using the app like a pro.

The Salesforce Navigation menu is where you should begin. You can toggle the navigation menu by selecting the menu icon on the top-left of the app (see Figure 4-7).

**REMEMBER**

The Navigation menu is customizable, so if the default configuration doesn't meet your organization's needs, you can change the items that appear and the order in which they do.

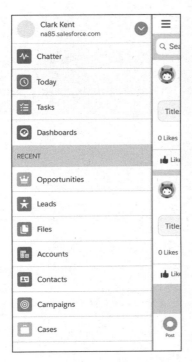

**FIGURE 4-7:**
Using the
Salesforce App
Navigation menu.

You can select the items that will always appear at the top of the menu, such as tasks or dashboards. This is called the *selected list.* The first item you choose for the Selected list will be the landing page for the app. In other words, that's what users will first see when they log in.

TIP

Keep user adoption in mind when setting up your Navigation menu. Put the items that users will use most often at the top of the list, because the Navigation menu is not user-specific and the entire organization will see the same Selected list.

Under the Selected list, you see a Recent list, which shows you the most recent objects you've accessed, either on the browser or mobile version of Salesforce.

Finally, the last section is the Apps menu.

REMEMBER

Anything that is represented as a tab in Salesforce can be visible to a user in the Navigation menu. Users can only see the tabs and items in the Navigation menu that they have permission to access via their Salesforce profiles.

To customize Salesforce navigation, go to the full site. click the gear icon, then Setup and follow these steps:

1. **Choose Apps ⇨ Mobile Apps ⇨ Salesforce ⇨ Salesforce Navigation.**

   The Mobile Navigation page appears.

2. **Use the Add and Remove arrows to move the items you want into or out of the Selected column. Use the Up and Down arrows to rearrange the order of the items in the list.**

   The item named Smart Search Items becomes your Recent list (discussed earlier) and expands into multiple items that you've recently accessed. Anything above the Smart Search Items element becomes part of the Selected list in the menu, and anything below it falls under the Apps list in the menu.

3. **When you're done, click Save to save your work.**

   Your navigation setup is complete! Now you can log in via your mobile device to see the changes you've made.

# Importing Your Contacts

One of the keys to making Salesforce productive for you from day 1 is to get your contacts into the system. If your contacts exist primarily in Microsoft Outlook, you may be better off synchronizing your data. Otherwise, Salesforce provides easy-to-use wizards that help you import contacts and accounts. See Chapter 9 for the details on importing, and see your administrator if your data goes beyond the limits of the Import wizard. (For example, if you have historical activity linked to contacts, you can't import those records by using standard wizards.)

# Working with Salesforce Remotely

For all companies, email is still a critical piece of the workday: It's how people communicate with customers and schedule meetings. For many companies, Microsoft Outlook is still the leading email software. Salesforce lets you synchronize with Outlook so that key conversations or meetings in Outlook can be reflected and saved in Salesforce. And if you're a road warrior as well, Salesforce provides various ways to log in from your mobile device and close that deal, without having to squint too much looking at that smaller screen.

It's important to make sure reps are productive and have the tools they need, no matter where they are, to get the job done. Integrating Outlook and Salesforce makes sure reps don't spend valuable time entering data twice in two different applications. Outlook Integration and Lightning Sync are the new and improved Outlook integration products replacing what was previously knows as Salesforce for Outlook. Outlook Integration and Lightning Sync work together to super charge your reps' productivity. Let's briefly look at both of these tools, their capabilities, and their added value.

Outlook Integration lets you associate important emails to Salesforce records. That alone means a few important things: first, no more switching between two applications. Second, no more manually logging emails or activity in Salesforce, and third, others on the sales team are able to see relevant emails and important details that may have been hiding in one person's inbox. The integration also works the other way — reps can view or update pertinent Salesforce data directly from their Outlook inbox and don't have to leave their emails or lose their train of thought.

Lightning Sync allows you to sync Contacts and Events between Microsoft Exchange and Salesforce automatically or manually – it's your choice. Admins can define sync settings for reps, such as which records to sync, which direction to sync (for example, syncing Contacts from Office to Salesforce or syncing them both ways), and what happens when a record is deleted in Outlook or in Salesforce. Regardless of the settings you choose, Lightning Sync allows reps the freedom to focus on sales and minimizes both duplicate data entry as well as the eventual errors that come with it.

TIP

If you're the administrator responsible for maintaining accurate data in Salesforce, encourage your company to adopt Salesforce as the system of record or "the single source of truth" for customer interactions. For example, tell users to make updates to accounts and contacts in Salesforce rather than in Outlook. Then have them configure Outlook Integration to allow Salesforce to win if a data conflict occurs between Salesforce and Outlook. By doing this, you can reduce common synchronization issues and influence greater Salesforce adoption.

In most cases, installing Outlook Integration and Lightning Sync is a simple process. If you connect to the Internet via a proxy server or if your company has a firewall, you may want to consult with your IT department.

IN THIS CHAPTER

» **Understanding common Salesforce record behaviors**

» **Efficiently detailing the record page**

» **Logging your work**

» **Emailing in Salesforce**

» **Finding help and setup options**

# Chapter **5**

# Working in Salesforce

I n Salesforce, there are common ways that records behave, and there are common things you can do when you're on a specific record. Even if different companies use Salesforce for very different business processes, there's still a fundamental commonality of creating a new record, and tracking something someone did, in order to get the benefit of collaboration and using Salesforce as a source of truth.

By managing activities in Salesforce, for example, you can better coordinate with your team, quickly assess what's going on in your accounts, and focus on the next steps to close deals or solve issues.

In this chapter, you find out how to create records, manage your activities, and send emails from within Salesforce. Finally, we cover where you can go for help.

## Managing Records

By using the + New drop-down option on any tab on the navigation bar on the top of any page in Salesforce, you can easily add new records into Salesforce. You may find yourself in the position of having deleted important records. Don't worry — Salesforce gives you a way to put them back in their rightful spots before anyone notices that they're missing.

## Creating records

To create a record (by using Contacts as the example), follow these steps (which can be applied to all + New *Items* on the navigation bar):

**1.** **From the navigation bar, click the drop-down menu to the right of the Contact tab and select the + New Contact option, as shown in Figure 5-1.**

A New Contact window appears in Edit mode.

**2.** **Complete the fields, as necessary.**

Make sure you fill in the required fields, which are the ones with the red asterisks to the left of the field name.

**3.** **When you're done, click Save.**

The Contact detail page appears. Here, you can begin tracking information.

**FIGURE 5-1:** Creating records by using the Create New drop-down list.

## Resurrecting records from the Recycle Bin

Occasionally, you delete a record and regret it. Don't panic — the Salesforce Recycle Bin gives you 15 days to restore recently deleted records, including any associated records (such as activities deleted in the process) and your credibility.

*Important:* As of the time of publication, the Recycle Bin feature is currently not available directly in the Lightning Experience. To access a deleted record, you will need to revert back to the Classic UI. Go back to the Classic UI by clicking your profile icon in the upper-right of the screen and selecting Switch to Salesforce Classic under the Options section. If you don't see the Switch to Salesforce Classic link, get ahold of your administrator — you may have had a permission taken away that allows you to see this link.

To restore a deleted record, follow these steps from Salesforce Classic:

**1.** **On your sidebar, click the Recycle Bin link.**

The Recycle Bin page appears. If you're an administrator, use the View picklist to view and restore records deleted within the last 15 days by other users.

**2.** Navigate the list as you would a normal list page until you find the desired record or records.

**3.** Select the check box(es) in the Action column corresponding to the record(s) that you want to restore.

You can click the Select All link to select all the records on the page.

TIP

**4.** When you're done, click the Undelete button.

The Recycle Bin page reappears, and a link to your restored record appears in the sidebar below Recent Items.

There is a maximum amount of space that the Recycle Bin can contain, before it starts automatically deleting the oldest files first, as long as they're at least two hours old. The space is 25 times your organization's total megabytes (MB) of storage, which you can find by choosing Setup ⇨ Administer ⇨ Data Management ⇨ Storage Usage.

TECHNICAL
STUFF

# Detailing the Record

After you create and save a record, the record appears on its own detail page (see Figure 5-2 for an example using the Contact object). You can use the detail page to update the record's detail fields or manage and track activities and common operations on the related lists displayed below the highlights panel. In this section, we show you how to navigate the detail page.

**FIGURE 5-2:**
Looking over the detail page of a new Contact record.

**TIP**

Some of the features that we describe in the following sections may not be enabled by default in your organization. If you can't locate what we're talking about, have your administrator choose Setup⇨Platform Tools⇨User Interface⇨User Interface to turn on any of these capabilities.

## Using links and buttons on the record page

From any record's page, you can use links and buttons to perform different actions. In LEX, Salesforce has moved record-specific buttons to the upper-right area of the highlights panel. Custom links appear in the Details subsection of a record. Go to any page and try these out:

>> **Edit a field.** From the Details subsection of a record, if you hover your mouse over any field and a pencil icon appears, you can double click that field to enter Edit mode for the record, so you can make that change (if you have permission to do so). Click the Cancel button to return to the detail page, or click Save to save the record.

>> **Edit a record.** Click the Edit button in the upper right area to edit several fields in the record (if you have permission to do so). The record appears in Edit mode. Click the Cancel button to return to the detail page, or click Save to save the record.

>> **Delete the current record.** Click the Delete button to delete the current record that you're viewing (if you have permission to do so). Click the Cancel button in the pop-up window if you change your mind about the deletion.

>> **Use related list quick links to jump to the corresponding related list.** This feature is not available by default in LEX, as the UI was re-designed to minimize vertical scrolling. Salesforce realizes that some of you have a lot of related lists to wade through (and may have a slight case of FOMO (Fear of Missing Out)), so related list quick links can still be added to your page layout. See Chapter 17, "Performing Common Configurations" to learn how to add the Related List Quick Links Lightning component to your Lightning record pages layouts. Once these links are visible on your page, note that the label for each link consists of the name of that type of record, as well as the number of records that are related. So, when you're looking at an Account detail page, instead of scrolling down the page to see whether any contacts exist, you can see how many exist right at the top. But wait, it gets better: You

can click the link and immediately jump to the part of the record page to where that related list is normally found.

» **View a printable version of the page in a new window.** Click the Printable View link in the upper right, and then click the Print This Page link in the upper-right corner of the window to print a copy of the entire page. Believe it or not, some users still like to print good old-fashioned hard copies that they can review while traveling (hey, we can't always assume great access to the Internet or a cellular connection).

## Modifying records with inline editing

To cut down on the number of steps you have to take when you update records in Salesforce, you can edit fields directly in detail pages.

**TECHNICAL STUFF**

Make sure that your administrator has enabled this feature.

Follow these steps to edit a field directly from the Details subsection of a record's page. Salesforce calls this *inline editing.*

1. **Hover your mouse over any field on a record that you own (or have permission to edit).**

   Figure 5-3 shows the email address of a contact within a company being updated.

   An icon appears to the right of a field, telling you whether you can edit that field. Here's what the various icons mean:

   - *Pencil:* This icon appears to the right of editable fields, which become highlighted.

   - *Padlock:* This icon appears to the right of fields that you can't edit.

   - *None:* You can edit a field that doesn't have an icon, but not with the inline editing feature. You have to edit the record the old-fashioned way, using the Edit button.

2. **Double-click an editable field and update the information in that field.**

3. **Move your mouse away from the field to complete editing that field.**

4. **After you finish editing all the fields you want for that record, click the Save button for the record.**

**TECHNICAL STUFF**

If you happen to change your mind after editing a field but can't remember what data was in there before, you have some hope before saving the record. Click on any whitespace away from the field, and the field you just edited will be highlighted in yellow to show that it's been changed. Click the Undo arrow icon just to the upper-right of the field (it looks like a left U-turn arrow) to revert that field's data back to what it was before editing.

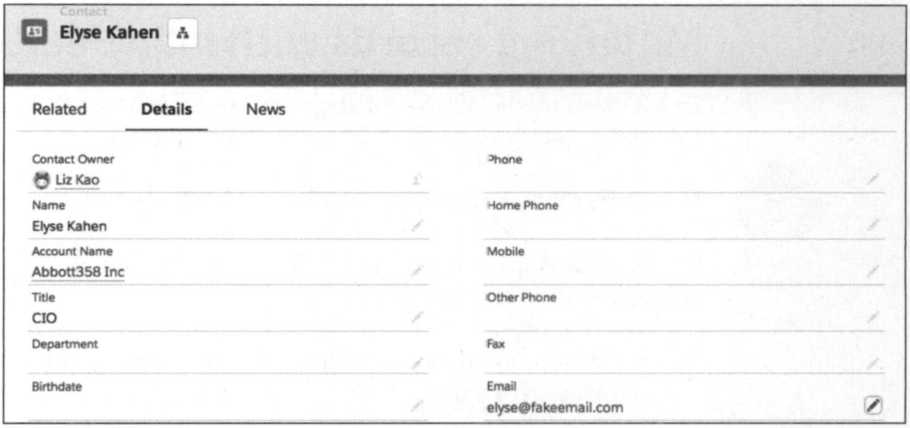

---

Contact

📇 **Elyse Kahen**  ⚛

Related    **Details**    News

Contact Owner
🔵 Liz Kao                                     Phone

Name                                          Home Phone
Elyse Kahen

Account Name                                  Mobile
Abbott358 Inc

Title                                         Other Phone
CIO

Department                                    Fax

Birthdate                                     Email
                                              elyse@fakeemail.com   ✎

**FIGURE 5-3:**
Editing a field inline.

---

## Capitalizing on related lists

*Related lists.* Say it three times so you don't forget the term. By designing the page with related lists grouped into sections called *cards*, Salesforce enables you to gain 360-degree customer visibility and ensure that more detailed information is only a click away. For example, if you open an Account record page for one of your major customers and look below the highlights panel, you can see a sample of Contacts, Activities, Opportunities, Cases, Notes, and so on grouped as related lists under the Related subsection. And if you don't see these cards, you have work to do.

## Looking things up with lookup hovers

On any record page, you can hover your mouse over any field that looks like a link with a dotted underline below the field's content, to get a pop-up preview of that other record's contents. Figure 5-4 shows a preview of the Account record by hovering over a Contact's company name.

A *lookup field* is any field that actually links to another record. A lookup field's content is underlined to show that it acts as a link to another record.

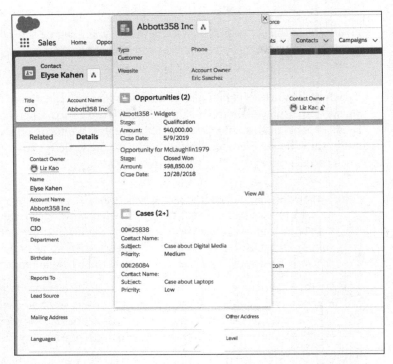

**FIGURE 5-4:** Hovering over a lookup field provides a preview of that record.

# Reviewing Activities

*Activities* in Salesforce are scheduled calendar events and tasks. In many ways, the Events and Tasks in Salesforce are just like the activities you use in Microsoft Outlook, Google Calendar, or any other productivity application. You can schedule events on your calendar, invite people to meetings, sync your Microsoft or Google calendar appointments with Salesforce, and add tasks to your to-do lists so that you don't forget to get things done.

However, Salesforce takes activities further: You can easily link Events and Tasks to other related records, such as Accounts, Contacts, and so on. You can view activities both in the context of a relevant item (for example, all activities that relate to an Account) and as a stand-alone from your Today's Events and Today's Tasks areas in the comfort and convenience of your home page. And, if you're a manager or in operations, Salesforce allows you to stay up to speed on your teams and how they're spending their time, and hopefully find some correlations between customer interactions and won deals.

You can use activities in Salesforce to track all the significant tasks and events involved in acquiring, selling, and servicing customers. Think about all the actions that you and your teams perform to accomplish your job — meetings, calls, emails, even the occasional physical letter — and imagine the value of having the pertinent interactions in one place at your fingertips. You can have such a place in Salesforce, and you can easily link your activities together in an organized fashion.

Salesforce features several types of activities that you can access from the Activity subsection displayed on many of the major records, including Accounts, Contacts, Leads, Opportunities, and Cases. In this chapter, we focus on Events and Tasks, but in the following list, we briefly explain all the various activity records you can track in Salesforce:

>> **Task:** Essentially a to-do. Use this activity record as your online yellow sticky note. It's an activity that needs to be completed, but it doesn't need a specific time or duration associated with it. For example, if you know that you're supposed to follow up with a Contact by researching some product information, you can create a task such as Confirm product minimum requirements.

>> **Event:** A calendared activity. An Event has a scheduled time, date, and duration associated with it. It can also have invitees associated with it, as well as be a recurring thing that happens on a regular basis. Examples of common events are meetings, conference calls, and tradeshows.

>> **Log a Call:** A task record of a completed call — but you don't have to use it always for calls. Use Log a Call during or after a call, or any completed Task, to make sure that you capture important details. For example, use it when a contact calls you and you want to record comments or outcomes from the discussion. This saves you a step from creating a new Task and then changing its status to Completed.

>> **Send an Email:** Logs an activity for an email that you send to a Contact or a Lead. You can send emails from Salesforce or a third-party email product, and capture that information directly inside Salesforce.

# Creating Activities

Before you can begin managing your time or activities in Salesforce, you need to know the easiest and most reliable way to add Events and Tasks.

## Creating an Event

When you want to schedule activities that have a particular place, time, and duration, use Event records. By using Event records, you and your sales teams can keep better track of your calendars.

You can create an Event from the Activity subsection of a record. The best method to choose often depends on what you're doing. If you're carving out meetings on a specific day, add Events from your calendar, which you can access from the Calendar tab on the navigation bar.If you're working on a customer deal, you might create the Event from an Opportunity record. The end result is the same.

**TIP**

If you're just getting accustomed to filling out records in Salesforce, create Events from the record that's most directly associated with the Event. By using this method, many of the lookup fields are prefilled for you. So, when you save, you ensure that you can find the activity quickly because it's linked to all the right records.

To create an Event from a relevant record (such as a Contact or Account record), follow these steps:

**1. Enter a name in the search field in the upper-middle part of every page. Select the record to which you want to link the Event.**

For example, if you want to schedule a meeting about an Account, you search for the Account name.

When you click Search, a Search Results page appears.

**2. Click the name of the particular record you want.**

The record's detail page appears.

**3. Go to the Activity subsection that's usually in the right sidebar below the highlights panel. Click the New Event subtab, as shown in Figure 5-5.**

A New Event page appears. If you created this Event from a relevant record, the name of the person or the related record is prefilled for you.

**4. Fill in the relevant fields.**

Pay close attention to the required fields highlighted with a red asterisk. Depending on your company's customization, your Event record may differ from the standard, but here are tips on some of the standard fields:

- *Assigned To:* Defaults to you. Use the 'x' icon to remove your name and type in another user's name, to assign the Event to another user.

- *Subject:* The Event's subject, which appears on the calendar. Click the magnifying glass icon. A drop-down list appears, displaying a list of your company's Event types. When you click a selection your selection appears in the Subject field (LK Note: this last sentence seems super obvious to me in 2019. . . . Can we remove it? "ok – Liz"). To the immediate right of your selection's text, customize the subject by adding a brief description.

- *Related To:* The standard Event record shows two drop-down lists that you can use to link the Event with relevant records, as shown in Figure 5-6. One relates to certain types of records — an Account, Opportunity, or Case. The other relates to a person — a Contact or Lead. First, select the type of record and then use the associated magnifying glass icon to select the desired record. For example, if you select Opportunity from the first drop-down list, you can use the Opportunity icon to find a specific account.

If you use the Related To fields on activities, you'll rarely have problems finding an activity later. For example, if you sell through channel partners, you might associate a meeting with a partner Contact, but you might relate the meeting to an end-customer Account. When you save the Event, it appears on the related lists of both records.

- *Time:* Allows you to specify the start time and end time. You can use basic shorthand and avoid unnecessary keystrokes. For example, type **9a** for 9:00 a.m. or **2p** for 2:00 p.m.

**5.** **Click Save.**

The page you started from reappears, and the Event appears under the Activity subsection within the Next Steps portion of the sidebar. The event also appears on the home page of the user assigned to the event, on the day of the Event.

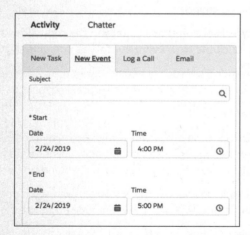

**FIGURE 5-5:**
Creating an Event.

**FIGURE 5-6:**
Linking the Event to related records.

**TECHNICAL STUFF**

Salesforce also allows syncing of select calendar Events from your Microsoft or Google calendars into Salesforce. You'll need to get your team responsible for setting up and maintaining emails involved in evaluating the options here. Reach out to your Salesforce account executive for more details and to see if this could work for your organization.

## Creating a Task

Some sales reps refer to Tasks as action items; others call them reminders or to-dos. Whatever your favorite term, use Task records when you want to remind yourself or someone else of an activity that needs to get done.

You can create a Taskfrom the Tasks tab of the navigation bar where you can access the + New Task option from the Task's drop-down menu or from the Activity subsection on any page within Salesforce. We use both methods, depending on whether we're planning out our weeks or strategizing about a particular Account, Contact, or other record.

To create a Task from the relevant record, follow these steps:

1. **Enter a name in the search bar for the record to which you want to link the Task and click the magnifying glass icon.**

   For example, if you want to set a Task to review a proposal that relates to an Opportunity, search for the Opportunity name.

2. **Click the name of the record you want.**

   The record's detail page appears.

3. **Select New Task from the Activity, as shown in Figure 5-7.**

   New Task related fields appear in the sidebar.

**TIP**

   When creating Tasks, go to the record that the Task is most directly related to before adding the Task. By taking this path, you ensure that your Task is easy to find because it's automatically associated with the correct record. For example, if you're creating a Task to follow up on an email to a Contact, you most likely add the Task from the Contact record.

4. **Fill in the relevant fields.**

   Like the Event record, your fields may vary, but here are some tips on adding a Task:

   - *Assigned To:* Defaults to you. Remove your name and type in another person's name to select them instead.

   - *Subject:* The Task's subject, which appears on the Today's Tasks section of the Assigned To's home page. Click the magnifying glass icon to see a drop-down list of your company's activity types. When you click a selection, the selection appears in the Subject field.

   - *Related To:* Shows two drop-down lists that you can use to link the Task with relevant records similar to the Event fields. First, select the type of record, and then use the associated magnifying glass icon to select the desired record.

   - *Status:* Defines the status of the Task.

   - *Due Date:* The date by which you expect the Task to be completed. This is typically optional. Clicking your cursor in this field makes a calendar window pop up; you can select a date from this calendar.

5. **Click Save.**

   The page that you started from reappears, and the Task displays under the Activity subsection within the Next Steps portion of the sidebar. The Task also appears in the Today's Tasks section of the home page of the user who's assigned to the Task.

**TIP**

Make sure that you set your Today's Tasks view on the home page so that your Tasks are included in the filter. The view defaults to Today's Tasks, which can confuse some people when they don't see a recently created Task in that area.

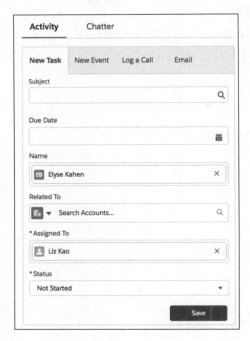

**REMEMBER**

Always link your Tasks with the relevant records in Salesforce. Otherwise, you run the risk of losing valuable customer information that might have been captured in that Task.

## Logging a call

Sometimes, you perform a task and just want to log the activity after the fact. For example, a Contact calls you on the phone, or you get stopped in the coffee room by your boss to talk about a customer issue. In these situations, instead of creating a Task, saving it, and then completing it, use the Log a Call feature.

When you click the Log a Call subtag, you're simply creating a task record that has a Completed Activity Status. To log a call, go to the record that the call relates to (an Account or Lead record, for example) and follow these steps:

1.  **Find the Activity subsection below the highlights panel and click the Log a Call subtab.**

    Log a Call fields appear in the sidebar.

2. **Fill out or modify any of the fields to log the call.**

   The Status field is preset to Completed, and thus isn't exposed, as shown in Figure 5-8.

3. **Click Save when you're finished.**

   The detail page that you started from reappears. The call record appears under the Activity subsection within the Past Activities portion of the sidebar.

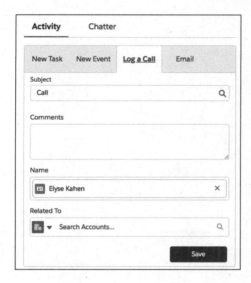

**FIGURE 5-8:**
Logging a call.

As an alternative to the Notes feature in Salesforce to track details of your interactions with customers and prospects, consider using Log a Call to record this type of information.

# Organizing and Viewing Activities

You can view your activities from the home page and from a specific record's Activity subsection where you see Next Steps and Past Activities.

After you create (or are assigned to) activities, you probably want to view them so that you can prioritize and complete them.

**TIP**

On the home page, change the default view in the Today's Tasks section to My Tasks or to Today, depending on how efficient you are, so that you can see all tasks that you still need to complete. The current default view, Today's Tasks, only shows you open tasks or ones where a due date is set for today, which we have found to not be many users' first choice.

If you're planning around a specific record, such as a contact or opportunity, you can view linked activities from the Activity subsection located on a sidebar of a record's page.

The Next Steps and Past Activities lists work hand in hand. An event record automatically moves from the Next Steps to Past Activities when the scheduled date and time pass. A task record remains on the Next Steps section until its Status is changed to Completed; then the record appears on the Past Activities section.

To view activities from a detail page, follow these steps:

1. **Open a saved record.**

   The detail page of the record appears. The highlights panel appears at the top, and the Related and Detail subsections are just below that.

2. **Note the Activity subsection in the right sidebar, also below the highlights panel.**

   See the Task and Event creation subtabs in this subsection. Below that, see the Next Steps and Past Activities section. If you already created related activities, activity links appear in the sections.

3. **Click the Subject of one of the activities.**

   The activity record appears. You can also expand details of the activity by clicking on the activity type icon to expand and hide more information.

# Updating Activities

Things happen: Meetings get canceled, and small tasks suddenly become big priorities. With Salesforce, you can perform many of the actions that a normal time-management tool would allow you to do, including delegating activities to other users, rescheduling, editing information, deleting records, and so on.

You can do the following basic functions by clicking the drop-down menu to the right of any activity record:

>> **Edit:** Update any of the fields in the record whose fields now appear, and make sure that you save.

>> **Edit Comments:** Add some more details or notes about what occurred during this activity.

>> **Delete:** Delete the record. A pop-up window appears in which you can confirm the deletion.

>> **Create a Follow Up Task:** Generate a related task. A New Task page opens, prefilled with information from the prior record.

>> **Create a Follow Up Event:** Schedule a related meeting. A New Event page appears, prefilled with information from the prior record.

>> **Change Status:** Update the status of an activity without having to go to another page.

## Assigning activities

Sometimes, you may create activities and assign them to others (intentionally, not because you're trying to shirk your duties). Sales development reps often do this as they set up meetings for their account executives. Salesforce lets you easily reassign tasks and events.

To assign an activity, locate the activity in the Activity subsection and follow these steps:

1. **Click the drop-down menu to the right of the activity, and select the Edit option.**

   A pop-up window appears, displaying the record in edit mode.

2. **Click the 'x' to the right of the Assigned To user to remove that user. Then search for People by typing a name in the field.**

   Salesforce will suggest some users to select as it tries to auto-complete and anticipate what you are typing.

3. **Use the Search field to search for the user or select the user from the list.**

4. **Click Save.**

   The activity record reappears within the Activity subsection, and the Assigned To field has been modified.

## Completing a Task

When you're done with a Task, you want to gladly get it off the list of things to do. You can mark a Task as complete from your Activity subsection's Next Steps area where the Task is displayed.

To complete a Task, follow these steps:

1. **If you're viewing the Task from the Next Steps section, click the check box to the left of the Task. If you're looking at the Task on the home page, also click the check box.**

   Both actions have the same result when clicked: The Task's name gets crossed off and the Status field changes to Completed. (Your company might have its own terminology for the Completed status.)

2. **From the Activity subsection, add additional comments and click Save.**

   Use the drop-down menu at the right of any Activity to select Edit Comments to add relevant new information. The detail page reappears, and the completed Task now appears under the Past Activities list.

# Understanding Email Fields in Salesforce

Email is a fundamental method for communicating with customers, prospects, and friends. By using email correctly, you can better manage your sales territory and be more responsive to customers. However, by not using email appropriately, you can leave a bad impression or lose a client.

If email is an indispensable part of your business, you and other users can send email from Salesforce and track the communication history from relevant records, such as Leads, Accounts, Contacts, Opportunities, and Cases. This capability is helpful if you inherit a major customer Account, because you can potentially view all the email interactions from a single account record.

In this section, we discuss options for sending a basic email, mass emailing, and using templates.

An email in Salesforce is an activity record comprising fields for the message and for the people you want to keep in the loop on the message.

The email record comes with standard fields that people commonly use when sending email. Most fields are self-explanatory, but the following list summarizes some additional fields:

>> **Related To:** Use this field to relate the email to an account, opportunity, campaign, case, or other standard or custom object record in Salesforce, depending on your edition. By completing this field, the email is stored under the Past Activities list of that record.

>> **To and CC:** Similar to writing an email from your corporate email, use these fields to type in primary and additional recipients. They don't have to be contacts or leads in Salesforce.

>> **Attach File:** Of course, you know what an email attachment is, but we want to let you know that the size limit is 10MB per email message within Salesforce.

# Setting Up Your Email

Before you begin emailing people from Salesforce, check out a couple of setup options that can save you time and headaches. In the following sections, we show you how to personalize your outbound email, and options to consider for creating personal email templates for common messages that you send to people.

## Personalizing your email settings

When you send an email via Salesforce, the recipient can receive the message just as if you sent the email from your standard email program. The email message appears as if it came from your business email address, and you can use a standard signature to go with your message. And if the recipient replies to your email, that reply email comes right to your standard email inbox. To pull this off, though, you need to personalize your email settings in Salesforce.

*Note:* Send emails from Salesforce judiciously. Salesforce provides this option to send low volumes of emails.

To set up your email, follow these steps:

**1.** **From the upper-right of any page, click on your user icon and choose Settings ⇨ Email ⇨ My Email Settings.**

The My Email Settings page appears in Edit mode.

2. **Modify the first two required fields, as necessary, to specify the outgoing name and the return email address.**

3. **Select the Yes radio button if you want to send a blind carbon copy (BCC) to your standard email inbox.**

   That way, you can still keep emails in customer folders in your email application.

4. **Modify the Email Signature field.**

   If you're personalizing your email settings for the first time, you might notice a default signature from Salesforce. This message appears at the bottom of your email in lieu of your signature.

5. **Click Save.**

   A confirmation message appears noting that your settings have been successfully saved.

# Building personal email templates

If you ask your top sales reps about sending email, they'll probably tell you that they don't reinvent the wheel every time they send certain messages to customers. It's a waste of their time, and time is money. Instead, they use templates and form letters to send the same message with less work.

In your standard sales process, you probably send a variety of emails to customers, including

>> Letters of introduction

>> Thank-you notes

>> Responses to common objections

>> Answers on competition

Although you do need to personalize a message to fit the specific details of a customer, you probably use certain effective phrases and sentences over and over again. Instead of searching for a prior message and cutting and pasting, you can create personal email templates and improve your productivity.

Over time, Salesforce and third-party vendors have created the ability to build and manage these templates outside of Salesforce, with tight integration back into Salesforce so those activities are still logged in the CRM tool. These tools have become quite sophisticated over the years, and are able to handle high volumes of emails, accommodating custom cadences and email sequences, all while tracking when a recipient has received and opened the email.

As the technology and vendors here continue to evolve, we do not discuss the implementation details in this book. We do recommend you speak with your Salesforce account executive to understand what options Salesforce provides, as well as do your own research in the growing category of what at the time of this publication are called "email productivity" or "sales productivity" tools. Make sure you check the AppExchange (`https://appexchange.salesforce.com`) for options that integrate with Salesforce.

# Sending Email from Salesforce

You can send an email to any Lead or Contact stored in Salesforce with a valid email address. By sending from Salesforce, you can ensure that you and your team members can keep track of critical outbound communications to customers and prospects.

You can initiate your outbound email from many different records in Salesforce, including Opportunity, Account, Case, Campaign, Lead, and Contact records. To create and send an email, go to the relevant record and follow these steps:

1. **Click the Email subtab on the Activity subsection.**

   Email-related fields appear, as shown in Figure 5-9. The Email is in rich-text format.

2. **Type the recipient's name in the To field. Salesforce tries to match the email address with an existing person in the system, whose names appear in a drop-down list while you type. If there is no record that matches that email address, you can still send an email to that recipient.**

   Add additional recipients as needed.

**TIP**

   If you send an email from the relevant Lead or Contact record, you can eliminate or reduce the effort for this step because the To field is prefilled. But remember to use the Related To field to associate the email to other records, such as an Opportunity.

3. **Use the Related To drop-down list to associate the email with the correct type of record, and then click the magnifying glass icon to the right of the adjacent field to find the exact record.**

   Depending on which record you started from, the Related To drop-down list might already be filled.

4. **Clicking the CC link or the BCC link lets you copy other contacts or users to the email.**

   A CC (or BCC) field appears. Type in email addresses or names, and Salesforce's auto-complete will work to try to show you which names to enter into the fields.

5. **Complete the Subject and Body fields of the message and then click Send.**

   The record that you started from reappears, and a link to a copy of your email appears in the Past Activities lists of the Activity subsection for that record.

**FIGURE 5-9:** Composing an email.

# Getting Help and Set Up

In the upper-right corner of any Salesforce page are three critical lifeline links you need to remember. First is Help & Training, then Setup, and then your Personal Settings. In this section, we describe each of the links and the insights they give you.

You'll be able to administer and customize Salesforce for your company from Setup.

- **>> Help & Training:** Clicking the question mark icon pops open a window that contains a variety of educational resources on all things Salesforce. Salesforce groups the information into general Salesforce overviews as well as specific guidance for the page that you're on. If you've still got questions, there's even a search bar for accessing documentation, and a link for getting technical support and providing customer feedback.

- **>> Setup:** Click the gear icon with the lightning bolt in the center to access a drop-down list of administrator-focused options. Choose the Setup option to open a new browser window that takes you to the Setup home, which is every administrator's home base.

- **>> Personal Settings:** Click the Astro avatar to access your profile and related drop-down menu options. If you click your name, you'll go to your profile listing. Clicking Settings allows you to update your personal information. You can also choose the display density in which you'd like to see the text and layout in Salesforce, in case you have good eyesight and want less whitespace on your Salesforce pages. And if you really, positively, absolutely have to switch back to the old Classic UI, you can do that from here, too.

# Chapter **6**

# Collaborating in the Cloud

E very one of us has been the new guy or gal at a company at some point in our lives. Even if you received a formal orientation and a review of the organizational chart (a luxury that you shouldn't take for granted), do you remember still having to meander around, finding that person who has the answers? Or maybe you're an old-timer who is extremely busy but always willing to answer a newcomer's questions because you remember how overwhelming it was when you first started.

Organizations have huge amounts of varying types of knowledge: formal and informal, documented and verbal, current and outdated. Very rarely is knowledge shared in one centralized location. Even when a company is pretty diligent about communicating, the sheer volume of information and the speed at which current information gets outdated can be overwhelming. Chatter bridges the gap between sharing useful information and information overload by allowing you to communicate quickly with colleagues, as well as keep track of progress and updates on topics as they happen.

In this chapter, we discuss how Chatter, when used correctly, works to eliminate all that information chaos by providing a central place where Salesforce users can update statuses, post and respond to questions, and see recent activity on records to easily collaborate in a private and secure environment. We walk you through setting up your profile, updating your status, and using groups and feeds so that your sales, marketing, and customer service organizations can work together even more effectively, all in the new and improved Lightning Experience.

**TIP**

At the time of this writing, Chatter has three license types. A Salesforce license already comes with full Chatter features, but there are also three different Chatter-specific licenses for colleagues who don't need to be in Salesforce, yet could still benefit from collaborating with people who work in Salesforce often. The free license just lets users see status updates from others, but they can't click into any customer relationship management (CRM) tabs, like Accounts or Contacts. The external license is like the free license, but it's intended for customers and other external users. You can add them to specific Chatter groups for collaborative projects, but they can't see your Salesforce data. Chatter Only (or Chatter Plus) is available at an additional charge for users who may only need to see Accounts and Contacts, and some custom apps or objects, but not Opportunities. All these options are for colleagues who don't need to be in Salesforce but could still benefit from collaborating with people who work in Salesforce often. If you're a daily user of Salesforce, your license comes with Chatter.

**REMEMBER**

Each profile, group, and status update you make is a record in Salesforce, which adds to your data and storage usage numbers. Salesforce has also set some limits on the number of posts and comments that are stored in Salesforce (and for how long). It's usually not an issue, but if your organization has a bunch of die-hard super-users (and what organization doesn't?), always check with your account executive for more details.

# Preparing to Use Chatter

When you get a new car, it's tempting to just drive away as soon as you're handed the keys, but taking a few minutes to read the owner's manual may serve you better. The same holds true for Salesforce Chatter. By spending a little extra time preparing, you can ensure a successful implementation of this powerful feature and ensure your standing as a Salesforce hero in your company.

**TIP**

Here are some key actions that we recommend for every Chatter implementation:

>> **Get key executives of your organization to use Chatter.** Engage executives early, help them update their profiles (more on that later), and show them how easy it is to follow other employees. They'll love the communication-improvement aspect of Salesforce Chatter and will encourage their employees to post regular updates.

» **Allow the most informational objects to be followed.** If you have a popular product or brand, you may get hundreds of leads a day in Salesforce. Being able to track Chatter on leads is important, especially if you can selectively choose which records to monitor. Other types of records (such as Products) probably won't change that often and, thus, don't warrant tracking via Chatter. As part of your preparation, you have to determine which objects make sense to track for your business.

» **Prepare for the change.** Your organization may not have processes in place to provide routine updates to management. People naturally resist change, especially change that embraces sharing what they're doing. When you put together your communications plan introducing Salesforce Chatter, be sure to focus on the timesaving aspect and reassure people that it's not a surveillance tool used by Big Brother. It's meant to encourage collaboration.

» **Lead by example.** Show users how to find and follow your profile. Then be sure to post status updates about the work you're doing so that they can get a feel for how it works. You can even create polls via Chatter to encourage participation.

» **Establish basic posting guidelines.** Your colleagues may already be used to an informal posting functionality of social networking sites, but before they post personal information in Chatter, set some basic guidelines. Here are some ideas to get you started:

- Keep Chatter updates related to business matters.

- Don't post anything you wouldn't want to be seen by your CEO, HR department, or peers.

- Never post confidential information that isn't widely available elsewhere in your organization.

- Keep statements constructive and professional. Leave the flame wars and boorishness to anonymous forums.

» **Provide training sessions and FAQs.** Education is the key to success for any Salesforce implementation. Training and documentation not only improve adoption but also ensure that users make fewer mistakes. The same holds true for implementing Chatter. It might seem easy to "just turn it on," but if people aren't all on the same page on when and how to use the tool, information that's posted won't be helpful, which will affect adoption rates.

An FAQ list is a basic question-and-answer document that your users can reference. In addition to the previous guidelines, you can include sample status updates (good and bad ones) and instructions on common tasks. See Chapter 5 to find out how you can create a reusable email template that includes your FAQs and guidelines.

>> **Continue adoption.** When new employees join your company, be sure to bring them onboard them with training, and review your FAQs and Chatter guidelines with them. This will ensure that they continue the success of your Chatter implementation and prevent any embarrassing mistakes.

# Understanding Key Chatter Terms

Here are some Chatter–related terms to familiarize yourself with:

>> **Profile:** A page about a specific person in your company who is using Salesforce. A profile can include the person's name, a short bio, contact information, and a photo, for example. The one for yourself is accessed from the top menu, via your name. That page is called My Settings, and we discuss how to update that in Chapter 3.

>> **Feed:** A Chatter feed shows a chronological list of activities performed by people or records within your company's Salesforce instance.

>> **Stream:** A collection of feeds that you can manually select. Think about this as your playlist of records, groups, people, or topics that you want an ongoing stream of updates on. You can create different streams for different purposes, so that you don't have to manually click into individual feeds. For example, create one stream for important Opportunities so you are notified on updates to them in one place. Or create a stream for a project you're working on and include the feeds of the people working with you, as well as the records, groups, and topics pertaining to the project.

>> **People:** A collection of people within your company who have Chatter profiles.

>> **@:** Pronounced *at,* type this symbol and then immediately the name of a co-worker whom you want to include in your post, in the hopes of giving him a specific heads-up or asking him to join in the conversation. If you have emails allowed and the user you are mentioning has opted to receive email notifications from Chatter activity, the user will get an email notifying him of that specific post. This also applies to groups, not just individual users.

>> **Following/Unfollowing:** The act of following (or unfollowing) a person or record to see (or no longer see) her feed updates. These can include comments, posts, and updates to certain fields within a record. Other people in your Salesforce organization can also choose to follow you.

>> **Post:** A type of update that you make about yourself that's added to your feed for others to see. Because it's called a *post,* you're usually posting an update to some work most likely associated with a record. Certain actions are posted in the feed automatically (such as status changes).

>> **Draft Post:** Similar to drafts you may be used to working with in email, these are posts that are saved or "held" until you're ready to send them off. To enable this feature, talk to your administrator.

>> **Bookmark:** You can bookmark Chatter posts in much the same way as you would bookmark a website you want to reference or read later. Think about this as the same as following above, but on a Chatter post level.

>> **Comment:** A response that you write based on feed activity. For example, if an Opportunity that people are following is finally won, your CEO could comment on the feed and say, "Congratulations, team!"

>> **Like:** A very quick way to say that you approve of a particular post or comment.

>> **Share:** A quick way to share a post with your followers or a specific group.

>> **File:** A document (up to 2GB in size) that can be attached to a post or comment. It can come from your computer or from within files you own in Salesforce.

>> **Group:** A way to collaborate with specific people. People can join these freely, or you can make them private so that people have to request entry or be invited, and its contents are not seen by nonmembers.

# Turning On Chatter

Chatter is automatically enabled for all new customers. However, if you subscribed a long time ago or turned it off, then before your company can begin using Chatter, your system administrator has to make some minor changes to your Salesforce configuration.

The first step in using Chatter is activating it in Salesforce Setup. Click the gear in the top right of your page and click Setup, and then follow these steps:

**1.** **Choose Platform Tools ⇨ Feature Settings ⇨ Chatter ⇨ Chatter Settings.**

The Chatter Settings page appears.

**2.** **Click Edit to make the page editable, then select the Enable check box.**

Several more sections appear.

**3.** **Review the fields that have defaulted to having the check box selected.**

- *Allow Group Archiving:* This allows groups without any activity over a 90-day period to be archived so that group clutter is minimized. Sometimes people create groups for one-time events; this option allows the organization to archive a group, which keeps this group information in the system without letting new users join or add to the conversation. You can search for them if needed.

- *Allow Records in Groups:* This allows the addition of Account, Contact, Lead, Opportunity, Contract, Campaign, Case, and custom object records to groups. You still need to include the Add Record action in the group publisher layout if you want users to be able to add records to the groups.

- *Allow Rich Link Previews:* When people post a URL, a preview of a photo or video from that URL is shown.

- *Allow Draft Posts:* This lets users create draft posts, essentially saving posts prior to publishing or deleting them. It also gives you access to the My Drafts feed, where users can see and manage these drafts.

- *Allow Customer Invitations:* This allows Chatter users to invite people outside of your company into your organization via a private group. They won't have access to anything outside of that group.

- *Enable Actions in the Publisher:* Allows you to add actions to the publisher layout, as well as the order in which they appear. You can add these actions on the home page, Chatter tab, and records themselves.

- *Allow Today Recommendations:* This enables Chatter feed recommendations within the Salesforce mobile app. The Chatter feed includes recommendations for users, such as suggesting groups to join.

- *Allow Users to Edit Posts and Comments:* This allows certain users to modify posts and comments. They must be authors of the post or comment, record owners, or Chatter moderators.

- *Allow Users to Compose Rich Text Posts:* Allows users to use rich text in their posts so that they can use formatting or bullets.

- *Allow Post Pinning:* This settings allows admins and group owners to pin up to three Chatter posts to the top of a group or topic feed. You can extend this ability to other users through their profile or a permission set.

**TIP**

If some of your users want external people to be invited into a private Chatter group, pause for a moment and think about that external user's user experience. Is this a great way to collaborate on a project? Will they mind having to log in to a different system on a regular basis to share information? What if they have their own instance of Salesforce — will they get mixed up logging into two organizations' Chatter conversations every day? Every situation is different, and you can't control 100 percent of it. But make sure that your employees know that adoption by the external person is highly dependent on the context and expectations set.

# Locating Chatter

After your administrator turns on Chatter, you'll start to notice it in lots of different places. You'll probably notice a Chatter tab when you log in to Salesforce on your home page. If you don't, just click on the App Launcher at the top left of your home page and search Chatter.

Figure 6-1 shows you what the Chatter home page looks like once you click on the Chatter tab and after you set up your profile. On the top left-hand side of the page, you see different views of Chatter that you can quickly select:

>> **What I Follow:** Click here to see a quick view of the latest from records or people you follow.

>> **To Me:** A collection of all the posts or comments that include an @mention of your name. You won't see any from records or feeds you don't have access to, though.

>> **Bookmarked:** All the posts that you've bookmarked.

>> **Company Highlights:** Think about this as a view of all the posts that are trending in your organization that you have access to.

>> **My Drafts:** This is where to go for a list of your saved posts that you haven't published yet.

Under these views, the next section is where you view your streams or create them if you don't have any. Check the Key Chatter Terms above if you forgot what streams are. The final section shows the latest groups you've visited.

The middle of the page shows you your Chatter feed activity, and what appears there depends on the view you select on the left-hand menu we just talked about. On top of the activity is a Chatter Publisher component, which you can use to publish posts, ask questions or poll users in your organization. Finally, the right side of the page shows Einstein (AI) recommendations as they pertain to Chatter, such as groups or individuals you should follow.

**FIGURE 6-1:**
Viewing your
Chatter page.

On record pages in the Lightning Experience, the Chatter feed is now nested in its own subsection. In Salesforce Classic, the Chatter feed is at the top of the record's page. Lots of collaboration can turn into lots of posts that users have to scroll past to get to the record details. In the Lightning Experience, the Chatter feed is tucked within the Chatter subtab, which is accessible from the "top of the fold" view in a browser. The feed's details are just a click away if you want to see them, and not taking up valuable visual real estate otherwise.

## Profiling Yourself

The first thing you should do when starting Chatter is to update your profile. When you click your name anywhere in the Chatter feed or click the avatar photo at the top-right corner of the page and then click the avatar photo in the drop-down that appears, you're taken to your Profile page. Your profile page is your work profile, displaying your profile picture, basic information about yourself (your background, contact information, and so on), a history of your status updates, the groups you're a member of, the files you've shared, the co-workers who follow you, and the co-workers and Salesforce records that you follow.

**REMEMBER**

Your profile is also what others see when they click your name, which means that profiles work like a company directory. Be sure that you don't include any information in your profile that you don't want *everyone* in your company to see.

To update your Profile page, refer to Chapter 4.

# Keeping Everyone Informed with Posts

Part of what makes Chatter work is letting your co-workers — even your boss — know what you're up to. In return, you can find out what they're doing. In this section, we show you how to post as well as how to comment on others' posts.

## Posting a status

Posts are what your followers see. You can update posts to let others know what you're working on, to ask questions, or to share files or website links. The inspiration comes from status updates on websites, such as Facebook and Twitter, that play an increasing role in people's personal lives. If you have a Facebook or Twitter account, you'll pick up Chatter in no time.

To make a post, follow these steps:

1. **Click the Chatter tab or open any record page.**

   Either option should have a Chatter feed in it.

   **REMEMBER**

   If you're on a record page, look for the Chatter tab and click on it. If it's not there, make sure Chatter is enabled for your organization and that your administrator has a Chatter Publisher lightning component on that particular record page.

2. **Type a post in the open field where it says, "Share an update."**

3. **(Optional) Attach a file to your update by clicking the paper clip icon under the post and selecting a document from within Salesforce using the filters on the left, or from your computer by clicking Upload Files at the top.**

   You may want to upload a file with a presentation you're working on that's relevant to your post.

4. **Click the Share button to publish your update.**

   Your post is published.

5. **(Optional) From the small drop-down list to the right of your post, select the Delete option to remove it.**

   If you ever make a typo or post something embarrassing, you can always delete that entry and make it disappear from the feed. That said, if email notifications are enabled, emails may have already gone out to users.

**6.** **(Optional) Click the Poll or Question tabs next to Post, to poll an audience or ask users a question, respectively.**

This works the same way as posting, but provides a different format to a regular post; such as a poll with multiple choice answers.

## Commenting on posts

When you're following people, you start seeing their posts in your Chatter feed. Chatter allows you to add comments to posts, thus creating and managing multiple conversations in an organized fashion.

To add a comment to someone's post, follow these steps:

**1.** **Locate the post in the Chatter feed.**

**2.** **Click the Comment link below the post.**

**3.** **Type your comment in the indented field that appears below the post.**

**4.** **Click the Comment button when you're done writing.**

Your comment appears indented below the original update, as shown in Figure 6-2.

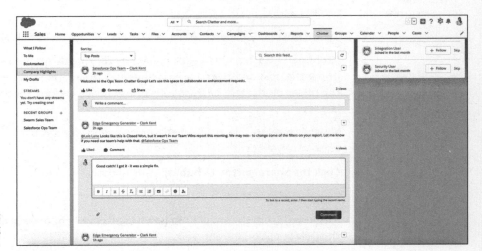

**FIGURE 6-2:**
Commenting on a post.

# Choosing What to Follow

Before you can follow anything, your administrator needs to enable Chatter on the objects you wish to follow. *Objects* are types of records. They're the words (for example, Accounts) that appear at the top of your Salesforce page; you can click these words, and then they look like highlighted tabs. (For a review of how to navigate the default objects in Salesforce, turn to Chapter 3.)

Your administrator and executive stakeholders should decide which objects to first turn on for following: typically, the one or two objects that your Salesforce users collaborate on the most, such as Opportunities.

## Configuring your Chatter feeds

After you determine which objects need to be followed, you can enable Chatter for those objects as an administrator. Click the gear in the top right of your page and click Setup, and then follow these steps in the Setup menu:

1. **Choose Platform Tools ➪ Feature Settings ➪ Chatter ➪ Feed Tracking.**

   The Feed Tracking page appears, as shown in Figure 6-3.

2. **Click the name of an object in the Object list on the left side.**

   The Fields In page for that object appears.

3. **Select the Enable Feed Tracking check box.**

4. **Select each check box for the fields that you want to track with Chatter.**

   Select fields that others will want to be notified about when a change occurs to that field, for example, Close Date, Next Step, Status, or Stage.

   You get a maximum of 20 fields on any given object that you can track with Chatter. You may be able to expand this number for an additional cost.

   **TIP**

5. **Repeat for other objects. When you're done, click Save.**

## Following people

When you first start Chatter, the feed activity will be empty (or nearly empty) because you're not following anyone. In this section, we show you how to follow people in your organization.

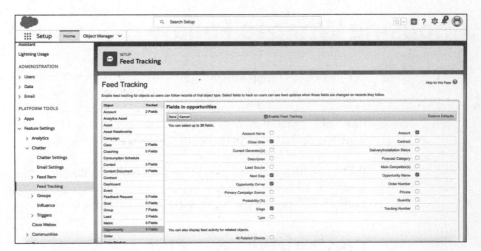

**FIGURE 6-3:**
Selecting fields on
objects to follow.

**TIP**

You can follow people, groups, and records in your organization that pertain to the things that interest you or that affect what you're doing so that you can join the conversation and keep tabs on important updates.

To follow people or records, follow these steps:

**1. Click the Chatter tab from the home page.**

The Main Chatter feed appears.

**2. From the feed, hover over the name of someone you'd like to follow, and click the Follow button, as shown in Figure 6-4.**

You are now following this person, and the link toggles to Unfollow in case you want to unfollow her in the future. Her posts now show up in your Chatter feed under What I Follow.

You can also use the global search bar at the top of any page to type the name of somebody specific you want to follow. The list of people automatically updates while you're typing. Look for key executives, peers, and other movers and shakers within your company.

Be picky about whom you follow first so that you don't get overwhelmed with all the updates you'll be getting in your feed.

**3. Click on any record.**

The record detail page appears.

4. **Click the + Follow button on the top right of the record page.**

   You are now following this record.

   When you click a person's name, you go to his or her Profile page.

**REMEMBER**

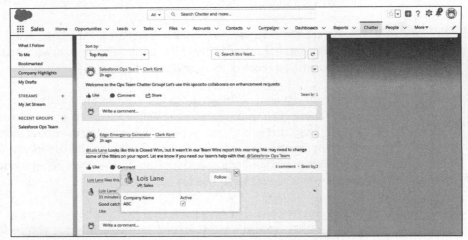

**FIGURE 6-4:**
Following people.

## Your secret is safe

Only internal users of your company's Salesforce instance can see your Chatter posts and comments, depending on where you enter that update. (Read through the earlier section for more information on how to update your status.)

As far as having outsiders or Google see your updates, you're safe because Chatter uses the built-in privacy and security functionality of Salesforce. Internal users can see whatever you post, if they have access to the record you're posting on or about. So if you post from your home page that you're looking for a notary, everyone can see that (what's the point if they can't?). But if you're on the Opportunity record for "Big Secret Government Deal" and make a post there asking about a notary, only people who can see that Opportunity will be able to see your post.

## Following feeds

One of the key differentiators of Chatter, as compared with other social networking sites — or other services that attempt to bring social networking into the workplace — is that you can also follow nonhuman things in your Salesforce database. Sounds crazy, right? This feature means that you can follow specific Opportunities, Accounts, Contacts, Leads, Price Lists, Cases, and any changes that are made to those records. You can even create or follow groups, focused on a single competitor, region, or vertical. Being able to choose what things you want to stay in the loop about makes Chatter highly relevant to what you need to be successful at work.

To follow a record feed, click the + Follow link under the record's name on the record's detail page.

**TIP**

If you created a stream, when you click the – Follow link, you'll see the option to follow the record's feed in the What I Follow view or to add the record's feed into the stream you created, as shown in Figure 6-5.

Whenever someone changes a tracked field in an Opportunity, for example, you know about it. If you're a sales manager, you can choose to follow a strategic Opportunity that one of your reps has been toiling over. The moment she updates that Opportunity Stage field to a Closed-Win, it appears in your feed. If you have key executives following that Opportunity, too, they can provide comments that amount to a virtual high-five for all to see.

When you follow a specific record, your profile photo appears as a follower of this object on the record's page so that others will know you're interested in this record.

**FIGURE 6-5:**
Following a record.

You can also add comments to specific records, just as you can with people you follow (see the earlier section, "Commenting on posts"). They appear in your feed on your home page and on the feed on the record's page.

REMEMBER

Only users with read access to a record will be able to see any posts that you make on that record. To read more about profiles and permissions, visit Chapter 20.

## Creating a Stream

As we mentioned above, a stream is a way to organize or group a selection of different feeds to see them in one place. Let's look at how to create a stream.

TIP

It makes sense to think about what logical feed groupings you need before creating your stream. For example, you can create a stream for a project you're working on that includes the feeds of people you're working with, Contacts and Accounts relating to the project, as well as a group that is also involved in the project. Once you've created that stream, you not only can check it to see the latest activity without clicking into individual feeds, but you also can get notified whenever changes take place to any of the items in the stream.

To create a stream, follow these steps:

1.  **Click the Chatter tab from the home page.**

    The Main Chatter feed appears.

2.  **On the left-hand side bar, click the + icon next to Streams.**

    A New Stream pop-up dialog box appears.

3.  **Enter the name of your stream in the Stream Name field.**

4.  **Under the Records to Follow field, choose the type of record to follow using the drop-down arrow, then start typing the name of the record you have in mind to search, as shown in Figure 6-6.**

    The record should appear as you type in the search bar.

5.  **Finally, if you want to be notified or not using the radio buttons, and click Save.**

    Your new stream is created.

# Being Part of a Group

Similar to finding people to follow, you search for groups to join. By following a group's feed, you can collaborate with a specific subset of people within your company on a regular basis.

REMEMBER

Posts made to a private Chatter group can be seen only by members of the group, system administrators, and those with the View All Data permission.

## Understanding Salesforce Chatter groups

Chatter groups in Salesforce are subsets of people who collaborate on a project, event, or idea. You can create a Chatter group for all sorts of different projects. For example, that company retreat may warrant a Chatter group to broadcast updates and answer questions. A specific branch or office could have its own Chatter group. Similarly, you can create Chatter groups for a wide variety of use cases — product lines, organization-wide competitions, and so on. Just make sure that these groups are kept professional and don't become a channel to talk about personal lives or your weekend plans.

## Joining a group

To find a group to join, follow these steps:

1. **Click the Chatter tab.**

   The Chatter feed appears.

2. **Click the Recent Groups heading in the left sidebar.**

   The Recently Viewed Groups list view appears.

3. **Click the drop-down arrow to the right of Recently Viewed, and select Active Groups.**

   A list of active groups appears. If you don't see any, either none have been created, they are no longer active, or they're private.

4. **Use the search bar to look for specific group names.**

   While you type, the list automatically changes to show the results of your search.

**TIP**

   If you don't find a group that you want to join, create a new one yourself. See the next section, "Creating a new group," on how to create a group from scratch.

5. **Click a group's name to view the Group detail page.**

   This provides more details about the group.

6. **Click either of these two links:**

   - *+ Join:* Join a public group.

   - *Ask Owner:* Ask the owner for permission to join a private group.

## Creating a new group

Communication is key when working in teams. With groups, you can set up private feeds where team members can discuss their work outside their normal feed. This feature is extremely useful for sensitive projects to ensure that online conversations remain secure. You can set up public groups as well for less-confidential discussion.

To set up a new group, follow these steps:

1. **Click the Recent Groups heading on the left sidebar of the Chatter tab.**

   The heading expands. The Recently Viewed Groups home page appears, listing existing groups.

2. **Click the New button on the right side.**

   The New Group dialog box appears.

3. **Type the name of your group.**

4. **Enter a description to further distinguish it from other groups. You can also add more information about it in rich text format in the Information field.**

5. **Select whether you want to have this group automatically archived after 90 days of inactivity.**

6. **Set the Group Access as Public or Private:**

   - *Public:* Anyone can join the group or see its feed.

   - *Private:* Only members, system administrators, and people with the View All Data permission can see and add posts to the feed.

7. **Select whether you want to allow customers, such as external users or those with Chatter profiles, to have access to the group. Additionally, you can check the Broadcast Only check box if only the owner of the group and managers should be able to post, whereas other members can only comment. Then click Save and Next.**

8. **Upload a photo for the group and make it more attractive to join. Click Next.**

9. **In the Manage Members section, select the folks you want to invite as members of your group, and click Done.**

   Your new group's page appears.

## Managing Chatter Notifications

There are two main ways you get Chatter notifications: in-app notifications and emails. Chatter notifications let you know whenever you're mentioned or when someone (or something) you're following has made a post.

The in-app notifications appear in the bell icon at the top right of every page, near your photo or avatar. A little red number appears or increases by one each time you're notified of a new Chatter activity, as shown in Figure 6-7.

The second form of Chatter notifications can be configured in Chatter Email settings in the Setup menu.

**FIGURE 6-7:**
Seeing your
in-app Chatter
notifications.

You can set your preferences as follows:

1. **Choose Your Photo or Avatar ⇨ Settings ⇨ Chatter ⇨ Email Notifications.**

2. **Select the Receive Emails check box to ensure that you receive emails about updates.**

3. **Select the appropriate check boxes corresponding to the events for which you want to be notified, and how often. Optionally, you can select how often you get emailed based on activity in groups you belong to, as well as selecting frequency on each group specifically.**

4. **Click Save.**

# Using Chatter Effectively

Here are a few ideas on how your company can benefit from Chatter if some people are reluctant to get onboard:

» **Help Sales sell smarter.** Follow key Accounts and strategic Opportunities. Ask others for references to help you close a specific deal. Create a group to team up to win against a competitor.

» **Market more effectively.** Get feedback on updated presentations and other marketing materials by attaching them to status updates. Share noteworthy press mentions. Follow leads to find out more about which types of prospects are converting.

» **Improve customer service.** Receive and provide help on cases. Discuss potential work-arounds and technical solutions in a private group. Collaborate on creating the most succinct answer to common customer issues.

» **Define a Chatter code of conduct.** If you have different generations of employees at your company, they're going to react very differently to this tool. Establish basic norms to ensure that this doesn't turn into yet another medium to post cat photos.

» **Install Chatter Desktop or Chatter Mobile.** Get proactive alerts on your computer screen whenever someone or a record you're following makes an update so that you're never out of the loop.

» **Skim posts from your mobile device.**

# 3

# Closing More Deals with Sales Cloud

# Chapter **7**

# Tracking Leads

O ften, we hear frustrated salespeople say, "We could hit our numbers if we just had enough Leads to fill our pipeline." Leads are the building blocks by which many companies drive their sales.

Loosely defined, a *Lead* is a person or a company that may be interested in your services. Some organizations refer to them as *visitors* because they haven't shared any information about themselves yet. Others call them *prospects* because a Lead has to be someone who has expressed interest in your service. Whatever your favorite terminology is, you can use Leads to efficiently follow up on sales inquiries, aggressively attack new markets, and vastly improve your sales pipeline.

In this chapter, you can discover all the basic tricks you need to convert Leads into revenue. You need to get your existing Leads into Salesforce, and update them when you follow up with them. Also, we discuss how to convert a Lead into an actual Opportunity that you can link to an Account and a Contact. For online marketing or email managers or administrators, we devote an entire section to how you can manage and maintain your Lead database.

# Introducing the Lead Record

A *Lead record* consists of a number of fields that you use to capture information about a potential Lead. A Lead record has two primary modes:

>> **Edit:** In Edit mode, you can modify the fields.

>> **Saved:** In Saved mode, you can view the fields and related lists.

The standard record comes predefined with several fields. Most of the terms are immediately clear, but if you want specific definitions, click the question mark icon in the upper-right corner of Salesforce to access Help & Training. Here are the most common standard fields:

>> **Lead Owner:** The person who owns the Lead. If no one owns the Lead, Salesforce can automatically place the Lead in a queue or assigns it to a specific individual (though we don't recommend that, because users take vacations, get sick, or leave the company, and should always have a backup). You can then assign the Lead to a group of users (for example, "Corporate Sales — West Region"), who can take Leads in the order in which they arrive in the queue.

>> **Lead Status:** One of three required fields on a Lead record. Lead Status is a drop-down list of values, and this field is critical if you want to follow a standard Lead process. We talk more about Lead status in the nearby sidebar, "Building an effective Lead process."

>> **Lead Source:** A standard, but not required, field on a Lead record. If you use it, you can define and group the sources of your Leads by using this field.

**REMEMBER**

Lead sources are the originators of Leads that come knocking at your door. These can be related to broad communication channels (a toll-free number, cold call, or web form, for example), more specific types of marketing venues (trade show, print ad, partner referral, and so on), or a blend of both. It's up to you. Always remember to balance your desire to get really granular data with the tolerance of the users who often have but a few seconds to customize this field (alongside other fields). And if you really want to track granular details of where Leads are coming from, seriously consider using Campaigns or a third-party marketing automation tool, described further in Chapter 15.

## BUILDING AN EFFECTIVE LEAD PROCESS

The key to a successful Lead program that contributes to sales is a well-constructed Lead process built into your Lead Status drop-down list. Salesforce provides a default list of four statuses: Open, Contacted, Qualified, and Unqualified. These statuses may appear straightforward, but they require definition and alignment with Sales because those four choices may not mirror your process or your terminology. The good news is that after you define the statuses that relate to your business, your administrator can quickly modify the values. The process starts with the Lead Status field, but it doesn't end there.

Here are some additional suggestions for how you might construct your lean, mean, Lead-generating machine:

- Create fields to capture qualification criteria, based on what your Sales and Marketing teams agree make a Lead qualified.

- Make it clear at what point in the process a Lead qualifies to be converted to an Opportunity.

- Decide who'll manage the Lead program and what that entails. As Marketing Operations teams grow, they may need to coordinate with the Digital Marketing, Demand Generation, other teams within Marketing, and teams outside, like IT. Make sure the right people have the sufficient permissions to nimbly administer the Lead database.

- Determine when a Lead should be deleted, marked as inactive, or archived.

- Set up queues, if it makes sense, to manage the workload and drive the competitive spirit.

- When you figure out your process, train your users so that everyone knows what's expected of him or her.

**TIP**

When you first get a Lead, you'll likely want to qualify that Lead to make sure that a sales opportunity really exists for you. For example, maybe you want to be certain that the Lead has the budget and a real interest and isn't just kicking tires. A *marketing-qualified Lead* (MQL) is a Lead that meets your sales and marketing's teams qualification requirements to hand over the discussion to a salesperson. Teams in the Marketing or Sales department can own this responsibility. Some organizations then require Sales to further qualify the Lead until they can accept that it's a sales-qualified Lead (SQL).

You'll have your own definition of what qualifies as a Lead, so jot it down, make sure there's agreement between your sales and marketing organizations, and then seek out someone to customize your Lead record. (See Chapter 17 for the how-to details on building fields, rearranging your layouts, and other design tricks.) You'll have greater success with Leads if you collect the right information, where "right" is the same between sales and marketing.

**REMEMBER**

Writing useful Help text and descriptions for each field you create is vital to a healthy customer relationship management (CRM) system. It may seem laborious at first, and you may write terribly unhelpful descriptions. But fast-forward 6 to 18 months, where sales and marketing teams experience above average rates of turnover, and you'll have new team members scratching their heads wondering why certain fields were created and no one can remember why. Do yourself and your teammates and future generations a favor: Write down who requested a field and for what purpose.

# Setting Up Your Leads

Before you can begin working your Leads, you need to add the Lead records into Salesforce. In the following sections, we show you three quick approaches for Lead creation, and if needed, how to share your Leads with the right people. If you want to capture Leads from your website, see Chapter 15 for details on generating Web-to-Lead forms.

## Adding new Leads

The best way to manually create a Lead is to use the + New Lead option from the drop-down list from the Lead tab on the navigation bar. To create a Lead using this method, follow these steps:

1. **Select the + New Lead option from the Lead tab's drop-down list.**

   A New Lead window appears in Edit mode, as shown in Figure 7-1. The only prefilled field is the Lead Status field.

2. **Fill in the fields as much as you can.**

   At a minimum, you must complete the Last Name and Company fields.

**TIP**

You can add a list of target companies as Leads, even if you don't yet know the names of the right people. In certain cases, you may have only the name of a company because you know you want to target it, but you don't yet know whom to call. You can work with incomplete information. In these cases, we recommend that you type **?** or **unknown** in the Last Name field so that you know this information is missing.

**3.** **When you're done, click the Save button or the Save & New button.**

Here's the difference between those two buttons:

- *Save:* When you click Save, the Lead record appears in Saved mode, and your changes are displayed in the fields.

- *Save & New:* Salesforce knows that salespeople commonly add multiple Leads before working them. When you click Save & New, the Lead is saved, and a New Lead page appears in Edit mode.

**FIGURE 7-1:** Filling out a Lead record.

**WARNING**

When entering or editing records, click the Save button or the Save & New button when you're done. Otherwise, you won't save the information that you just typed for that record.

## Cloning an existing Lead

If you're developing relationships within a particular company and you want to enter multiple Leads for that company, you can save time by cloning Leads. For example, say that you already created a Lead record for Sergey Brin at Google. When you talk to his assistant, he courteously refers you to Larry Page. In this case, cloning can save you many extra steps.

To clone a Lead record from an existing Lead, follow these steps:

1. **Click the Clone button at the top right of the Lead record.**

   A new Lead window appears in Edit mode. All the information is identical to the previous Lead record.

2. **Edit the information on the new Lead, where appropriate.**

   Pay attention to what's prefilled because you want to avoid inaccurate information on the new Lead record.

REMEMBER

3. **Click Save when you're done.**

   The newly created Lead reappears in Saved mode.

## Importing your Leads

If you already have a file of Leads, you probably want a faster way to get them into Salesforce than entering them manually. You need special permissions to import Leads (as well as other types of records), so if you're able to do this, find your administrator, tell her what you're trying to do, and have her provide you with the "Import Leads" permission.

TIP

Although you can import up to 50,000 Leads at once, test an import with 5 or so Leads first, just to make sure that you know what you're doing. After the test data is imported, review your new Lead records to make sure that they contain all the information that you want to have brought in. Delete the test records, refine your import file, and then run through the final import.

WARNING

If you're a new salesperson who just came from a competitor and you happened to bring all your Leads with you to upload into your new company's CRM system, hold up. Dumping tens of thousands of pieces of unreviewed data into your nice CRM system is terrible practice. You're just moving potentially dirty data from an old home into a new one. The new Leads may also set off a domino chain of workflows that involve other teams. Think that's someone else's problem? Just wait until people start going through it and finding quadruplicates, old job titles, and other pollution. Instead, take a more measured approach. Can you name the top 50 companies that you should be targeting? See how many Leads are from any of those companies, and start with that as an upload. Broaden your range slowly.

To import Lead files, follow these steps:

1. **On the Leads home page, click the Import button at the top right of the page.**

   The Data Import wizard appears, providing you with a process to import your records, plus helpful hints on how to prepare your data for a smooth first-time import, such as to make sure the field values you want to import can match fields in Salesforce, and to not import too many records at once.

2. **In your existing Lead file or system, compare your fields against the Lead fields in Salesforce. Map all your fields between your current system and Salesforce.**

   If you can map all the necessary fields, move to the next step. If not, add fields to the Lead record by customizing Salesforce. (See Chapter 17 for simple instructions on adding fields.)

   **TIP**

   While someone is mapping the fields from your current system to Salesforce, you should also be talking with your company about cleaning up that data. Now's a good time to discuss which of your current system's fields are still needed in the new world. Some fields may have been used several years ago, but no one's been filling them in since you can remember, and no one's bothered to remove or hide them from the current system. Even worse, no one can recall what those fields were for, or maybe you have multiple fields with very similar names! Also, you could have lots of duplicate or partial records. Talk with your company and your Salesforce consultant about best approaches to cleaning up this information.

   **TECHNICAL STUFF**

   *Mapping* is a technical term for matching one field to another field, typically in different databases, to properly move data. For example, in Microsoft Outlook, you type a corporation's name into the Company field. In Salesforce, you typically use the Account Name field. These two different labels have the same meaning. Mapping is the process by which you decide that data from the Company field in Outlook should correspond to the Account Name field in Salesforce.

3. **Export your file.**

   You may have Leads in an existing database or spreadsheet, such as Microsoft Excel, Oracle CRM On Demand, or Microsoft Dynamics. Most systems like these have simple tools for exporting data into various formats. Select the records and the fields that you want. Then, export the file and save it in a .csv format. If your Leads are already in spreadsheet format (such as Excel), just resave the file in .csv format.

**4.** **Review your Lead data.**

You've probably heard the old adage "garbage in, garbage out." Regardless of whether your company spent some time with initial housecleaning before this step, it's important to review the data again at this point. Clean up your information before you bring it into Salesforce so that you can save yourself the effort later.

**5.** **When you're done with the preparation, from the Data Import wizard, confirm that you want to import Leads by clicking that option under the "What kind of data are you importing?" column.**

A green checkmark appears and you proceed to the next step, as shown in Figure 7-2. The progress bar moves along to the second step.

**FIGURE 7-2:**
Uploading the
Lead file.

**6.** **Complete the fields in the next step of the wizard.**

The wizard next asks what you want to do in your import. You choose whether you're adding new records, updating existing ones, or a combination of both.

Assuming that you already prepared your file, follow these steps:

a. *Select the matching type.*

If you want Salesforce to avoid importing duplicate records, choose whether you want to identify a duplicate Lead by matching Salesforce ID, name, or email. If a Lead record with the matching criteria already exists in Salesforce, that record is updated with the information in your file.

b. *Apply an assignment rule if you want Leads to route directly to assigned reps.*

If you don't use an assignment rule, all the Leads that you import are assigned to you unless you otherwise specify a Lead owner in the file. (See the section "Creating assignment rules for automatic routing," later in this chapter.)

*c.* Select the check box if you want to use assignment rule settings to send email notifications to the record owners.

*d.* Select the check box if you want assign all the imported Leads to Campaigns.

*e.* Select the check box if you want to trigger workflow rules and processes to new and updated records.

See Chapter 17 for tips on improving workflow.

*f.* When asked where your data is located, either drag your file from your computer's desktop to the "Drag CSV file here to upload" section, or select one of the file options depending on the file's original source (like CSV, Outlook CSV, Gmail, and so on).

**7.** **When you're done with this part of the wizard, click Next.**

The Edit Field Mapping page appears for this object.

**8.** **Map the fields between your file and Salesforce and then click Next.**

The Edit Field Mapping page displays all the Salesforce Lead fields in a column that correspond to the fields in your file. Simply go through the list of fields and select the field from the corresponding file that you're importing that maps to the Salesforce field, as shown in Figure 7-3. Any column headings in your source file that don't have an obvious Salesforce equivalent will be identified with the word *Unmapped* in red letters. Click the word Map or Change in the Edit column if you want to manually make the mapping yourself or change an existing mapping.

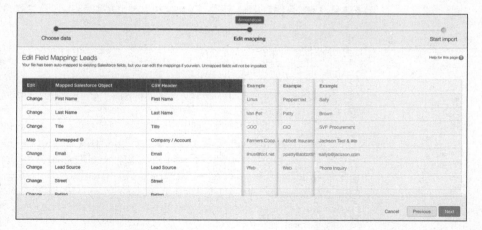

**FIGURE 7-3:**
Mapping the Lead fields.

After you click Next, the Review & Start Import page appears if you have no possible errors. Otherwise, this step may bring up warnings about problems with the data or let you know about fields that you haven't mapped. If you discover an error, you can click the Back button and refine your mapping, or even close the wizard so that you can improve your import file. You may have to start over, but at least you avoid importing bad or incomplete data.

A summary of information about the import is displayed, confirming what fields will and won't be imported, and what type of import you'll be doing.

9. **When you're satisfied with the summary, click the Start Import button.**

   A pop-up window appears to let you know that the import has started. Click OK to close that window and get sent to the Bulk Data Load Jobs page, which identifies the progress of the import.

10. **Check the Lead records that you imported.**

    Salesforce sends you an email after your file has been successfully imported. To check your handiwork, click the Leads tab to go to your Leads home page. In the View drop-down list, select Today's Leads to see a list of the Leads that were created today. Click the link for a Lead that you just imported and review the information for accuracy.

Importing Leads is one of the fastest ways for you to set up your Leads in Salesforce so that you can begin working them.

## BREAKING INTO UNCHARTED WATERS

A leading Internet performance-monitoring company wanted to sell its services to a variety of new, untested markets. This Salesforce customer had a stronghold in financial services but wanted to extend its client base to other Fortune 500 companies. Because of the specific nature of its business, the actual names of the decision makers that it wanted to target was publicly unavailable.

Marketing simply imported the Fortune 500 list and set the Last Name field as Unknown. Then, the company used Salesforce and a team of sales development reps to generate Leads and set up appointments between actual buyers and the company's field sales reps. In just a few short months, this use of Salesforce dramatically helped improve qualified Lead generation and increased the pipeline and new bookings while breaking ground in new markets.

# Accepting Leads from a Queue

If you're a rep assigned to a queue, you can access the queue in the View drop-down list on the Leads home page. The queue list page looks just like a regular list page, but you can use it to grab and claim Leads. (See the section "Making use of Lead queues," later in this chapter, for details on setting up queues.)

To pull Leads from a queue and make them your own, go to the Leads home page and follow these steps:

1. **Select the queue name from the View drop-down list.**

   The queue list page appears.

2. **Select check boxes in the Action column to the left of Leads that you want to claim.**

   Your manager may have specific guidelines. This is your chance to click into some records and try to pick the hottest Leads.

3. **Click the Accept button in the upper-right of the page.**

   The queue list page reappears, minus the Lead(s) that you selected.

TIP

Another way to keep your Leads organized is to make sure that multiple versions of the same person don't show up in Salesforce. This can wreak havoc as people update activity information on different records for the same person. Salesforce detects whether duplicate records already exist and merges them for you. Read the next section to see how to identify duplicate Lead records.

# Following Up on Leads

After you receive a new Lead, you want a quick way to follow up and determine what you caught: a strategic one, a warm one, or just another person kicking tires. Your company may already have a standard Lead qualification process, but the following sections talk about some of the ways that you can use Salesforce to pursue Leads.

## Qualifying Leads

Below the highlights panel of a Lead record, you will see a section that looks like a timeline, as in Figure 7-4. This is a "path", which is part of Salesforce's Lightning Experience. It's meant to show you a visual cue of your particular record's progress along a linear lifecycle. Each milestone is a stage. In the case of Leads, you track a Lead's status as you determine whether they are qualified or not. You can also interact with those stages by clicking on them to update your record to that particular stage.

**FIGURE 7-4:**
Identifying a
Lead's path.

## Tracking Leads

How can you remember all the interactions that took place with a Lead? Some of us have a hard enough time remembering what we did yesterday, let alone three weeks ago with 200 Leads. The Activity subsection, located below the Lead path on a Lead record, can help you capture all that information so that it's at your fingertips the next time you talk to a Lead.

If you're looking for typical ways that salespeople use Activity lists on a Lead record, read the following list for an example:

>> **Log a Call:** The next time you respond to a Lead and want to record what you said, click the Log a Call subtab and enter the details.

>> **New Task:** You plan to call the Lead back next Friday when you know that the gatekeeper is on vacation. Click the New Task subtab and set a tickler for yourself for Friday. (See Chapter 5 for details on how to fill out a new Task record.)

>> **Send an Email:** You get through to the Lead, and he asks you to send him an introductory email about your company. Click the Send an Email subtab to send and track the email directly from Salesforce. We talk more about sending email through Salesforce in Chapter 5.

>> **New Event:** The Lead agrees to a demo. Click New Event and schedule a meeting so that you don't forget.

TIP

At some point, you may decide that a Lead can't become a qualified Opportunity at this time. In that case, you can archive the Lead by changing its status. Archiving inactive Leads allows you to get a sense of how many Leads are still being worked.

# Converting qualified Leads

When you decide that a Lead is actually a qualified Opportunity, you can start using Salesforce's full Opportunity tracking system. To do so, you must convert the Lead to an Opportunity. This conversion gives you two benefits:

>> **It allows you to track multiple Contacts within an Account, which you can do more easily than tracking a single individual Lead.** In other words, if you have ten Leads from Microsoft, they aren't linked with each other in Salesforce. But, by converting a Lead, you create an Account called Microsoft and you link all the Microsoft co-workers as Contacts for the same Account.

>> **Your goal is to ABC (always be closing), so the sooner you can start managing opportunities and not just Leads, the healthier your pipeline and wallet.** For a qualified Lead, your sales process begins where your Lead process ends.

**REMEMBER**

When deciding whether to add names of companies or businesspeople as Leads or as Accounts with Contacts, remember that the Leads module of Salesforce is non-relational from Lead to Lead. If you're serious about going after a particular company, and the interrelationships of business contacts will be important, we recommend that you add the target as an Account, rather than as a Lead.

To convert a Lead to an Opportunity, follow these steps:

**1. Click the Convert button on a Lead record that you want to convert.**

The Convert button is located at the top right of the Lead record. Alternatively, you can click the Converted stage within a Lead path, and then Select Converted Status to confirm the selection. A Convert Lead window appears (see Figure 7-5).

**2. Complete the required fields.**

Required fields are highlighted in red. Here's a summary:

- *Account Name:* If Salesforce doesn't find an Account that closely matches the Company field from your Lead, it defaults to wanting to create a new Account record. In the event that it does find a match, select an option from the list of matches, or search for matching Accounts yourself, depending on whether you want to create a new Account or associate the Lead to an existing Account.

- *Opportunity Name:* If you want to create an Opportunity, complete this field by giving the Opportunity a name. (We typically recommend that the name of an Opportunity be the Account name followed by a hyphen and then a summary of the product interest — for example: Amazon – New Hardware.) You don't have to always create an Opportunity record when you convert a Lead. Sometimes, the Lead that you're converting is associated with an existing Opportunity. In these situations, select the Don't Create an Opportunity upon Conversion check box to avoid creating a new Opportunity.

- *Record Owner:* If the Lead owner remains the record owner, don't change the selection. If the owner changes, remove the owner by clicking the 'x', and then click the magnifying glass icon and choose from the list of users.

- *Converted Status:* Salesforce prefills this field with the default value that your company has chosen for a qualified Lead. Don't change this field unless your company has multiple selections for a qualified Lead.

3. **When you're done, click the Convert button.**

   If Salesforce finds a Contact record that matches your Lead, you can decide to associate it with the existing Contact record. Otherwise, a Contact record appears for your former Lead. That Contact is linked to an Account corresponding to the Lead's Company field, and all associated records from related lists are carried over. If you chose to create an Opportunity in Step 2, you can see the Opportunity on both the Account and Contact record's Opportunity related lists. The confirmation page displays what corresponding records have been created.

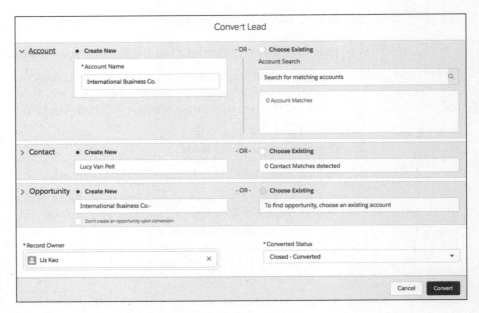

**FIGURE 7-5:** Converting a Lead.

# Maintaining Your Lead Database

If you're a system administrator or a lead manager who has the right permissions (we specify those permissions in the following sections), one of your greatest challenges is managing what hopefully will become a large pool of Leads.

Lead databases can become unwieldy over time, so you need to keep them clean. For example, say that you work for a company that regularly collects Leads from industry conferences. Someone who hadn't read this book ended up importing a lot of Leads into Salesforce without any review beforehand. After a year, your Leads database may have many duplicates and plenty of garbage. Salesforce provides a number of simple tools to make short work of cleaning up your Leads and other tasks.

The biggest problems we see with Leads involve creating a regular cadence around assigning, identifying duplicate records, merging them together (also known as *deduping*), transferring, archiving, and deleting. We know: You hate to get rid of anything. However, sometimes it's necessary and relatively painless.

As technology around artificial intelligence and machine learning evolves, data quality will be critical for Sales and Marketing teams to get the most value of these tools. As we said earlier, "garbage in, garbage out," and the smartest technology in the world may try to help you with your messy data. At the time of this writing, we have seem that a methodical and disciplined approach to data cleanliness is the right prevention to a lot of headaches downstream.

## Making use of Lead queues

If you have a sales team made up of multiple people (often called sales development reps [SDRs]) responsible for harvesting Leads collectively, you may want to set up Lead queues. For example, some companies hire SDRs to handle Leads on a first-come, first-served basis. You may just find that your reps work harder if they all have an equal chance to go after a fresh pool of Leads.

If you're an administrator or user who has permission to customize Salesforce, you can set up Lead queues. Follow these steps:

1. **Choose Setup ➪ Users ➪ Queues.**

   A Queues page appears.

2. **Click New to create a new queue.**

   The New Queue page appears in Edit mode, as shown in Figure 7-6.

3. **Name the queue and specify the Lead object to associate with this queue.**

4. **Add members to the queue.**

   Members can be users, groups, or roles in your company who'll be part of the queue. For example, you may label the queue Western Field Sales and then choose users who make up the Western Sales team.

5. **When you're done, click Save.**

   You can now use this queue when you organize and reassign Lead records.

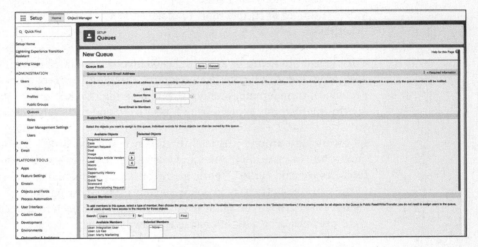

**FIGURE 7-6:**
Creating a new
Lead queue.

REMEMBER

Lead queues can be viewed in the same place on your Leads home page where you view your Lead views. The name of the Lead queue is automatically added to the drop-down list for the Lead views. Pretty neat, huh?

## Finding and merging duplicate Lead records

You probably know that duplicates frequently occur with Leads. For example, if you capture Leads from your website, the same visitor may fill in your web form multiple times, even with the best of intentions. Instead of wasting your time or upsetting the existing Lead, check first for duplicates.

If your company has enabled the Duplicate Management feature, Salesforce will be on the lookout for potential duplicate Leads based on default matching criteria (that you can also customize for your business), as shown in Figure 7-7. Before following up on a new Lead, look on the record to see if Salesforce has found any potential duplicates. Click the View Duplicates link to open up the Potential

Duplicate Records window to see whether a matching Lead or Contact record already exists. Depending on your permissions, you can select the matches to merge all the records, or you can just select an existing record to proceed with your work on it.

If you're not sure which action to take, work with your Demand Generation team to get on the same page as to how to handle duplicate Leads. This helps avoid any embarrassing conversations when interacting with a Lead ("Doesn't your CRM system tell you that I'm an existing customer?!"), and also helps Marketing ensure the person is getting the right types of Campaigns directed to where they are in their buyer's journey with your products.

When you merge duplicate records, the remaining record inherits not only the information you select but also linked records on related lists.

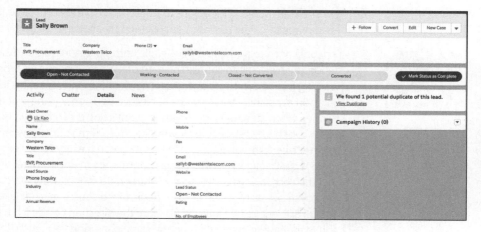

**FIGURE 7-7:**
Finding duplicate Leads.

**REMEMBER** To merge Lead records, you must be the Lead owner of the records, the Lead owner's manager (that is, the Lead owner must be subordinate to you in the role hierarchy), or a system administrator. You must also have Duplicate Management enabled.

To find and merge duplicate Leads, follow these steps:

1. **Go to a Lead record that you suspect or know has duplicates.**

2. **Click the View Duplicates link from the page section that confirms how many potential duplicates have been found.**

   A Potential Duplicate Records window appears. By default, Salesforce looks for a duplicate with a matching first and last name, company or email address, and phone number. The window shows any matching Lead, Contact, Account, or Opportunity records, based on the default matching criteria.

3. **Review the duplicate Lead records and select a maximum of three records to merge.**

   In Salesforce, you can merge only three records at a time.

4. **Hit Next to continue to compare the fields of the Leads you selected.**

   A Compare Leads window appears, displaying, side by side, the selected records and their fields.

5. **Compare the information and select the radio buttons to choose the values that you want to retain.**

   **TIP**

   At the top of each column, you can also choose to keep all the values from one record by clicking the Select All link.

6. **When you finish reviewing, click Next to confirm the merge request.**

   The Confirm Merge step appears, prompting you to validate that you want to perform the merge. Click Merge Leads to perform the action, and the merged Lead reappears. Any records from related lists are kept.

   **REMEMBER**

   If people need to pause and think while under pressure to qualify a ton of Leads, they're going to choose the path of least resistance and proceed with working a Lead even if it's already got a ton of duplicate matches in your Salesforce instance. Minimize the subjective decision making that needs to happen when an end-user is reviewing conflicting criteria within matching Leads. Do this by establishing some clear rules with your teams so they don't get frustrated spending time trying to re-research everything. For example, if there is contradictory employee size information in duplicate records, establish that the tiebreaking field is the one whose data most closely matches the employee size as reported in a pre-determined source of truth (like LinkedIn, or Dun & Bradstreet). Finally, make sure the direction comes from both Sales and Marketing so everyone is on the same page, and your end users don't get contradictory instructions.

## Creating assignment rules for automatic routing

If your company generates a lot of Leads, assignment rules can help distribute the workload and get Leads to the right users. Assignment rules give you a better chance to keep Leads from becoming stagnant. A Lead *assignment rule* is a feature that lets the administrator define who should receive a Lead and under what conditions. For example, if your reps have sales territories defined by states or countries, you can use those states or countries to dictate who gets what Leads.

To create a Lead assignment rule, follow these steps:

1. **Choose Setup and type in Lead Assignment Rules in the Quick Find search box at the top of the left sidebar of the Setup home.**

   If you haven't yet set the default Lead owner, the Lead Settings page appears, asking you to select the default Lead owner. The buck stops with this person or queue, as far as Lead routing goes. After you make this selection, Salesforce returns you to the Lead Assignment Rules page.

2. **Click New to create a new assignment rule.**

   The New Lead Assignment Rule page appears in Edit mode.

3. **Enter a title in the Rule Name field, select the check box if you want to make it the active assignment rule, and click the Save button.**

   The Lead Assignment Rule page reappears. You can have only one active rule at a time, but the rule can have multiple entries. Click the rule name to go to the detail page for that rule.

4. **Click New in the Rule Entries related list.**

   A Rule Entry Edit page appears.

5. **Complete the steps as follows:**

   a. *Enter a number in the Order field to set the order in which the rules will be evaluated.*

   b. *Select criteria to define the rule.*

   See Chapter 17 for details on selecting criteria. In this case, you might enter **State Equals CA, AZ, WA**.

   c. *Use the drop-down list and Lookup icon to select the user or queue.*

   d. *Use the Lookup icon to choose an Email Notification Template.*

   You can set the assignment rules to send email alerts to recipients of new Leads.

6. **When done, click the Save button or the Save & New button.**

   Here's what happens when you click each button:

   - *Save:* When you click Save, the New Lead Assignment Rule page reappears.

   - *Save & New:* When you click Save & New, a new Rule Entry Edit page appears, and you can repeat Steps 5 and 6 until you finish.

# Transferring Leads

You may need to transfer Leads for a variety of reasons. For instance, after you set up your Lead records in Salesforce, you need to give them to the right people on a different team. Or maybe some reps just weren't following up, so you took their Leads away after swatting their noses with a rolled-up newspaper.

To transfer Leads, you must be an administrator or a user with Manage Leads and Transfer Leads permissions. If you want to reassign many Leads at the same time, take these steps:

1. **From the Leads home page, select a view from which you can see some Leads that you want to reassign.**

   The list page appears.

2. **In the Action column of the Lead list, select the check boxes to the left of the Lead records that you want to assign to someone else.**

3. **Click the Change Owner button at the top right of the page.**

   The Change Owner window appears.

4. **Select the user or queue that you intend to reassign Leads to, and then click Submit.**

   The Lead list reappears, and the Lead owners have been changed. The new Lead owner can be optionally notified via email of this ownership change. Just select the Send Notification Email check box before clicking the Save button.

**TIP**

If you're an administrator, you can use the Mass Transfer Records tool in Setup to accomplish the same goals of reassigning en masse. See Chapter 21 for details on mass-transferring Leads.

If you're reassigning one Lead at a time, you can transfer ownership directly from a Lead record. Follow these steps:

1. **On the Lead record, click the Change Owner button in the upper-right of the record. Or, from the Details subsection, to the right of the Lead Owner field, click the Change Owner icon, which looks like a silhouette of a person.**

   The Change Lead Owner window appears.

2. **Select the user or queue that you're assigning the Lead to.**

   You use this same page when you're assigning multiple Leads.

3. **(Optional) Select the Send Notification Email check box to notify the new owner of the reassignment.**

4. **When you're done, click Change Owner.**

   The Lead record reappears, displaying your ownership change.

## Changing the status of multiple records

An administrator or a user who has Manage Leads permissions can change the status of multiple records at the same time. This feature comes in handy if, during a process, a lead manager reviews Leads prior to assigning them to reps.

To change the status of multiple Leads at the same time, follow these steps:

1. **From the Leads home page, select a view.**

   The list page appears.

2. **In the Action column of the Lead list, select the check boxes to the left of the Lead records that require a status change.**

   To select all the Leads in this view, select the check box that resides along the column header, which selects all the Leads on this page.

   For example, if you're eyeballing a list of Leads from a trade show, you might select obviously bogus Leads.

3. **Click the Change Status button at the top right of the page.**

   The Change Status window appears.

4. **Select a status from the New Status drop-down list and click Save.**

   The Lead list reappears.

If you require industrial-strength deduplication tools, a number of proven technology partners handle deduplication within Salesforce, plus a variety of other data management tasks. You can check out these offerings on the AppExchange directory by searching for "data cleansing" in the search bar.

## Mass-deleting Lead records

Periodically, be sure to delete records that are unqualified or of no value to your company. You must be an administrator to mass-delete records.

**TIP**

Some companies add a To Be Deleted value to their Lead Status field to denote garbage. Then, periodically, the administrator deletes those records.

If you want to delete multiple records at a time, follow these steps:

1. **From the Setup home, type Mass Delete Records into the Quick Find search box on top of the left sidebar. Select Mass Delete Records.**

   The Mass Delete Records page appears.

2. **Click the Mass Delete Leads link.**

   The Mass Delete Leads page appears, including a three-step deletion wizard.

3. **Review the steps and then type the search criteria for the Leads that you want to delete.**

   For example, if you want to delete unqualified Leads, enter a filter in which Lead Status Equals Unqualified.

4. **Click the Search button.**

   The page reappears, displaying your results at the bottom of the page.

5. **Select all records or just the records that you want to delete by selecting the appropriate check boxes.**

   To select all the search results for deletion, click the Select All link at the top of the list.

6. **Click the Delete button after you complete selecting the records for deletion.**

   The search results are updated to omit the record(s) you deleted.

**TIP**

When deleting records, always be cautious, but don't overly stress out. When you delete records, that information is placed in your Recycle Bin, and you can access records for 15 days. Just remember that the Recycle Bin, as of the time of this publication, is not visible in the Lightning Experience. It is visible though, in the Classic UI. Once you've switched to the Classic, to undelete a record, click the Recycle Bin link on your sidebar, find the record, and undelete it. Then, count your blessings and breathe into a paper bag until the panic attack subsides.

# Chapter **8**

# Using Accounts

Who are your customers? What do you know about them? What are their top compelling business problems? If you have trouble answering any of these questions, pay close attention to this chapter. Here, we discuss how to use Salesforce to manage your Accounts.

In Salesforce, an *Account* is a company that you do business with or have done business with in the past. Accounts can include all types of companies — customers, prospects, partners, and even competitors. Among the top reasons why companies implement any customer relationship management (CRM) tool is that they need a centralized place where they can store Account data, to prevent themselves from searching all over the place for critical customer information. With Salesforce, you can keep all your important Account information in one place so that you and your team can apply that knowledge to sell more and keep customers happy. For example, if you work for a pharmaceutical company, you can use the Accounts area to manage your territory of hospitals, clinics, and top offices and capture everything from call reports to business plans.

In this chapter, we describe all the ways you can use Accounts to manage and track companies. First, you need to get your important company lists into Salesforce and organize them according to the way that you work. Then, you can find out how to make the best use of the Account record to profile your companies. Finally, you can discover how to capitalize on the Account-related lists to gain a 360-degree view of your customers and ensure that no one drops any balls.

# Getting Familiar with the Account Record

You use an *Account record* to collect all the critical information about the companies with which you interact. That Account record is supported by other records (Contacts, Opportunities, Cases, Activities, and so on) that collectively give you a complete view of your customer. From this vantage point, you can quickly take in the view from the top, but you can also easily drill down into the details.

Here's a short list of valuable things you can do with Accounts:

>> Import and consolidate your lists of target Accounts in one place.

>> Enter new Accounts quickly and maintain naming consistency.

>> Create parent/child relationships that describe how companies' divisions or subsidiaries relate to each other.

>> Realign sales territories.

>> Segment your markets with ease.

>> Eliminate paper-based business planning.

>> Assign Account teams to better serve your customers.

>> Track your top customers and deemphasize nonstrategic ones.

>> Define the movers and shakers within an Account.

>> Monitor information from your Account's social network.

>> Manage your channel partners.

## Understanding standard Account fields

An Account record comprises fields that make up the information on a company that you're tracking. A record has two modes:

>> **Edit:** You can modify fields.

>> **Saved:** You can view the Account fields under the Edit tab and the Account's related lists, which are located under the Related tab.

An Account record also comes preconfigured with a set of fields commonly used for Account management. Most of the standard fields are self-explanatory, but in the following list, we highlight certain terms that warrant greater definition:

- >> **Account Owner:** This required field identifies the person in your organization who owns the Account. An Account record has only one owner, but many users can still collaborate on an Account.

- >> **Account Name:** This required field represents the name of the company you want to track.

- >> **Account Site:** The Account Site field goes hand in hand with the Account Name field when you're distinguishing different physical locations or divisions of a company. This field, although not required, is very important if your company sells to different locations of a customer with decentralized buying patterns. For example, if you sell mattresses to HappyDaze Hotels but each HappyDaze hotel buys independently, this field is useful for classifying different sites.

- >> **Type:** This is one of the fields on an Account record that classifies the relationship of an Account to your company. The Type field consists of a drop-down list of values, which can prove critical if you want to differentiate types of companies. For example, if you work for a software company that uses value-added resellers (VARs) to sell and service your products, you may want to select Reseller as one of your drop-down list values.

- >> **Rating:** Use this drop-down list to define your internal rating system for companies that you're tracking. Salesforce provides default values of Hot, Warm, and Cold, but you can replace these with numbers, letters, or other terms based on how you want to segment companies.

**TIP**

See Chapter 18 for instructions on customizing Account fields, such as the Type and Rating picklists.

## Building parent/child relationships

If you sell into different locations or divisions of a company and you're currently challenged by how to keep this information organized, use Account hierarchies to solve your problem. In Salesforce, you can link multiple offices of a company together by using the Parent Account field on an Account record. And you can create multiple tiers to the hierarchy if your customer is organized that way.

To establish parent/child relationships, follow these steps:

**1.** **Create Accounts for the parent and subsidiary companies.**

   If you need help with this step, turn to Chapter 5 for information on how to create new records.

**TIP**

   You can skip this step if the Accounts are already created. However, you may want to type a term such as **Headquarters** or **HQ** in the Account Site field to signify which Account s the parent.

2. **Click the link in your Recent Items list in the left sidebar for the subsidiary Account (a *child Account*) that you want to link and then click Edit.**

   If it's not in the Recent Items list, search and find the child Account you want to link and click Edit.

   The record appears in Edit mode.

3. **Click into the Parent Account field, and search for the parent Account by typing the name of the Account.**

   A list of search results appears as you type, with a list of recently viewed Accounts.

4. **From the list of results, click the name of the company to select the parent Account (as shown in Figure 8-1).**

   Your selection appears in the Parent Account field.

5. **(Optional) To further denote the child Account, use the Account Site field.**

   Some companies use city, state, country, division, and so on, depending on how they organize their Accounts. For example, if Big Box Office Supplies, Inc., has locations in Dallas and Atlanta, you could type the city into the Account Site field for each child Account so that you can tell which is which.

6. **Click Save.**

   The child Account detail page appears.

7. **To view the Account hierarchy, click the View Hierarchy link to the right of the Account Name in the header of the child Account record.**

   An Account Hierarchy list page appears and like other lists, you can click an item to go to a specific Account.

**FIGURE 8-1:**
Select a sample parent Account.

# Performing Actions with Account Related Lists

Fields on an Account record are useful for storing important data specific to a company. But where do you go to capture all the critical interactions and relationships when you're working an Account? To keep track of these details, use the related lists located on the Account detail page.

Many of the actions on Account related lists are common to other modules. For example, major modules, such as Accounts, Contacts, Opportunities, and Cases, all have related lists for Open Activities, Activity History, and Notes & Attachments. Instead of being redundant, we point you to Chapter 5 for details on using related lists to track Tasks and Events. In the following sections, we describe certain related lists that are especially pertinent to the Account record.

## Displaying an Account's Opportunities

Over the course of managing an Account, you'll hopefully uncover specific Opportunities to sell that company your products or services. You can use the Opportunity related list to quickly perform the following tasks:

» Stay aware of all open Opportunities that you and your team are pursuing on an Account.

» Add new Opportunities and link them automatically to the Account.

» Edit and delete Opportunity records.

» Gauge the progress of an Account by quickly seeing all open and closed Opportunities at their various sales stages and amounts.

See Chapter 10 for the scoop on managing Opportunities.

## Viewing Cases

Account health is much more than measuring the growth of sales for a customer. After selling, sales reps want to stay informed of customer service issues so that they can continue to keep their customers satisfied, resolve issues early, receive warnings about potential landmines, and track potential upsell Opportunities. Use the Cases-related list to view all the open and closed customer service Cases that relate to an Account.

**TIP**

If your company relies on a channel sales team to manage partners, distribute Leads, and bring in revenue, consider using Salesforce Communities, which is available in Enterprise and Performance editions for an extra charge. This partner relationship management (PRM) application gets your partners on board with using Salesforce to manage all the details of their activities with your company and your joint deals. Go to Chapter 12 for a more in-depth discussion.

## Tracking your Account teams

If you work with large companies, you probably know that it takes a team of people to win complex deals and maintain large Accounts. The Account Owner field may identify the primary person in charge, but often you need to know who to go to for a specific purpose, or maybe the Account owner is just out sick. Account teams lets you list all the individuals at your company who work with an Account and detail their specific roles.

1. **Enter the Setup menu by clicking the gear icon at the top right, then Setup, and search for Account Teams in the Quick Find search bar on the left-hand sidebar and click it.**

   The Enable Account Teams link appears.

2. **Click Enable Account Teams.**

   The Account Team Setup page appears.

3. **Select the Account Teams Enabled check box (as shown in Figure 8-2), and then click Save.**

   The Page Layout Selection page appears, allowing you to select all the Account page layouts to which you want to add the Account Teams related list. If you have Account types (and layouts) that never require team collaboration, don't add the related list to these.

4. **Select the Account page layouts to which you want to add the Account Teams related list and click Save.**

   The Account Team Setup page appears, where you can choose to define team roles for your organization. This step is optional.

Now that Account Teams are enabled for your organization, to give credit to your team and make sure that others know whom to call, go to an Account record and follow these steps:

1. **Scroll down to the Account Team related list under the Related tab.**

   If you don't see the Account-Team-related list, have your administrator activate the feature in Setup.

FIGURE 8-2:
Enabling Account
Teams.

2. **Click the Add Team Members button to add team members.**

   The New Account Team Members page appears, as shown in Figure 8-3.

3. **Use the Team Member lookups to select fellow users of Salesforce who work on this Account.**

   You can always go back and add more later.

4. **(Optional) Specify the sharing access you want to give for this Account, its Opportunities, and its Cases.**

5. **Select the appropriate role in the Team Role drop-down list.**

6. **Click Save.**

   You're returned to the Account record's detail page with your Account team listed.

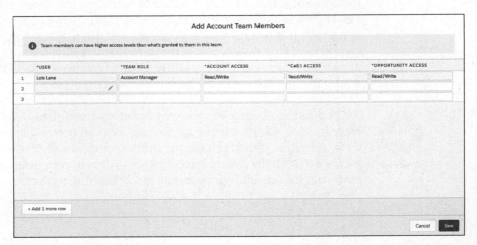

FIGURE 8-3:
Add Account
team members.

# Maintaining Your Account Database

The more you use Salesforce for Account management, the more important it is to maintain it over time.

In the following sections, we show you simple tools for keeping your Account database up to date.

## Increasing Account accuracy with Lightning Data

Everyone has his or her own way of entering a company name, but when each sales rep uses his own method, it leads to duplicate Account records. Instead of arguing over whose method is best, you can use Lightning Data to provide you with the correct name.

Lightning Data provides top-quality data from Dun & Bradstreet and is available on the Salesforce AppExchange for an added charge. You can use it to automatically clean your Account records, providing you with up-to-date information for 83 Account fields. Sales reps can also use Lightning Data to instantly import new Accounts and Contacts into Salesforce. Whether you're augmenting your existing data or starting from scratch, Lightning Data can provide the data you need without ever having to leave Salesforce.

## Deleting Account records

If you (or a subordinate) own Accounts that need to be deleted, you can delete them one at a time by using the Delete button on the Account records. The one caveat here is that some companies remove your permission to delete Accounts altogether. If this is the case or if you want to delete many Accounts at one time, consult with your system administrator. System administrators are the only users in your company who have the ability to mass-delete records. (Kind of startling to realize that geeks have all the power, isn't it?)

**WARNING**

When deleting Account records, remember that you're also deleting associated records. So, if you're deleting an Account, you can potentially be removing Contacts, Activities, Opportunities, and other records linked to the Account. You can rectify a mistakenly deleted record within 15 days of your deletion by retrieving it from your Recycle Bin, but be careful before deleting records.

IN THIS CHAPTER

» Customizing the Contact record

» Creating and updating Contacts

» Putting your Contacts in order

» Viewing Contact-related lists

» Building organizational charts

Chapter **9**

# Developing Contacts

I f you've been selling for more than a few years, you probably have a big golden list overflowing with business contacts. And if you're just starting out, you probably wish you had one. But how much do you know about those contacts? Where do you keep track of the personal and business information that you've collected throughout the years?

Salesforce enables you to plan, manage, and capture all the important interactions that you normally have with your prospects and customers. Just imagine the value that keeping this shared information in one place can have for you and your teams.

By using the Contacts section in Salesforce, you can effectively keep all your most important Contacts together in one place, easily link them with the Accounts they work for, gain insight into the relationships between contacts, and capture the critical personal drivers of each Contact that are so key to your selling success.

In this chapter, we discuss how to use Salesforce for your Contact management needs. You can also find out how to build your Contact database by adding information directly or by importing your existing files. Later in the chapter, we describe how to organize your Contacts lists so that you can quickly find the people you want to talk to. We also show you how to maintain the integrity of your Contact data by editing Contact records, merging duplicate records, and deleting old records. These tasks allow you to start putting your Contacts to work for you.

# Understanding the Contact Record

A *Contact record* is the collection of fields that consists of the information about a person you do business with. Unlike a business card or a Lead record in Salesforce, however, a Contact is linked to an Account. Like other records, the Contact record has two modes: an *Edit* mode, in which you can modify fields, and a *Saved* mode, in which you can view the fields (under the Details tab) and the Contact's related lists (under Related).

A Contact record comes preconfigured with a standard set of fields commonly used for Contact management. The exact number isn't important because your company might add or subtract fields based on the way you want to track your Contacts. Most of the standard fields are self-explanatory, but in the following list, we highlight a few fields that are less obvious:

>> **Contact Owner:** This is the person in your organization who owns the Contact. A Contact has only one owner, although many users can still collaborate on a Contact.

>> **Reports To:** This lookup field on the Contact record allows you to organize your Contacts hierarchically.

>> **Lead Source:** This drop-down list defines where you originated the Contact.

>> **Email Opt Out:** This check box reminds you whether a Contact should be emailed.

>> **Do Not Call:** This check box reminds you whether a Contact can be called.

REMEMBER

Privacy is a big issue with companies and the selling tactics they employ. Nothing damages a customer relationship more than a Contact who's contacted when he or she has asked not to be. To protect your Contacts' privacy, be diligent about the Email Opt Out and Do Not Call fields. Users in your company should always check the Contact record before calling or marketing to a Contact.

# Customizing Contact Information

After you complete the standard fields, you never have trouble knowing where to reach your Contacts. Whether they take your call is another question, though.

Think about all the personal or professional information that you commonly collect on your best Contacts. For example, if Michael Jordan is your client, you may like to know that he loves golf and fine cigars and has five kids. And he's always driven to be number one.

**TIP**

Ask yourself these questions while you customize your Contact record:

>> What professional information is important in your business (for example, prior employers or associations)?

>> What personal information can help you build a better relationship?

>> How do you evaluate the strength of your relationship with the Contact?

>> What probing questions do you commonly ask all contacts? (For example, what are their current initiatives and business challenges?)

We always advise keeping it simple, but if any specific fields are missing, write them down and seek out your system administrator. (See Chapter 17 for the details on how to build fields and other design tricks.) Salesforce can help you remember important details about your contacts, and you can use that information to build better relationships.

# Entering and Updating Your Contacts

Your Contact database is only as good as the information it contains, so Salesforce has multiple ways for you to get your contacts into the system. You can either start from scratch and manually create new Contact records, or if you already have contacts on a spreadsheet or in another tool, you can use Salesforce's simple wizard to import your Contacts within minutes. In the following sections, we discuss quick and simple ways to get started and how to update records.

## Entering new Contacts

Because Contacts belong to Accounts, the best, most reliable way to create Contact records is by starting from the relevant Account detail page. From the Account detail page, you can then add a Contact by using either the New Contact button on the top of the page or the New button on the Contacts related list. The layout may be different but the result is the same in both situations, and Salesforce automatically prefills the Account lookup field. By doing this, you can always find your Contact, and your Contact's activities also appear in a list on its Account detail page.

To create Contacts by using this best practice, follow these steps:

1. **Search for the Account, and then click the appropriate Account Name link on the Search Results page.**

   The Account detail page appears.

2. **Click the New button on the Contacts related list.**

   A New Contact pop-up appears in edit mode, as shown in Figure 9-1.

3. **Fill in the fields as much as you can or as required.**

   The Account field is prefilled with the Account you were working from.

4. **When you're done, click one of the following buttons:**

   - *Save:* After you click the Save button, the Contact detail page appears. On this page, you can click the Edit button whenever you need to modify information on the record.

   - *Save & New:* Clicking this button saves the current Contact record and automatically opens a new, blank Contact record in Edit mode.

   The new Contact appears in the Contact recent list on the Account.

## Importing your Contacts and Accounts

If you already have contact lists in another database (such as Excel), you can use the Data Import wizard to create multiple Contact records in Salesforce and be done in no time. The Data Import wizard is located in the Setup menu or by click-ing the Import button on the Accounts or Contacts home page.

When you import Accounts, you can import just companies and their associated information, or you can import companies and their related Contacts in one action. Which route you take really depends on your existing data and what you want in Salesforce.

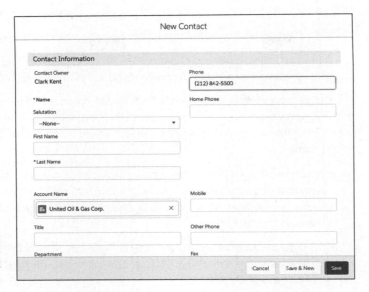

**FIGURE 9-1:**
Completing fields
on a Contact
record.

To import your Contacts and Accounts automatically, follow these steps:

1. **Click the Contacts tab, and then click the Import button.**

   The Import Accounts & Contacts wizard appears, which includes three steps for importing records, plus helpful hints.

   You can import 50,000 records at a time using the Data Import wizard.

2. **In your existing contact tool or file, compare your current fields with the fields in Salesforce. Add fields to the Account or Contact objects by customizing Salesforce.**

   If you can map all the information you currently have to fields in Salesforce, move on to Step 3. If you have to add fields to Salesforce to match fields, see Chapter 17.

3. **Export your file.**

   You may have Contacts and Accounts in an existing database, such as Zoho CRM, Microsoft Dynamics, Microsoft Access, or Microsoft Outlook. Most systems like these have simple tools for exporting data into various formats. Select the records and the fields that you want to export. Then export the file and save it in a comma-separated values (CSV) format. If your Accounts are already in spreadsheet format, such as Microsoft Excel, just resave the file in the CSV format.

4. **Review and prepare your data in Excel.**

   Refine your Accounts and Contacts before bringing them into Salesforce or clean them up after the import — it's up to you. Some sales reps prefer to make changes on a spreadsheet first because they're more accustomed to spreadsheets.

When preparing your import file, keep these points in mind:

- *Enter your column headers in the first row.* We recommend renaming column headers to be consistent with the field names in Salesforce. For example, you could rename the Company field from Outlook as Account Name.

- *To import data for your entire company (available as an option only to system administrators), add a column for Record Owner to signify who should own the record in Salesforce.* Otherwise, as the person importing, you own all the records from the file.

- *To differentiate locations of a company (for example, Sony in Tokyo versus Sony in New York), add a column for Account Site and update the rows in your file to reflect the different sites.*

- *Link Accounts in the import file by adding columns for Parent Account and Parent Site and by filling in fields as necessary to reflect the hierarchy.*

- *Make sure that a Type column exists and that fields are filled to correspond to the types of companies you track (customers, partners, prospects, competitors, and so on).*

- *To import Contacts and Accounts at the same time, add a column for the billing address fields if those addresses are different from the Contacts' mailing addresses.*

For more hints on importing, click the Help and Training link and check out the Training and Support information in Salesforce by searching for the keyword *Importing*.

**TIP**

When you're figuring out how to import data into Salesforce, we recommend testing an import with five or so records first, just to make sure that you know what you're doing. After importing the test data, review your new records to make sure that they contain all the information you want to have brought in. Delete the test records, refine your import file, if necessary, and then run through the final import.

5. **After preparing the file, in the Data Import wizard page choose Accounts and Contacts under the Standard objects tab in the left window and choose what you want to do with them.**

   You can add new records, update existing Salesforce records, or update and add new ones at the same time.

**6.** Click Add New Records and choose the unique identifier for the records.

If you want Salesforce to avoid importing duplicate records, choose whether you want a duplicate Contact to be identified by matching name or email (an email address is typically more unique" than a name). If a Contact record with the matching criteria already exists in Salesforce, Salesforce updates that record with the information in your file.

**7.** Drag and drop your CSV file into the right window, as shown in Figure 9-2, and click Next when you're done.

The Edit Field Mapping page appears, where you can edit your data mapping.

**8.** Map the Contact fields between your file and Salesforce, and when you're done, click Next.

If you're importing only Accounts, skip this step. Otherwise, just go through the field mapping, click the Change link to modify the auto-mapped fields, and click the Map link to map your unmapped fields to Salesforce, as shown in Figure 9-3.

**TECHNICAL STUFF**

Mapping fields is simply the process by which you associate a field from one database with a field in another database so that your data appears in the right fields. For example, if you're importing your Contacts from Outlook, you want data from the field called Company in Outlook to map to the field called Account Name in Salesforce. Take your time when making the mappings. Pay attention to which screens are for Account-specific fields and which screens are for Contact-specific fields.

**9.** Review your selections and import to make sure you didn't forget anything, and when you're ready click Start Import.

This step basically warns you about problems with the data or lets you know about fields that haven't been mapped. If you discover an error, you can click the Previous button and refine your mapping, or even close the wizard so that you can improve your import file. You might have to start over, but at least you avoid importing bad or incomplete data.

When you click Start Import, an Importing page appears to confirm that your import is in progress.

**10.** Click OK and later check the records that you imported.

Salesforce sends you an email after it successfully imports your file. To check your import, just use the global search bar to search any Contact name from your imported list and ensure it comes up. Click the link for a Contact that you just imported to double-check that the information is accurate.

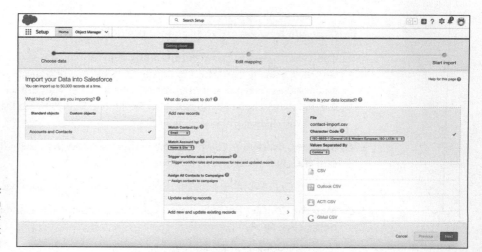

**FIGURE 9-2:**
Using the Launch wizard to prepare for your Contact import.

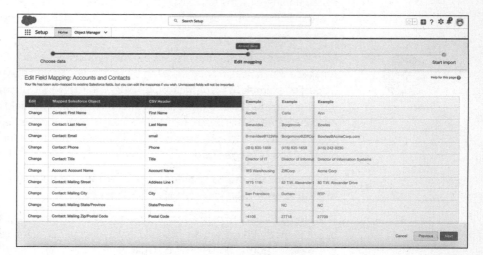

**FIGURE 9-3:**
Mapping Contact fields.

If you're importing both Accounts and Contacts, scroll down on an applicable Account to verify that all the right Contacts are linked from your import file. Click into a specific Account and Contact record and check to see that the information matches your import file.

## Researching your Contacts in the news

Visiting a company's website may tell you about its location and phone number, but it probably won't give you the latest scandal plaguing your customer. For more detailed and timely insight on your customer's organization, industry, competitors, and executives, you can enable News on the Contact record.

Formerly known as Account Insights, News is a Salesforce feature that shows you relevant news articles right on your Contact record. It is an Account object feature, which you can enable in Account Settings. Once enabled, News shows up in a separate tab within the Tab component on your Lead, Contact, and Account pages. Read more about how to enable this feature in Chapter 18.

## Updating Contact fields

While you work with your Contacts, you may need to modify Contact information. To update a Contact, follow these steps:

1. **Type the name of your Contact in the Global Search field at the top of any Salesforce page and click Search.**

   A Search Results page appears.

2. **Click the desired Contact Name link.**

   The Contact detail page appears.

3. **As with any record, in the Detail tab, double-click any field that has a pencil icon to its right to edit that field.**

   If a field doesn't have an icon at the right of the field, click the Edit button at the top of the record to make changes. You may have to click the drop-down to the right of the buttons at the top to reveal Edit. A padlock icon means that you can't edit that field.

4. **Update the fields as necessary and then click Save.**

   The Contact detail page reappears.

## Cloning an existing Contact

If you want to add a Contact that's similar to an existing record, cloning can save you keystrokes and time. To clone a Contact, go to the existing Contact and follow these steps:

1. **Click the Clone button at the top of the Contact record.**

   You may have to click the drop-down to the right of the buttons at the top to reveal Clone. A new Contact pop-up in Edit mode appears. All the information from the previous record is pre-populated for you.

**2.** **Edit the information on the new Contact record, where appropriate.**

Pay attention to what's prefilled because you want to avoid inaccurate information on the new Contact record.

**3.** **When you're done, click Save.**

You created a new Contact without altering your existing Contact.

# Organizing Your Contacts

When you have all or a portion of your Contacts entered in Salesforce, you can begin to organize them to suit the way you sell.

In the following sections, we show you how you can use list views and other tools from the Contacts home page to provide greater focus for you and your sales teams. We also show you an important feature of the Contact record that lets you build powerful organizational charts (also called *org charts*) for Contacts of an Account. (See Chapter 17 to find out how to use standard and custom Contact reports.)

## Using Contact list views

A *Contact list view* is a list of Contacts that match certain criteria. When you select a list view, you're specifying criteria to limit the results that you get back. The advantage of using a list view versus searching is that you can use the list view over and over again. For example, if you like to send a card on a Contact's birthday, you can benefit from a preset list view for this month's birthdays.

The Contacts home page comes with several predefined list views, including

>> **All Contacts:** Provides a list of all the Contact records entered into Salesforce. Depending on the way your company has set up your security model, you may not see this view or its results.

>> **Birthdays This Month:** Generates a list of Contacts whose birthdays land in the current month (assuming that you collect that information).

>> **New This Week:** Generates a list of Contacts that have been created since the beginning of the week.

>> **Recently Viewed Contacts:** Allows you to look at a list of Contacts that you've recently viewed.

You use a predefined Contact list view in exactly the same way that you use any list view (detailed in Chapter 17) or the predefined list view for any other record.

## Creating custom Contact views

If you want special lists for the way that you track your Contacts, we recommend building custom list views, just as you do for any other record. (For an example of how to create a custom view, see Chapter 17.) For example, if you sell medical equipment, and once per month you like to call your Contacts who are dentists, you can create a list view to simplify your work.

# Developing Organizational Charts

Having 20 Contacts associated with an Account is great, but you may not be any further along in understanding the pecking order. In practice, sales reps have been building org charts to strategize on Accounts ever since someone thought up org charts, but often, the charts resided on whiteboards and PowerPoint presentations. (And whiteboards are tough to lug around.) By using the org chart feature in Salesforce, you can quickly define the reporting structure for your Contacts and use that structure to more easily identify your relationships with your customers.

To build an org chart in Salesforce, follow these steps:

1. **Add all the Contacts for an Account.**

   See the section "Entering and Updating Your Contacts," earlier in this chapter, for details about adding records.

2. **Go to the Contact record for a person who's low on the totem pole and then click the Edit button.**

   The record pop-up appears in Edit mode.

3. **Type the name of the Contact's boss in the Reports To field and then select the correct Contact or refine your search until you can select the right Contact. Alternatively, if you don't have the Contact's boss in Salesforce yet, you can select the + New Contact option at the bottom of the list to create him or her.**

   The Reports To field is prefilled with the selected Contact, as shown in Figure 9-4.

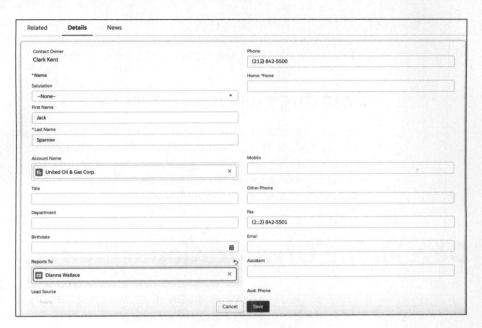

**FIGURE 9-4:**
Selecting
the boss.

4. **Click Save.**

   The Contact detail page appears.

5. **Click the Contact Hierarchy icon that appears to the right of the Contact Name in the header of the page to display the hierarchy.**

   An Org Chart list page appears, and like other lists, you can click a link to go to a specific Contact.

TIP

Some sales reps run into certain challenges based on the way they create the org charts in Salesforce. One such challenge is gaps; you just may not know or even care about the entire reporting structure. By getting creative and building placeholder Contacts, you can avoid pitfalls. For example, if you sell to both the business side and the technology side of a customer, create a Contact record called "IT Organization" and another called "Business Organization" and then align your Contacts accordingly. This technique also works well for *orphans*, where you know one Contact in a department and don't want to leave the Contact out of the org chart for the entire Account.

IN THIS CHAPTER

» **Demystifying Opportunities**

» **Creating new Opportunities**

» **Changing Opportunity records**

» **Organizing Opportunity lists and Contact roles**

» **Using Chatter to follow Opportunities**

Chapter **10**

# Tracking Opportunities

Your sales pipeline is the lifeblood of your business. It's the list of deals that can help you achieve your sales targets. But try as you might, you can probably never close every deal in your pipeline. Things happen: Budgets get slashed, projects get tabled, you lose to a competitor, decision makers change. So, you need enough deals to give yourself the chance to hit and exceed your revenue goals in a given time frame.

An *Opportunity* in Salesforce is a sales deal that you want to track to an ultimate conclusion (ideally, a win). The Opportunity record has tools to help you efficiently track and close a sale. By using Salesforce, you can manage more Opportunities at the same time and pursue each Opportunity with greater precision. For example, if you're a Salesforce sales rep, you can use Opportunities to follow a standard process, link distribution partners, associate products, strategize against competition, record your actions and other notes, and more. And you don't have to waste precious time updating a pipeline spreadsheet. Instead, you or your manager can generate the current pipeline with the click of a button.

In this chapter, we show you the techniques and best practices for using Opportunities to track sales. First, you find out the most reliable way to create Opportunities. Then we discuss how to view them in the manner that makes sense to you. You can also discover how to update your records so that your information is current and how to use Chatter to follow Opportunities.

# Getting Familiar with the Opportunity Record

An *Opportunity record* is the collection of fields that make up the information on a deal you're tracking. The record has only two modes: In Edit mode, you modify fields; in View mode, you view the fields and the Opportunity's related lists.

An Opportunity record comes preconfigured with several standard fields. Most of these fields are self-explanatory, but be sure to pay attention to these critical ones:

>> **Amount:** This field displays the intended best-guess amount of the sale. Depending on the way your company calculates the pipeline report, you might use numbers that include total contract value, the bookings amount, and so on.

>> **Close Date:** Use this required field for your best guess as to when you'll close this deal. Depending on your company's sales process, the close date has different definitions, but this field is commonly used to track the date that you signed all the paperwork required to book the sale.

>> **Expected Revenue:** This read-only field is automatically generated by multiplying the Amount field by the Probability field.

>> **Forecast Category:** This field is typically hidden, but every Opportunity automatically includes a value. Each sales stage within the Stage drop-down list corresponds to a default forecast category so that higher-probability Opportunities contribute to your overall forecast after they reach certain stages.

>> **Opportunity Owner:** This person in your organization owns the Opportunity. Although an Opportunity record has only one owner, many users can still collaborate on an Opportunity.

>> **Opportunity Name:** This required text field represents the name of the specific deal as you want it to appear on your list of Opportunities or on a pipeline report.

TIP

When naming Opportunities, you and your company should define a standard naming convention for the Opportunity Name field so that you can easily search for and distinguish Opportunities from a list. We recommend that the Opportunity name start with the Account name, then a hyphen, and then the name of the customer's project or the product of primary interest. This naming convention makes for readable reports later on.

>> **Private:** If you want to keep an Opportunity private, select this check box to render the record accessible to only you, your bosses, and the system administrator.

>> **Probability:** The *probability* is the confidence factor associated with the likelihood that you'll win the Opportunity. Each sales stage that your company defines is associated with a default probability to close. Typically, you don't need to edit this field; it gets assigned automatically by the Stage option that you pick. In fact, your administrator might remove write access from this field altogether.

>> **Stage:** This required field allows you to track your Opportunities, following your company's established sales process. Salesforce provides a set of standard drop-down list values common to solution selling, but your system administrator can modify these values.

>> **Type:** Use this drop-down list to differentiate the types of Opportunities that you want to track. Most customers use the Type drop-down list to measure new versus existing business and products versus services, but your system administrator can modify it to measure other important or more specific deal types, such as add-ons, upsells, work orders, and so on.

REMEMBER

When customizing your Opportunity fields, take into consideration the patience and attention spans of your end-users. Keep the record as simple as possible to ensure that all your important fields actually get filled in. If you add many fields, you might make the Opportunity record harder to use, which then puts user adoption of Salesforce at risk. At the same time, you'll have greater success with Opportunities when you can easily capture what you want to track.

# Entering Opportunities

Before you can begin using Salesforce to close Opportunities, first you must get the records into Salesforce. The best method for creating a new Opportunity is to start from the relevant Account or Contact record, which guarantees that the Opportunity associates to the correct record, making the Opportunity easily trackable. And if you add the Opportunity from a Contact, you link both the Account and the Contact at the same time.

To create an Opportunity, go to the relevant Account or Contact detail page and follow these steps:

1. **Select the New button on the Opportunities related list under the Related tab.**

   A New Opportunity pop-up appears in edit mode (see Figure 10-1). The Account Name field is conveniently filled in for you.

2. **Fill in the fields as much as you can or as required.**

   At a minimum, you must complete the required fields. Depending on how you set up your Opportunity record, you might have to fill in additional required fields, all of which are highlighted in red. See the section "Getting Familiar with the Opportunity Record," earlier in this chapter, for more details on common required fields.

3. **Click Save when you're done.**

   The Account detail page reappears with the new Opportunity in the related list.

TIP

If you have the good fortune to need to enter multiple Opportunities, one after another, instead of clicking the Save button, click the Save & New button. A new Opportunity record appears in Edit mode. You have to fill in the Account Name field, but this technique can save you time.

**FIGURE 10-1:** Completing Opportunity fields.

**TECHNICAL STUFF**

If your company has legacy databases that contain deal information and you want this data to be in Salesforce as Opportunities, you can't use an import wizard to migrate your records like you can with Leads, Accounts, and Contacts. If this is a current challenge, seek out your technical staff, system administrator, Salesforce rep, or a Salesforce consultant. With business guidance, a person with the technical know-how can use the Data Loader to import Opportunities and other records into Salesforce, which can help you avoid wasting time manually re-inputting Opportunities. See Chapter 21 for additional tips and tricks on migrating data.

# Modifying Opportunity Records

After you add Opportunities to Salesforce, you can make changes to your records when deals progress, stall, or fade away. In the following sections, we cover three common practices: editing, sharing, and reassigning.

## Updating Opportunity fields

In the course of working with your Opportunities, you inevitably collect information that you want to save directly in the Opportunity record. Every time you capture important data on your Opportunity, remember to update your record by following these steps:

1. **Click the Edit button on the Opportunity.**

   You can also hover your mouse over the specific field that you want to edit. If a pencil icon appears to the right of the field, double-click the field to edit it. (If you see a padlock icon instead, that means the field is not editable, on purpose. Move along and pick another field to update.)

   Alternatively, if you're already in an Account or Contact record that's linked to the Opportunity, scroll down to the Opportunities related list and click the downward-pointing triangle to the right of the desired Opportunity and click Edit. The result is the same. The Opportunity Edit pop-up page appears.

2. **Update the fields, as necessary, paying particular attention to keeping fields such as Amount, Close Date, and Stage up to date.**

   Nine out of ten times, those fields play key roles in your company's sales pipeline reports. By keeping your information up to date, you and other users can get a true measure of the Opportunity's progress.

3. **When you're done, click Save.**

   The Opportunity is saved and the fields that you edited are changed.

**TIP**

You can keep track of certain critical updates to your Opportunity record by using the Stage History related list. Anytime you or one of your team members who has read-write access to your record modifies the Stage, Probability, Close Date, or Amount field, you can quickly scan this at the bottom or side of the Opportunity record page (depending on how your pages are set up) to see who modified the record and when. See Chapter 17 for more detail on creating, updating, and cloning records, and Chapter 22 for more information about using and customizing reports.

## Rolling up Opportunity data onto the Account record

The Opportunity record carries a great deal of quantifiable information about an Account, such as how many licenses were sold, the amount of a deal, and so on. By collecting and aggregating key Opportunity field information onto an Account record, a sales rep can quickly see how valuable a particular customer is by viewing the total number of licenses a customer currently has, how much total revenue a customer has closed with your company, and the highest deal closed with that customer, to name a few examples.

You can aggregate this summary information in two ways:

» You can run a report that summarizes this information for you. (See Chapter 22 for more details on creating reports.)

» Your Salesforce administrator can choose which Opportunity fields you want to have summarized automatically on the Account record.

**TECHNICAL STUFF**

Roll-up summary fields can only be created on the master object of a master-detail relationship. Remember that you are rolling up values from a set of related records up to their parent, such as a group of Opportunity values related to the same Account.

To create a custom roll-up of your Opportunity data onto the Account record, go to the Setup menu and in the left-hand sidebar, search for Object Manager in the Quick Find search bar, click it, and then follow these steps:

**1.** **Click the Account object.**

The Account Object Manager page opens.

**2.** **On the left-hand sidebar, click Fields & Relationships.**

A list of Account fields appears.

3. **At the top right of the page, click the New button to create a new field on the Account object.**

   The New Custom Field wizard opens.

4. **Select the Roll-Up Summary radio button and click Next.**

   The New Custom Field wizard opens.

5. **Enter the name of what you're summarizing in the Field Label field, hit tab, and click Next.**

   The Field Name field automatically populates itself based on what you enter in the Field Label. In this example, we typed Total Deals Closed, hit the Tab key to populate the Field Name, and then clicked the Next button.

6. **At the Define the Summary Calculation step, from the Summarized Object picklist, select Opportunities.**

   Identifying the summarized object tells Salesforce which records from which objects you want to be combined and summarized onto the Account record.

7. **Select the roll-up type from the selection of radio buttons in the Select Roll-Up Type section in the middle of the page, and then click Next.**

   This selection tells Salesforce how you want the field of your choice to be summarized. You can choose a count of records, the sum, the minimum value, or the maximum value. If you choose any of the latter three options, you also have to identify which field in the Opportunity you want to be summarized by using the Field to Aggregate picklist to make their choice.

   You can filter out certain criteria in your result set.

   If you want to summarize only records that meet certain criteria, select the Only Records Meeting Certain Criteria Should Be Included in the Calculation radio button to reveal a set of filter criteria. For example, you may want a sum of all the Amount fields for Opportunities in which the Closed status equals True. (Figure 10-2 shows an example of defining the field calculation.)

8. **Select which profiles should be able to view the new field and click Next.**

9. **Select on which page layout(s) the field should be displayed and click Save.**

# Tracking your deals on the Opportunity kanban board

Lightning Experience provides an option to display your Opportunity list views in the format of a columnar kanban board, where each column represents a certain Opportunity stage and applicable deals in that stage.

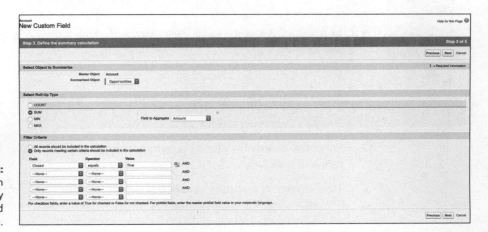

**FIGURE 10-2:**
Defining an
Opportunity
roll-up field
calculation.

**TECHNICAL STUFF**

*Kanban* refers to an engineering process originally used in Japan by Toyota that optimized inventory levels. The general system of moving a card through various stages, represented visually by columns, until its completion, has been adopted in other industries because it provides a visualization of progressing to a goal.

To visualize your Opportunities on a kanban board, as shown in Figure 10-3, follow these steps:

1.  **From the navigation bar on the left side of the screen, click Opportunities.**

    A list of recently viewed Opportunities appears.

2.  **Click the downward-pointing triangle to the right of the Recently Viewed Opportunities list name.**

    A list of standard and custom list views appears.

3.  **Select a list view so that it displays on the screen.**

4.  **On the right side of the list view header area, click the icon that looks like a small grid.**

    The Display As drop-down list appears.

5.  **Select Kanban from the Display As drop-down list.**

    The list view changes to a kanban board, where each Opportunity is represented as a card, nested under its current Opportunity stage. The board also shows a summary of all Opportunity Amounts for that particular stage.

6.  **(Optional) Move an Opportunity to a different stage by hovering over its card, and then clicking and dragging it to its updated column.**

    The Opportunity's stage is updated, and the sum of the Opportunity Amounts in the affected columns changes to reflect the move.

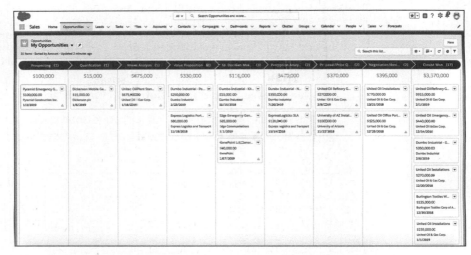

**FIGURE 10-3:**
Viewing an
Opportunity
kanban board.

## Visualizing your deal using Sales Path

To help coach users within a sales organization and foster proper usage of Sales-force, Leads and Opportunities now offer a Sales Path in the Lightning Experience. This guides reps through each required stage of the deal until it's closed. It also gives sales trainers and managers a narrative of what a user should accomplish in a particular stage of his process. This can include what fields should be filled out, instructions, and links to resources. Of course, this means your business has to have some business process to reflect within the system! For an example of a Sales Path item, see Figure 10-4.

**FIGURE 10-4:**
Receiving
guidance along
the Sales Path.

## Defining Contact Roles

Depending on your sales process, at some early point, you need to identify the decision makers who'll influence the buying decision. Contacts and their titles often don't tell the whole story about decision makers, influencers, and the chain of command within an Opportunity.

In the Lightning Experience, Contact Roles are available on Contracts and Opportunities and must be defined independently. To better define the buying influences on an Opportunity, go to an Opportunity record and follow these steps:

1. **Click the Manage Contact Roles button on the Contact Roles related list.**

   The Contact Roles page appears for that specific Opportunity, displaying a list of the available Contacts linked to the related Account (see Figure 10-5).

**Manage Contact Roles**

PRIMARY CONTACT (OPTIONAL)

| | *CONTACT | ROLE |
|---|---|---|
| 1 | Jack Sparrow | Decision Maker ▾ |
| 2 | | --None-- |
| 3 | | Business User |
| | | ✓ Decision Maker |
| | | Economic Buyer |
| | | Economic Decision Maker |
| | | Evaluator |
| | | Executive Sponsor |

+ Add 1 more row

Cancel    Save

**FIGURE 10-5:** Selecting the Contact Role.

2. **For each relevant Contact, use the Role drop-down list to select the appropriate role.**

   Salesforce comes preconfigured with a standard list of Contact Roles, but your company can customize this drop-down list if you need to modify the list of values. You don't have to classify a role for every Contact on the list; you can just leave the Role default value of None.

   If the right role for your Contact doesn't appear, advise your system administrator to customize the Opportunity Contact Role Picklist Values.

**REMEMBER**

3. **(Optional) Select the primary Contact.**

The primary Contact typically refers to the person who's currently your point of contact. One of the benefits of selecting a primary Contact is that you can list who the primary Contact is on a basic Opportunity report.

4. **(Optional) Click into the empty fields in the Contact column to find and add other Contacts who are critical to your Opportunity. Alternatively, select + New Contact to create a new Contact.**

TIP

If you work with multitier selling models or if you collaborate with business partners on your deals, use Contact Roles to add Contacts who aren't employees of an Account. For example, if your customer's legal gatekeeper works for an outside law firm, you can use the Contact Roles related list to highlight the attorney's role.

5. **When you're done, click Save.**

The Opportunity detail page reappears, and your Contact Roles related list is updated to reflect Contacts involved in the Opportunity. If you need to add more Contact Roles, click the New button in the Contact Roles related list again.

## Using Opportunity teams

Depending on how you do business, you can identify Opportunity Teams so that all members working a deal can access the same record. An *Opportunity Team* is a set of users in your Salesforce instance that can collaborate on a single Opportunity. You can also create default Opportunity Teams if, for example, you typically work on deals with the same account manager and presales representative from your territory.

To enable Opportunity Teams, go to Setup, and in the Quick Find search bar, type Opportunity Teams. Then select Opportunity Team Settings and click the Enable Team Selling check box, as shown in Figure 10-6.

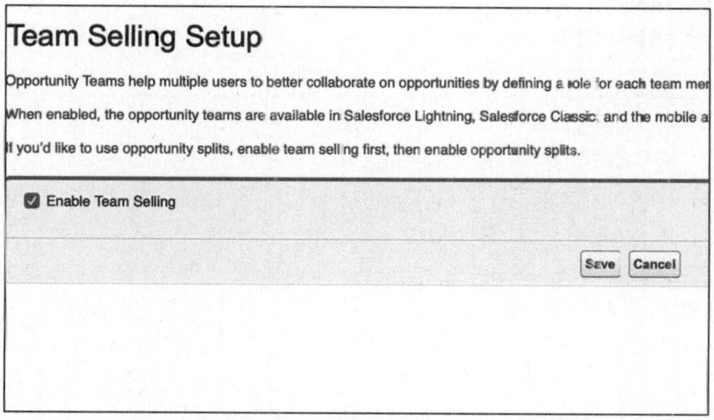

### Team Selling Setup

Opportunity Teams help multiple users to better collaborate on opportunities by defining a role for each team mer

When enabled, the opportunity teams are available in Salesforce Lightning, Salesforce Classic, and the mobile a

If you'd like to use opportunity splits, enable team selling first, then enable opportunity splits.

☑ Enable Team Selling

Save | Cancel

**FIGURE 10-6:**
Enabling
Opportunity
Teams for your
organization.

Now you'll see the page layout selection page, where you can select any and all Opportunity layouts to which you can add the Opportunity Team related list.

## Associating an Opportunity Team to your Opportunity

Now that you have Opportunity Teams enabled for your organization, you can create default Opportunity Teams or just create an ad hoc team and associate it with the Opportunity you're working on.

To create a default Opportunity Team that you typically work with, click your photo or the avatar photo at the top right of any page and then the Settings link to get to your personal settings. Then follow these steps:

**1.** **In the Settings menu on the left, select Advanced User Details.**

The Advanced User Details page appears, with information about your profile.

**2.** **Scroll down to Default Opportunity Team and click Add.**

The Add Members page appears, where you can select the users you want to add to your default team, their level of access to the Opportunity, and their team role, as shown in Figure 10-7.

**TIP**

You can choose to automatically add the default team to any Opportunities you create or are reassigned to by selecting the corresponding check box on the Add Members page.

**3.** **Click Save when you're done.**

The Advanced User Details page reappears with your default Opportunity Team.

Clark Kent
Add Members

Your default opportunity team should include the users that normally work with you.

Automatically add my default opportunity team to opportunities that I create or open opportunities that are transferred to me
Update open opportunity teams with these members

| | | | Save | Save & More | Cancel |

| User | | Opportunity Access | Team Role | |
|------|------|---------------------|-----------|------|
| Lois Lane | 🔍 | Read/Write ⬍ | Account Manager ⬍ |
| | 🔍 | Read/Write ⬍ | --None-- ⬍ |
| | 🔍 | Read/Write ⬍ | --None-- ⬍ |
| | 🔍 | Read/Write ⬍ | --None-- ⬍ |
| | 🔍 | Read/Write ⬍ | --None-- ⬍ |

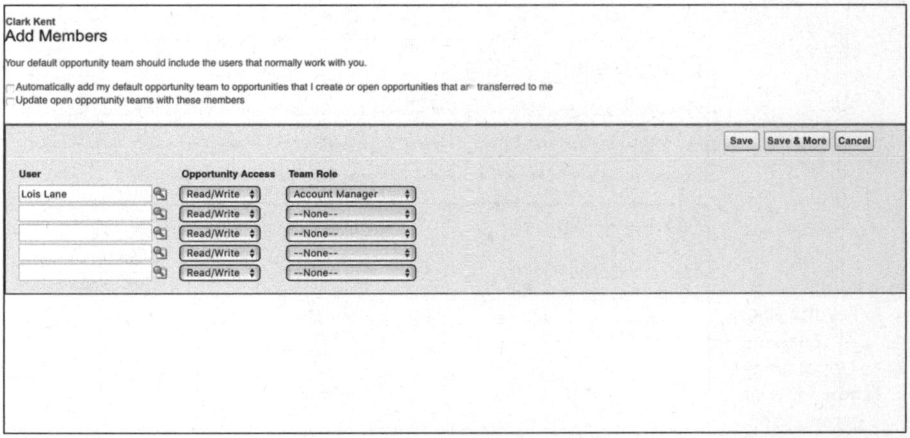

**FIGURE 10-7:**
Adding members to your default Opportunity Team.

To associate your default team to an Opportunity, navigate to the Opportunity record you own, scroll down to the Opportunity Team related list, and click Add Default Team.

If you don't have a default team, or just want to associate other users to the Opportunity, click the Add button on the Opportunity Team related list, and select the users, roles, and level of access there.

# Following Opportunities with Chatter

If you work as part of a sales team or just have a lot of deals to keep track of, Salesforce can bring you the news on your Opportunities as it happens. You are automatically set to follow updates on any Opportunity you create, but sometimes, you don't want to hunt down what's happening on someone else's Opportunity.

You can follow an Opportunity record by following these steps:

**1.** **From the Opportunity home page, click a recently viewed Opportunity.**

The Opportunity page appears, with Chatter as one of your tabs, as shown in Figure 10-8.

For more information on how to use Chatter, see Chapter 6.

**FIGURE 10-8:** Following an Opportunity.

2. **To follow the discussion on this Opportunity, click the Follow button on the top right of the page.**

   The Follow button turns into a Following button with a checkmark next to it that you can click if you want to unfollow the record. If you have a stream, a drop-down appears so that you can select where to follow the record first — in a stream or via the feed. For more information on feeds and streams, see Chapter 6.

   Now when there's Chatter activity on this Opportunity, it appears in your Chatter homepage feed (or stream), too.

IN THIS CHAPTER

» **Defining Products and Price Books**

» **Using Products and Price Books**

» **Creating Products**

» **Establishing and updating Product schedules**

» **Maintaining Product lists and Price Books**

Chapter **11**

# Tracking Products and Price Books

A *Product,* as its name implies, is a product or service that you sell to customers. Products are the individual line items that make up an *Opportunity.* Depending on your goals for Salesforce, you may not need to immediately incorporate Salesforce's Product-type features into your Opportunities. But if you sell multiple products and services and you struggle with product-level visibility, Salesforce provides powerful and easy tools to implement solutions.

Using Products in Salesforce benefits sales reps and people in operations, product marketing, management, and development throughout your organization. Sales reps can quickly locate the correct price of a product and select Products for Salesforce to automatically calculate an Opportunity's amount. With this increased accuracy, sales operations, and deal desk teams review deals with fewer errors in them, which helps expedite the approval, quote-generation, and contract-signing processes of a sale (which also should make the seller happy). Finance, Accounting, and Legal department members that review deals also can benefit from increased product and contractual language accuracy in standard sales deals. Marketing, management, or development professionals can get vital sales information to support strategic business planning, new product development, and product life cycle management.

In this chapter, we show sales teams how to use Products and Price Books with Opportunities (if your administrator has already set that up). Before setting up Products and Price Books, though, administrators first need to do some advanced planning. Confirm which department is in charge of organizing and maintaining Products and Price Books. Try to get agreement on how frequently these will be updated and in what way they will be updated. (Do you create a new Price Book for each year, or do you just update the list price for relevant Products in specific Price Books? These updates won't affect Products on existing Opportunities, so figure out what business process best suits the realities of your company.) We discuss how to create a Product catalog, consider schedules, and build Price Books. We then show you how to maintain Products and Price Books on an ongoing basis to facilitate your sales goals.

# Discovering Products and Price Books

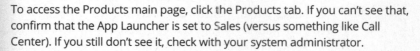

You need to know two key and interrelated terms before you can begin planning your product strategy in Salesforce:

>> **Products:** Individual items that you sell through your Opportunities. All Products belong to one universal product catalog, called the Standard Price Book. After you create a Product, though, you can associate it with one or multiple Price Books with identical or different prices. For example, you may use multiple Price Books if you use one set of prices when selling to qualified nonprofit agencies and a different set of prices when selling to companies in the private sector.

A Product can have an associated *schedule* based on quantity, revenue, or both. If you sell Products and break out schedules to forecast basic revenue recognition or for no-frills planning, you can use Salesforce to reflect important schedules for Products linked to Opportunities.

TIP

To access the Products main page, click the Products tab. If you can't see that, confirm that the App Launcher is set to Sales (versus something like Call Center). If you still don't see it, check with your system administrator.

>> **Price Book:** A collection of Products and their associated prices. A Product with its associated price is a *Price Book entry*. You can also create custom Price Books based on your unique sales model.

You can associate a Price Book, add Products, and build schedules on an Opportunity through the Products-related list on an Opportunity detail page.

**REMEMBER**

An Opportunity can have only one Price Book assigned to it, which then determines the prices of whichever Products comprise the deal.

## Defining standard Product fields

A Product record consists of a number of fields that you use to capture information about a product you sell. If you're involved in tracking products for your company, most of the standard fields are obvious. If you want specific definitions, click the Help link in the upper-right corner of Salesforce.

Here are some important pointers on understanding the standard Product record fields:

» **Product Name:** The name of your Product. Make sure to use titles that are clear and familiar to your sales reps and customers.

» **Product Code:** An internal code or product ID used to identify your Product. If your existing Products and product codes reside in a financial database and you want to plan for integration, make sure that the product codes are consistent.

» **Product Description:** Text to distinguish Products from each other. If you're in product management or marketing, describe your Products so that they're obvious and useful for your sales teams.

» **Product Family:** The category of the Product. Use this drop-down list when building reports that reflect sales data by product category. For example, if you work for a technology value-added reseller (VAR), you may want to reflect your pipeline by families that include hardware, software, services, training, and maintenance. You can set up Products in Salesforce so that each Product automatically maps to a product family.

» **Active:** This check box must be selected to make the Product available to your users who will be looking at a list of products to add to an Opportunity.

» **Quantity Scheduling Enabled:** Select this check box to enable quantity scheduling for a Product. This is usually chosen to determine when a Product is delivered. If you don't see this check box, your administrator hasn't enabled it.

» **Revenue Scheduling Enabled:** Select this check box to enable revenue scheduling for a Product. This is usually chosen to determine when a Product is paid for. If you don't see this check box, your administrator hasn't enabled it.

## Understanding the different types of pricing

Salesforce allows you to customize your pricing based on the way you sell. If you use Products in Salesforce, your company has three different options for pricing:

>> **Standard Prices:** Default prices that you establish for your Products when you set up your Standard Price Book.

>> **List Prices:** Prices that you set up for custom Price Books.

>> **Sales Price:** Price of a Product determined by the sales rep when he adds a Product to an Opportunity. (See the following section for details on adding Products to Opportunities.)

TIP

You'll hear the terms *Products* and *Opportunity products* referenced when you start using Salesforce Products and Price Books. What's the difference? Products are the base level things that your company sells. Products can be assigned to various Price Books and given different list prices within those Price Books. Opportunity products are the specific Products (and prices) that are associated with and unique to a specific Opportunity. Opportunity products should reflect the negotiated price and conditions for that specific Opportunity.

# Using Products and Price Books

Sales reps can add Products with specific prices to their Opportunities, and Salesforce automatically calculates the Amount field on an Opportunity record. If you're a sales rep selling multiple products and managing multiple Opportunities at the same time, you can take the frustration out of remembering what you offered to a customer. If you're a sales manager, you can segment your pipelines and forecasts by product lines. And if you're in product management or marketing, Products in Salesforce can give you real insight into product demand from your markets.

## Adding Products to Opportunities

To take advantage of Products, your company must first set up a Product catalog, as well as one or more Price Books. See the section "Building the Product Catalog," later in this chapter, for the how-to details on setting up your Products and Price Books. After this is done, sales reps can add Products to an Opportunity by going to a specific Opportunity and following these steps:

1. **From the Opportunity record look at the right sidebar to locate the Products related list, click the drop-down to the right of the section name, and then click the Choose Price Book option.**

   A Choose Price Book pop-up appears. If your company has made only one Price Book available to you, you can bypass this step and start with Step 2.

2. **Select the appropriate Price Book from the Price Book drop-down list and then click Save.**

   The Opportunity record appears again.

   On an Opportunity, you can use only one Price Book at a time.

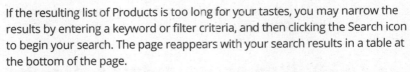

3. **From the Productsrelated list (in the right sidebar), click the drop-down to the right of the section name and selectthe Add Product option.**

   An Add Products pop-up appears, as shown in Figure 11-1. This shows all the Products in your selected Price Book.

   If the resulting list of Products is too long for your tastes, you may narrow the results by entering a keyword or filter criteria, and then clicking the Search icon to begin your search. The page reappears with your search results in a table at the bottom of the page.

4. **Select the check boxes next to the Products that you want, and then click the Next button.**

   An Edit Selected Products page appears with your selections and fields for you to provide line item details. The Sales Price field is prefilled with the default sales price from the Price Book that you selected.

5. **Fill in the line item details.**

   You must, at a minimum, fill in the Quantity and Sales Price fields for each selected Product. The Date field is typically used to reflect an expected shipping or delivery date for the Product. It could also be used to determine the contracted start date of a service.

6. **When you're done, click the Save button.**

   The Opportunity record reappears. Notice that the Amount field on the Opportunity record has changed based on the total from the Products you added.

If you need to change the details on your Product selections in the course of the sales cycle, you can do this easily on the Products related list of the Opportunity record.

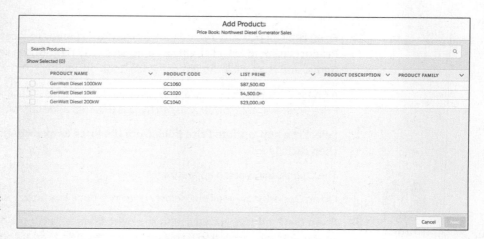

| | PRODUCT NAME | ⌄ | PRODUCT CODE | ⌄ | LIST PRICE | ⌄ | PRODUCT DESCRIPTION | ⌄ | PRODUCT FAMILY | ⌄ |
|---|---|---|---|---|---|---|---|---|---|---|
| ☐ | GenWatt Diesel 1000kW | | GC1060 | | $87,500.00 | | | | | |
| ☐ | GenWatt Diesel 10kW | | GC1020 | | $4,500.0 | | | | | |
| ☐ | GenWatt Diesel 200kW | | GC1040 | | $23,000.00 | | | | | |

**Add Products**
Price Book: Northwest Diesel Generator Sales

Search Products...

Show Selected (0)

Cancel

**FIGURE 11-1:**
Finding your
Products.

**REMEMBER**

If you find yourself unable to modify the sales price on your Products, you may want to politely confirm the intent with your sales manager. Some companies lock in the sales price for sales reps so that they must adhere to a predefined discount approval policy.

## Adding and updating schedules on Opportunities

If you manage Opportunities in which your products or services are delivered over time, you can create basic schedules for your Products by quantity, revenue, or both. By using schedules, you and your users can benefit in multiple ways:

>> **If you're on a sales team:** You get a better gauge on revenue recognition, which could be significant if that affects compensation.

>> **If you're in product management:** You can better forecast and plan for the number of units that you'll have to deliver in future quarters.

>> **If you're part of a services organization:** Schedules updated by reps provide a real-time gauge in planning your resources and projects.

**REMEMBER**

If your business sells some sort of subscription service or has a lot of product offerings that are dependent on other products you choose (like when configuring the components of a personal computer) you may need something more advanced that works with Salesforce's standard product features. There are in-house add-ons and third-party vendors that accommodate more complex deal needs, including Salesforce CPQ and Zuora.

**REMEMBER**

Your system administrator must first set up your products with scheduling. (See the section "Setting Up Schedules," later in this chapter, for more specifics on schedules, and see Chapter 17 for the details on common Salesforce configuration actions.)

After scheduling is enabled for a Product, set up a Schedule by going to the Opportunity record and following these steps:

1. **Click the desired Product name from the Products related list in the right sidebar of the Opportunity record page.**

   An Opportunity Product page appears, with a Schedule related list subtab and a Details subtab.

2. **Click the Related subtab to see the Schedules related list. Click the Establish Schedule button in the Schedule related list section.**

   An Establish Schedule page appears. If you see a Reestablish Schedule button instead of an Establish button, you have an existing schedule already. Clicking Reestablish Schedule deletes the old schedule and creates a new one by taking you to the Establish Schedule page.

3. **Complete the fields and click Save.**

   Your fields may vary, depending on whether the Product is set up for quantity, revenue, or combined scheduling. When you click Save, a schedule appears based on your choices.

4. **Review and modify the schedule.**

   If the revenues or quantities aren't equal over the periods that you first established, select Edit Schedule to type over the values in the schedule. For example, these amounts may not be equal if your customer has negotiated varying types of ramped payments, or more payments during certain times of the year to accommodate for heavier seasonal business.

5. **When you're done, click Save.**

   The Opportunity Product page reappears with the schedule you established.

Over the course of an Opportunity, if terms change, you can adjust the schedule on a Product by clicking the buttons on the Opportunity Product page. To access an Opportunity Product page, go to the relevant Opportunity record, find the Products related list in the right sidebar, and click the desired Product. The Opportunity Product page for the selected Product appears with a Schedule under the Related subtab. You can do the following with the schedule:

>> **Modify the schedule.** Click the Edit Schedule button.

>> **Delete the schedule.** Click the Delete Schedule button.

>> **Establish the schedule all over again.** Click the Reestablish Schedule button.

## Searching for Products

You can search for specific Products easily by using the Search This List search tool on the Products home page.

**TIP**

Instead of searching from the Products home page, you can search for Products from your main home page. Just make sure to toggle the default "All" to "Products" to hone in quickly on your particular Product.

# Building the Product Catalog

If you have a vested interest in your product strategy, be aware and take advantage of all the options that Salesforce provides for customizing Products and Price Books. The more you plan ahead, the better you can implement Products and Price Books for how your sales teams sell. As you make Products and Price Books active, your sales reps can start associating Products to their Opportunities. This make require a few conversations between leadership in Sales Operations, the Finance team that manages billing or orders, and/or the team that acts as a deal desk.

## Planning products for success

For products, consider the characteristics of your products outside the standard realm that you want to analyze. In most companies, the product management or marketing teams own and maintain these records in coordination with finance. You should pull together a cross-functional team made up of sales, marketing, finance, and product management users to decide what you want to achieve from products in Salesforce. Then work with your system administrator to customize the Product record to meet your specific needs. For more details on customization, see Chapter 17.

For pricing, consider whether to have set pricing on your Products or whether you prefer to keep the pricing simple at the beginning. The maturity of your organization and its billing and sales operations processes will play a factor here, too. Some customers of Salesforce, for example, set the prices on their Products at $0 or $1 and then depend on their sales reps to fill in the sales prices when they prepare an Opportunity. For organizations with a large amount of sales reps, this can place an undue burden on the deal desk team (and potentially cause delays in the sales cycle) as they work to correct typos or unauthorized discount rates. Some companies invest time and effort in creating actual standard or list prices on Products to provide guidance to their sales reps.

# Adding Products to the Product catalog

Before your sales reps can begin linking Products to their Opportunities, you need to add the Products to Salesforce.

To add a Product, log in to Salesforce and follow these steps:

1. **From the Products tab in the Navigation bar, click the drop-down icon and select the + New Product option.**

   A New Product page appears, as shown in Figure 11-2.

2. **Complete the fields.**

   Your exact fields may vary, but see the section "Defining standard Product fields," earlier in this chapter, for info on the standard fields.

3. **When you're done, click Save.**

   The Product detail page for your new Product appears with related lists for standard prices and Price Books.

**FIGURE 11-2:** Add a Product to the Product catalog.

# Changing Product details in the Product catalog

Over time, marketing, finance, or product managers may need to update details about a Product. You can make most of your changes to a Product from its record page. Go to a specific Product and take a look at this list of actions that you can perform. (You must have "edit" permissions on Products to perform these steps. See Chapter 21 for details on granting the right permissions to the right people.)

>> **Edit the Product record.** Click the Edit button. For example, if the name of your Product changes, you can change the Product Name and then save and automatically update all Opportunities that include that Product with the modified name.

>> **Delete the Product.** Click Delete and then click OK in the dialog box that appears. In circumstances in which you're no longer offering a Product but it's linked to Opportunities, it's better that you deactivate or archive the Product rather than delete it.

>> **Deactivate the Product.** Click the Edit button, deselect the Active check box, and then click Save. Take this path if you might offer the Product in the future.

>> **Delete and archive the Product.** Click Delete and then click OK in the dialog box that appears. If your Product is linked to Opportunities, a Deletion Problems page appears with suggested options. Click the Archive link if you're still intent on removing the Product but not altering the existing Opportunities.

TIP

If you want to keep your sales reps informed of any changes to your Products (for example, if a Product is no longer offered or if its name changed), you can use Chatter so that any changes to a Product's status or its name are reported in a Chatter feed. Interested users need to just follow the actions of the person who makes those changes (usually someone in Sales Operations), or they can follow the specific Product, too. (See Chapter 5 for more information on setting up Chatter and its feeds and following users and records.)

# Setting Up Schedules

If your company wants to track annuity streams, stay aware of key shipping dates, or estimate when revenue will be recognized on Products, you can also set up schedules on all or some Products.

## Enabling schedules for your company

Your administrator first needs to enable schedules before you can add them on specific Products.

**TIP**

If your company wants to track shipping dates with Salesforce, you need to enable *quantity scheduling*. If your company wants to measure revenue recognition or anticipate upcoming payments, be sure to enable *revenue scheduling*. If your company wants to do both, you'd enable both types of scheduling.

To set up schedules, follow these steps:

**1. Choose Setup ⇨ from the Quick Find search box, type in Product Schedules Settings to quickly locate that option to click.**

The Product Schedules Settings page appears, as shown in Figure 11-3.

**2. Select the appropriate check boxes.**

You can choose to enable schedules based on quantities, revenue, or both. You can also choose to enable schedules for all Products.

**REMEMBER**

**3. When you're done, click Save.**

The Setup Home page reappears.

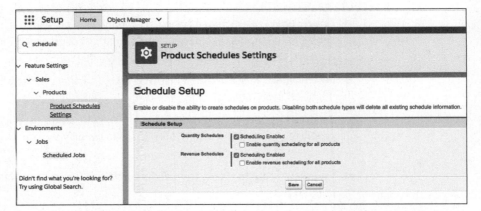

**FIGURE 11-3:** Enable schedules for your company.

## Adding and updating a default schedule

After schedules have been enabled, you can create default schedules on existing Products or while you're adding new Products.

By creating default schedules, you can simplify repetitive tasks for sales reps. With this setting, a default schedule is created when a sales rep adds a Product to an Opportunity. A sales rep can still reestablish a Product schedule on an Opportunity. The product date determines the start date for the installments.

**TIP**

If you sell a basic service with different payment plans, consider creating a unique Product for each payment plan and then using default revenue schedules. By doing this, you can simplify the data entry for the rep and reduce the chance of error. On the flip side, this is more tedious work for usually an operations team to maintain. You will need to weigh the benefits and tradeoffs with the realities of your organization and the people responsible for maintaining this data.

**REMEMBER**

If your Product has both quantity and revenue default scheduling, quantity scheduling is calculated first and drives the total amount. Then revenue scheduling divides the amount.

# Managing Price Books

Some companies require just one universal Price Book. Many other companies, however, want custom Price Books based on their unique selling needs. Examples include Price Books that are based on the following:

>> **Geography:** For a global company, the Japanese sales team might sell a subset of the products sold by its North American counterpart (and at different prices and in different currencies).

>> **Partner tiers:** In some companies that sell via partners, strategic partners might get preferential pricing.

>> **Sales teams:** If your company is divided into sales teams that sell different products, you can use custom Price Books to simplify the product selection for groups.

>> **Volume discounts:** Some companies build Price Books based on volume purchases.

>> **Seasonality:** Some companies change their pricing based on seasonal buying patterns. You can use custom Price Books to communicate pricing changes to your sales reps during these periods.

If the standard Price Book meets your objectives, keep it simple. Otherwise, in the following sections, we show you how to set up your Price Books.

## Adding to the Standard Price Book

Every time you add a standard price to a Product, you automatically associate it with the Standard Price Book. You can do this while you're creating Products, or you can add the standard prices after you've built the Product records.

The easiest time to add a standard price is while you're creating Products. To use this method, start creating a Product record as you normally would (see the section "Building the Product Catalog," earlier in this chapter). After clicking Save, follow these steps:

1. **From the Related subtab of the Product, find the Price Books related list and click the Add Standard Price button.**

   An New Price Book Entry page appears, as the Product s being associated with the universal Standard Price Book, as shown in Figure 11-4.

2. **Complete the List Price field and click Save.**

   The Product record page's Related subtab page appears, and a list price displays for the Standard Price Book.

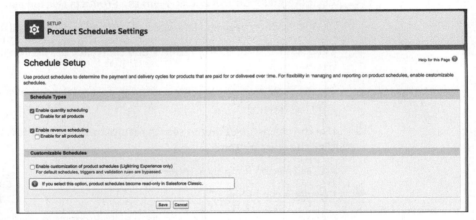

**FIGURE 11-4:**
Add a standard price.

## Creating a custom Price Book

To create a Price Book, you need to be an administrator or have permission to manage Price Books.

To create a Price Book from scratch, go to the App Launcher, and click the Price Books link. From the Price Books record page, follow these steps:

1. **A Price Book page appears with a default view of recent Price Books.**

   You can modify the view to show All Price Books.

2. **Click the New button on the Price Books record page.**

   A New Price Book pop-up appears in Edit mode.

**REMEMBER**

3. **Complete the fields.**

    Select the Active check box if you want to make the Price Book available.

4. **When you're done, click Save.**

    The Price Book detail page for your new Price Book appears with a Products related list under the Related subtab.

## Adding Products to a custom Price Book

After the Price Book has been established, you can add Products to it. A Product listed on a Price Book is also referred to as a *Price Book entry.* To add Products to an existing Price Book, go to a Price Book and follow these steps:

1. **Click the Add Products button from the Products related list.**

    An Add Products page appears with a search tool and a list of all Products.

2. **Enter keywords and filter criteria, and then click the Search icon to narrow your search.**

    The Product Selection page reappears with a list of Products based on your search criteria.

3. **Use the check boxes on the search results to choose Products and then click the Next button.**

    An Edit Selected Price Book Entries page appears.

4. **Complete the fields.**

    You can select the Active check boxes to make Products immediately available in the Price Book.

5. **When you're done, click.**

    After you save the Product, the Price Book Related subtag reappears, and your selected Products have been added to the Products related list.

## Making global changes to Price Books

Maintaining accurate and up-to-date product and price lists is challenging, especially if you have an extensive product catalog and/or complex pricing. If you're responsible for such a daunting task, you can make mass edits from the Products record page to save time.

## Changing activation on Price Books

At times, you'll want to make a Price Book unavailable to sales reps. Maybe you had to raise prices on a family of products or you stopped selling a product line. You probably need to preserve the current Price Book because existing customers and some prospects are still being associated with those products and prices, but new customers will need to be tied to the new catalog. Rest assured that you can deactivate one or more Price Books almost instantly so that sales reps won't be able to tie new Opportunities to old information.

To deactivate a Price Book, go the Price Books home page and follow these steps:

1. **Create a custom Price Books list view to meet your needs.**

   In this example, click the gear icon and select New under List View Controls to create a new custom view that filters your Price Books by those that are active. Call it the Active Price Books view. To learn how to create a custom list view, see Chapter 17.

2. **On the Active Price Books custom list, uncheck the Active check box next to a Price Book that you want to make unavailable.**

   The custom list view reappears, and the selected Price Book is no longer visible in this list because it is no longer active. A Save button now appears at the bottom of the page for you to commit your changes.

## Cloning Price Books

On occasion, you may want to create a Price Book that closely resembles an existing Price Book. Instead of starting from scratch, you can clone from an existing Price Book and then make changes, as necessary.

To clone a Price Book, follow these steps:

1. **From the Price Books record page, select a Price Book.**

   The Price Book page appears.

2. **Click the Clone button.**

   A New Price Book page appears.

3. **Type a unique name in the Price Book Name field, and give it a description in the Description field.**

4. **Select the Active check box when you want the new Price Book to be available to others for use.**

5. **When you're done, click Save.**

   The new Price Book page appears. Note that the Product from the existing Price Book have not been replicated over into the cloned Price Book.

## Deleting Price Books

**WARNING**

You can delete Price Books, but if the Price Book is associated with existing Opportunities, beware. In those circumstances, we recommend the following actions:

» Deactivate (rather than delete) the Price Book so that the linkage between Opportunities and Products stays intact.

» Delete the associated Opportunity records first, and then delete the Price Book.

» Archive the Price Book entries prior to deleting. Then, even if you delete the Price Book record, the Products associated with Opportunities are retained.

If you still want to delete a Price Book, on the Price Books home page, click the drop-down link for a particular Price Book, and select Delete. A Delete Price Book confirmation page appears. To proceed, click Delete.

If you select a Price Book that isn't associated with Opportunities, you return to the Price Book home page with the lists of Price Books. If a Deletion Problems page appears, follow the suggestions provided in the preceding bulleted list and on the Deletion Problems page.

# Chapter **12**

# Managing Your Partners

B ecause Salesforce can get sales reps and managers onboard to track all their Opportunities and sales-related activities, the big pipeline picture should be getting clearer for everyone. *Partners* — which might also be known in your business as third-party companies, your indirect sales force, value-added resellers (VARs), systems integrators (SIs), original equipment manufacturers (OEMs), wholesalers, or distributors — can also be accurately managed in Salesforce almost as if they were full-time dedicated company sales reps. It used to be difficult to create and maintain unique messages and branding for specific groups of partners. Not anymore.

The Lightning-enabled version of Salesforce Partner Relationship Management (PRM) is built using features that leverage Salesforce Communities, which allow your non-employees to access a snippet of your Salesforce instance. Salesforce PRM (which may go through several name revisions since the writing of this book) allows partners to do any of the following, depending on the nature of your business and how you interact with your partners:

» Receive Leads to pursue, based on manual or automated assignment logic (similar to how you assign Leads to your direct sales force)

» Register Leads to claim first dibs with a prospective customer (and to curtail any potential other partners from pursuing conversations with that prospect)

» Request and receive marketing development funds from their channel manager

>> Manage their Opportunities to provide visibility to their channel managers (and so the partners's pipeline isn't black box at the end of the quarter)

>> Access the latest marketing content from the vendor

>> Onboard with training materials

>> Submit and resolve support issues pertaining to the vendor relationship

A detailed discussion of Salesforce Communities, which is the foundation on which the Salesforce PRM user experience is based on, could take up a whole book on its own. In fact, many of the details are covered in *Salesforce Service Cloud For Dummies*, by Jon Paz and TJ Kelley (Wiley), so in this chapter, we provide a high-level overview of what life is like for partners and channel managers. Then we discuss how a channel team manages its partners with Salesforce. For partners asked by their vendors to use this application, we discuss how you will most likely receive access to the community. Finally, we give channel managers and administrators some business process-related pointers on how to set up a partner-focused community.

**REMEMBER**

The details we describe here pertain to the Lightning-compatible version of Salesforce PRM. If you are still in Salesforce Classic, there is an older approach to enabling Salesforce PRM that is no longer being enhanced. If you really want to learn more about that, you can look for this chapter online at the Dummies.com website where access to the 6th Edition of this book may still be referenceable.

# Understanding the Partner Life Cycle

Using an indirect sales force of partners to help sell your products allows you to quickly and cost-effectively expand your company's reach into markets that you might otherwise not have the resources to tackle. Some industries that are more partner intensive include high-tech, insurance, and manufacturing. In this section, we set the stage for two types of business users and describe how Salesforce PRM can help.

Here are some helpful Partner terms:

>> **Vendor:** The company that's using and administering Salesforce and for whom the channel managers work.

>> **Channel managers:** The employees within your company who manage a set of partners.

>> **Channel conflict:** There are a couple ways to interpret this phrase. One way is based on what happens when your direct sales force and your indirect sales force find the same prospect to woo and start bickering about who's entitled

to that Lead. Another common scenario is when two partners in the same territory approach the same company, and then debate ensues when both come to the channel manager with potential deals (and want exclusive access to that prospect). Conflict occurs, especially if the vendor has not established clear rules on how account ownership is claimed, and the channel manager isn't in frequent-enough communications with the partners to vouch for any of their assertions. Both scenarios are clear signs that your current system is ineffective.

>> **Deal registration:** Minimizes channel conflict. These programs get your partners registering deals with you (the vendor) to reduce the chances of other partners or the direct sales force competing for a deal.

>> **Lead distribution:** The act of assigning Leads to partners for follow-up. Your channel manager could do this manually by sending partners emails, but this may not be scalable for your industry, and there's a possibility of delay if the channel manager's inbox isn't too organized, or she gets distracted and forgets to send it over to the partner.

>> **Market development funds:** Budget requested by or provided to the partner from the channel manager to assist in promoting the vendor's offerings through a targeted campaign. This allows for "through-partner" marketing, by which the vendor helps the partner market to the desired target audience.

>> **Communities:** Customizable web portals hosted by Salesforce that allow users to access Salesforce. Your company can set up multiple communities for partners, in addition to employees or customers. When doing more research about Communities, make sure to focus on Partner Communities versus the more high-volume, typically B2C-focused Customer Communities.

>> **Partner accounts:** Specially designated Account records that are used by channel managers to manage partner organizations, partner users, and partner activities. These will be the Accounts whose related interactions will be visible to the designated partner when the log in to the Partner Community.

>> **Partner users:** Salesforce users with limited capabilities and visibility into your instance of Salesforce. They're associated with a specific partner Account and access Salesforce via a community interface.

## Understanding a day in the life of a channel manager

Channel managers manage relationships with various types of partners and partners-in-waiting. The channel team does whatever it can to empower its indirect sales force with the right selling tools, sticks, and carrots, to make sure that the relationship is win-win.

With Partner Communities, channel managers now have access to Salesforce dashboards, Leads, Opportunities, Accounts, Campaigns, and Content records where they can track how their partners are doing, as well as their budgets and fund claims for marketing programs. Dashboards provide a graphical snapshot of the channel's performance so that you can see how much revenue the channel is bringing in. Leads are potential business that come either from a partner or to your company and are automatically or manually reassigned to the best partner for the job. Opportunities are the deals sourced or nurtured by your partners. Regular Accounts can be resellers, distributors, agents — any type of partners that your business tracks. Partner Accounts, as defined earlier, represent organizations associated with the prospects and customers that your partners manage. Channel managers can also use Salesforce Content to publish copies of sales tools, price lists, or product information for partners. As the vendor who owns the underlying Salesforce instance, your company gets to decide what subset of all this information is available to your partners.

## Creating partner Accounts and Contacts

First, you should make sure that all your partners are represented as Accounts in Salesforce, with the respective channel managers owning the partner Account records. This allows channel managers to monitor and record all activities related to partners in their territory. Create Contacts below these Accounts to represent your partner users; their email information will be used to create their limited login to the Salesforce Partner Community.

REMEMBER

Before proceeding with this, we note two assumptions:

>> Your administrator has already enabled a Partner Community for your PRM solution, and you've been given the green light to proceed with doing this. If you see the buttons listed below, it could be remnants from a previous generation at your company. If you're not sure, make sure you check with your administrator or sales manager.

>> Your company has decided how to fund these partner users' access to the Partner Community. Each partner user gets a special Partner Community-related license. When vendors first think about using Salesforce PRM, it's really important to get alignment on which organizations are paying for these licenses. Sometimes a vendor assumes a partner will pay for it, and the partner assumes the vendor will pay for it. We discuss organizational considerations later in this chapter.

To create a new partner Account, follow these steps, after confirming the Account doesn't already exist in your Salesforce instance:

**1.** Select the + New Account option from the Account drop-down list on the navigation bar.

2. **Click the Enable as Partner option from the Quick Action button in the upper-right of the Account record.**

3. **Associate partner users to this partner Account record by adding them as Contacts.**

4. **From the Account record, create a new Contact. Once the record is created, click the Enable Partner User Quick Action button for your partner user to receive his or her login and password notification via email.**

   A New User page appears, allowing you to confirm user details before saving the record and generating a password for the user.

## Assigning Leads to partners

By assigning Leads to partners, channel managers ensure an organized way of seeing what potential business their partners are working on.

Leads may be assigned to partners by manually switching the record ownership, by assigning partner Leads to a broad or specific queue (also known lovingly as the "shark tank"), or by adopting a round-robin method, in which Leads are routed evenly to a number of queues. Partners then have access to the queue to grab Leads. (You can keep them from getting too greedy by setting a ceiling on how many Leads they can accept to work on at one time.) Additionally, Lead assignment rules may be set up by your administrator to automatically assign Leads to partner users or partner queues based on certain rules.

To manually reassign a Lead to a partner user, follow these steps:

1. **On the Lead record's Details subtab, next to the Lead Owner field, click the Change icon (which looks like a person's silhouette partially encircled by a small clockwise-pointing curve arrow).**

   The Change Lead Owner pop-up page appears.

2. **From the Search People search field, begin typing the name of the Partner User. The person's name should appear as the search field auto-completes. Select that name to have it appear in the search field.**

3. **(Optional) Select the Send Notification Email check box to notify the partner about the Lead.**

4. **Click Change Owner.**

   The Lead record reappears with your ownership change. The new partner owner instantly receives a customizable email if you selected the Send Notification check box, and the Lead appears in his Lead Inbox the next time he accesses the Partner Community.

You may also reassign Leads in bulk (see Chapter 7).

## Reducing channel conflict with deal registration

Without a well-thought-out set of PRM rules of engagement, companies often run into channel conflict when their direct sales and indirect sales forces (or multiple partners) butt heads over who found which Lead first. As the channel manager, you often have to waste time arguing with your manager over who has dibs, while the prospect waits for the internal bickering to stop. This isn't an efficient way to close a deal, and it's frustrating for the customer to often hear multiple messages (or even price quotes!) from what's supposed to be a united front. In addition, if the partner loses out on that opportunity, you've just lost some of her trust in how supportive you really are in her efforts — so why should she reveal her pipeline data early or adopt your processes?

By taking the time to design a deal registration process, concisely and consistently communicate the status of deal registrations to partners, efficiently carry out the approval for all submissions, and then be able to measure related conversion and close ratios, you can eliminate channel conflict. The deal registration capabilities of Salesforce PRM help provide clarity on what your deal registration processes are from start to finish, which can increase adoption of your partner program and help increase partner sales because the channel conflict inefficiencies disappear. However, this setup can be successful only if you channel management invest the time to think out your deal registration process. If you have a hard time explaining it or whiteboarding it, how do you think your partners feel?

TIP

Here are some key questions to ask before establishing any deal registration program:

>> How would you describe your deal registration process, from start to finish?

>> What do partners get for registered deals? Exclusivity? A rebate? A different tier or status?

>> What do you think would increase deal registrations?

>> What information do you need when a deal is registered? Balance your quest for knowledge with the partner's patience in filling out fields.

>> What's your process for approving deal registrations?

>> What criteria do you evaluate to determine who officially owns a deal?

>> Does this approval process work the same for all partners? For which categories would it be different?

>> What metrics matter to you?

## Managing Your Channel with Salesforce Partner Communities

After your administrator has set up your organization with a Salesforce Partner Community, the channel team can easily access it from the App Launcher in the upper-left of your Salesforce window, on the same row as the navigation bar. From there you can more easily view your partners, and their specific Leads and Opportunities separate from the rest of the ocean of records housed in your Salesforce instance.

# Understanding a day in the life of a partner

A partner's perspective is the flip side of the relationship managed by the channel manager. For example, one type of partner could be reselling your company's products. That partner works in a territory that's managed by a channel manager.

With Salesforce PRM, partner users can now access a limited view of your Salesforce information via a Partner Community. The Partner Community provides a centralized view of Leads to pursue, Opportunities in your pipeline, vendor materials to help with the sales cycle, and optional areas to help with additional responsibilities, such as making fund requests. Partners get to see Leads specifically assigned to them or grabbed from a general "shark tank" partner queue in which first come is first served. Additionally, partners can receive other key targeted messages on the website, update their company's information for the vendor to see, and email their channel rep, as needed. Figure 12-1 shows a sample Partner Community that you might set up for your partners.

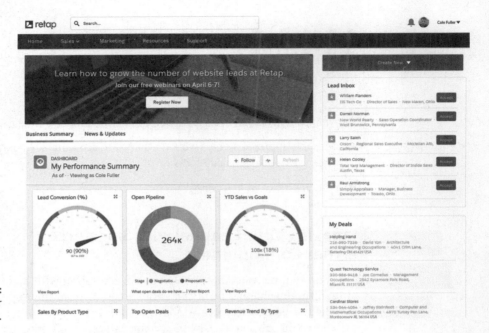

**FIGURE 12-1:**
Viewing a Partner
Community.

## Accessing Salesforce Communities as a Partner

You can strengthen your vendor relationship by accessing your vendor's instance of Salesforce from a web portal and getting first-hand access to Leads, Accounts, Opportunities, and other tabs to manage your deals. You can get Leads assigned to you in real-time — no waiting forever after a trade show ends to see which Leads to pursue. You can also provide your channel managers with real-time updates on the status of deals that you're trying to bring in. That way, if you need some assistance, your channel manager can view all deal-related activity that occurred up to a certain point and provide you with the appropriate resources to close the deal. In the following sections, we give you a quick overview of accessing and navigating your Partner Community.

As a partner sales rep, you'll receive an email from your vendor's Salesforce administrator after he's ready for you to start accessing the community. The email welcomes you to the community and provides you with everything you need to log in.

In this email, click the appropriate link to log in directly to your community and change your temporary password. Remember to bookmark the URL for easy access later. After logging in and changing your password, you're brought to the home page for your Partner Community. Every time you log in to the Partner Community, you begin at your home page. You'll see that the Partner Community is organized into a series of tabs (refer to Figure 12-1). The look of your portal may resemble your vendor's branding or your own. What you have permission to see is determined by your vendor.

### Viewing and updating your Leads

A partner will see a Lead Inbox tab (or My Leads . . . it really depends on how the vendor has chosen to customize your community), which contains Leads that have been assigned to the partner directly or to a general queue. The queue allows channel managers to make Leads available to their partners on a first-come-first-served basis while also avoiding multiple partners working on the same Lead. After you claim a Lead from the queue, no other partner can claim it.

**REMEMBER**

Play nicely. The Salesforce platform is very customizable, and your vendor could set up rules for how many Leads each partner can claim so that a partner with an itchy trigger finger doesn't take away all the goodies.

### Managing your Opportunities

When a Lead has progressed far enough in the sales process, you convert it into an Opportunity. You can manage your existing Opportunities and create new ones from the My Deals tab.

# Preparing for Your Salesforce PRM Implementation

Before setting up Salesforce PRM, your Salesforce administrator should meet with channel sales management to confirm your PRM needs and desired business processes to replicate. Proper planning can help prevent a lot of later drama, so it's best to get answers upfront, and identify those "parking lot" issues that executive sponsors and champions should work to resolve before any technology solution is applied. Additional considerations to consider are also listed below. Discuss the following questions:

>> What percentage of your sales force is indirect versus direct?

>> What types of partners do you work with? Where is this information kept today?

>> Do you message differently to each type of partner?

>> What are the objectives, challenges, and participation benefits for each type of partner in your program?

>> What key challenges are the channel sales team currently facing, that you want Salesforce PRM to address?

>> How are your channel territories broken out?

>> How do channel managers distribute Leads to their partners today? What logic do they follow (if any)?

>> How are channel conflicts resolved today?

>> How are channel managers tracking partners' sales and marketing activities today?

>> How do channel managers put together their channel forecasts? How long does it take, and how accurate is the information?

>> Have you confirmed funding for the additional license costs that would be needed for your partner users?

>> What actions do you want your partners to be able to do, from the Partner Community (for example, receive or register Leads, request market development funds, manage their opportunity pipeline, submit support requests, download marketing assets, review on-boarding materials)? Prioritize and stack rank the importance of having these options for your partners.

>> What corporate branding guidelines must a Partner Community adhere to?

>> What key KPIs are partners and channel managers responsible for, today? How is that currently being tracked? What insights would management like to be tracked today, but find challenging to report on?Make sure that you set an appointment with your Salesforce.com customer success manager for some additional advice on using Salesforce PRM for your particular indirect sales management needs. Chances are, if answers to these questions show that your business relies heavily on an indirect sales force, yet your visibility into the channel pipeline is as clear as mud, you probably need Salesforce PRM.

Again, the information we give you is meant to prepare you to successfully implement Salesforce PRM. The details of all the cool features that you can activate are more thoroughly discussed within *Salesforce Service Cloud For Dummies* by Jon Paz and TJ Kelley (Wiley).

# 4

# Providing Support with Service Cloud

Manage your customer service case load with Service Cloud.

Use different communication channels to improve your customer service.

Explore your options for providing multichannel support.

IN THIS CHAPTER

» **Understanding service and support processes**

» **Creating Cases**

» **Using Case queues**

» **Resolving Cases**

» **Communicating the outcome**

Chapter **13**

# Tracking the Support Life Cycle with Cases

alesforce provides robust customer service functionality in its Service Cloud product. The module is used to track and resolve Cases, using a variety of features that allow agents to respond to Cases as efficiently as possible. But it's more than that as well.

With Service Cloud, you have all the tools at your fingertips to efficiently deliver excellent customer service while managing the costs of operations. In days and weeks, versus months and years, you can start and manage a fully integrated customer service strategy that supports the many channels that customers use to communicate with you. Service Cloud also provides the ability to handle web chats from customers looking for help on your website, the ability for customers to log in to a private community where they can submit new Cases and check up on existing ones, and a console where agents can minimize the number of clicks and additional pages they have to open to see information about a customer.

In this chapter, we introduce you to basic customer support functionality in Salesforce, starting with its core concept: the Case. We first discuss fundamental support agent processes for handling new Cases; then we cover how to manage the growing caseload. For more extensive knowledge of Service Cloud and implementing its various features, check out *Salesforce Service Cloud For Dummies,* by Jon Paz and TJ Kelley (Wiley).

# Walking through a Day in the Life of a Service Agent

Salesforce follows a general process when it comes to managing Cases. Service agents (you may call them *support reps*) commonly perform these tasks on any given day. The specific tasks may be different in your company, but you probably see some similarities:

>> Responding to inbound emails and calls

>> Taking new Cases from assigned queues

>> Validating that the inquiry is coming from an authorized Contact

>> Creating a Case to begin tracking efforts to resolve the issue

>> Working the Case backlog, including researching solutions

>> Managing service-level agreements (SLAs)

>> Communicating the resolution to the customer

At its core, customer support is all about accepting questions and answering them in a timely and consistent manner, while providing high levels of customer satisfaction. How you handle your responses — and the scale on which you handle them — are more complicated issues.

TIP

If all your company's Salesforce users have full licenses, and you just need to capture a fairly manageable influx of basic Cases, you can do that without having to purchase full-blown separate Service Cloud licenses.

## Understanding the Case Record

A *Case* is a record of a customer service inquiry (you may call them *tickets*), as shown in Figure 13-1. Similar to other common records, such as Accounts and Contacts, you capture Case-related information from a single detail page. And to manage all your Cases, Salesforce comes out of the box with all the tools that you need for routing, queuing, and escalating Cases, plus complying with SLAs, if that applies to your company.

A Case record comes preconfigured with standard fields and two icons commonly used for Case management. Most of the standard fields are self-explanatory, but in the following list, we highlight key fields that are less obvious:

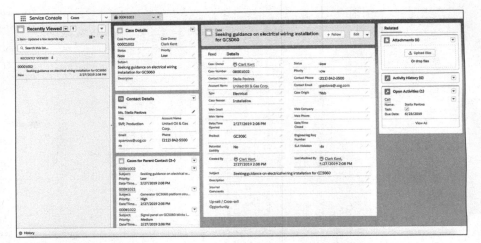

**FIGURE 13-1:**
Introducing the
Case record.

>> **Status:** This field defines the important statuses in your Case process.
It comes preconfigured with a basic process, but you should modify the
values to fit your process. If you're an Enterprise or Unlimited Edition user,
you can use this field to distinguish multiple support processes appropriate
to the different kinds of Cases you want to track.

>> **Case Number:** When you create a Case, Salesforce automatically assigns a
sequential number used for tracking.

>> **Type:** Use this picklist field to define the type of Case. Salesforce presets this
list with selections that include Problem and Question, but you can modify the
picklist to match your categories.

>> **Case Reason:** Use this picklist field to specify the reason the Case was opened.
Many companies track this field to identify areas of customer service that they
can improve. Of course, you can also modify this list to suit your needs.

>> **Case Origin:** Use this field to record from which channel the Case originated —
for example, by phone, email, or web. Many companies report on this field to
understand and improve the methods by which customers interact with service
and support agents.

>> **Internal Comments:** When editing a Case, use this field to jot brief comments
to communicate internal messages, as needed. Customers or people outside
your company will not see this field by default.

You may also hear the term *Case feed*. The Case feed borrows functionality from
Salesforce's Chatter feature so that users can better collaborate around resolving
a particular Case. Internal discussions about a Case appear on the Feed tab, next to
the Details tab, which contains field details, as shown in Figure 13-2. This layout
is meant to give agents quick access to Chatter discussions about the Case or
record details, with a minimum of page scrolling.

**FIGURE 13-2:**
Using Chatter
on Cases from
within the
console.

You may have also heard of the *console.* The console is an easily customizable user interface that serves as a helpdesk so that your agents can quickly see a personalized view of your customers and navigate to information. Speed is critical when interacting with a customer, and Salesforce provides as much information as possible to an agent without having to click off the screen to get to the right details. For simplicity's sake, our images in this chapter show you Cases within the console view, as we consider the Service Cloud Console to be the new default for agents.

# Creating a Case

One of the main responsibilities of an agent is handling new inbound inquiries. Writing notes on a little sticky square that you attach to your monitor may not be the best way to track information, especially if you have terrible handwriting. In the following sections, we discuss how to begin the Case management process in Salesforce so that the right information is tracked for the right customers.

## Validating the Contact

The first step in creating a Case is validating the company and Contact information to see whether any special circumstances or SLAs exist. This is less of a technological innovation than a general business best practice. You can't have just any random person taking up your precious time, can you? This information should reside in custom fields on the Account record. For example, to do this in response to an inbound call, log in to Salesforce and follow these steps:

1. **Type the company name (or Account number — whatever your company uses to identify its customers) into the global search bar from the home page (or wherever you are) and then click Search.**

   The Search Results page appears. You should see the Account name listed.

   If the Account name is not listed, you should have some business processes in place to determine how to verify that the person or business calling in is, indeed, a customer.

2. **Click the Account Name field.**

   The Account record appears. Verify the business's information on this record that helps you identify that you're allowed to support this company. You might verify an address or an Account number. You should confirm those processes first before using Cases.

3. **Look at the Contact detail list to locate the person with the problem.**

   Again, depending on your company's policies, you may or may not have specific customer Contacts authorized to call you for support.

4. **Click the Contact Name field.**

   The Contact record appears. Verify information on this record that helps you identify that this person is permitted to call for support. If the Contact record doesn't already exist, create a new Contact record. For more information, turn to Chapter 9.

## Entering new Cases

After you qualify the customer, you have to associate a Case to each new issue you receive. Because Cases are associated with ontacts, the best, most reliable way to create Case records is by starting from the relevant Contact detail page. From the Contact detail page, you can add a Case by clicking the New button on the Cases related list, which will automatically prefill the Contact lookup field. By doing this, you can always find your Case, and your Case activities will be listed on the overall Contact detail page. You can also select the add icon (+) from the Global Actions list on any page and fill in the Contact information yourself, as shown in Figure 13-3 below.

To create Cases by using the best practice, follow these steps:

1. **From the Contact detail page, click the New button on the Cases related list.**

   The Edit mode of a new Case appears.

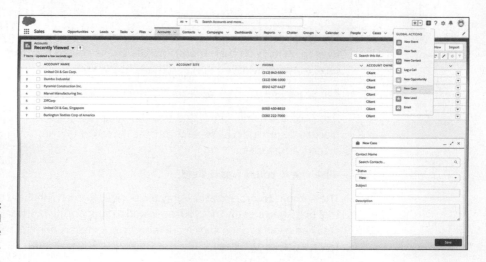

**FIGURE 13-3:**
Using Global
Actions to create
a new Case.

2. **Fill in the fields as much as you can or as required.**

   Notice that the Contact Name and Account Name fields are prefilled with the person and company you were working from.

3. **When you're done, click one of the following buttons:**

   - *Save:* Brings up the Case detail page.

   - *Save & New:* Saves the current Contact info and automatically opens a new, blank Contact record.

   - *Cancel:* Go back to the Contact record without creating the Case.

TIP

To clone a Case, click the Clone button at the top-right of the Case record (you may have to use the drop-down arrow to find it). If it's the day of a new product or feature release, and many customers are reporting the same problem, the Clone button will come in handy for you. Just remember to still skim the new copy that was cloned, to make sure you change certain fields (like the Contact), to be relevant for each customer. This is similar behavior across other records in the Salesforce family.

TECHNICAL
STUFF

You can also set up Salesforce to generate a new Case from an email sent to a specific address (like support@yourcompany.com), also known as the Email-to-Case feature. You have a few options, depending on your company's email requirements. Or, you could always have a Web-to-Case form set up (similar to the Web-to-Leads form that we discuss in Chapter 15). For details on how to set up Email-to-Case, see *Service Cloud for Dummies*.

# Managing Cases

As a service or support agent, one of your key goals as a Case owner is to address and resolve many customer issues as quickly as possible. Ideally, the need for speed is balanced with some defined processes to ensure a sense of order. Over time, your caseload will build up as different Cases take different lengths of time to resolve. You'll work off the Cases home page, which you access by clicking the Cases tab at the top of the page. There you'll be able to see the most recent Cases and adjust your views so that you can see the Cases that are most relevant to you. For example, maybe you handle all the Platinum requests for the West Coast and just want to see those. In the following sections, we discuss how to manage your growing caseload.

If your company has several agents resolving Cases for a variety of products and services, your administrator may set up *Case Queues* to automatically funnel Cases to the right pairs of eyeballs. For example, you may use your website to collect both product and billing inquiries. Case queues would allow support agents to grab new Cases from the product queue, while accounting operations staff can monitor the billing queue. Queues ensure that everyone has an equal chance at the latest Cases.

Case queues are accessed from the same location as Case views — the Case View drop-down list on the Cases home page.

To choose a Case from a queue, follow these steps:

1. **From the Cases home page, select the view that corresponds to a queue that you're supposed to monitor.**

   The list page appears.

2. **To the left of the Case list, select the check boxes for the Case records that you want to accept and begin working on.**

   If you don't see an Accept button you're probably looking at a list view instead. See Chapter 17 for more information on list views.

3. **Click Accept to take ownership of these Cases.**

   A message appears stating you've accepted the Cases and are now their owner. You've now claimed these Cases from the general pool of new Cases.

# Communicating the Outcome

After you research your Case and find the right solutions for it, you must communicate this resolution to your customer before you officially close the Case. Make sure that your administrator has created appropriate Case resolution emails for your support team.

## Emailing customers from a Case

You can use a standard email quick action directly from your Case feed to send emails to your customers. This increases the efficiency with which the support team can answer questions. To see this, first you must enable Email-to-Case in your org, by going to the Setup menu, and following these steps:

**1.** **Search Email-to-Case and click on the menu item in the left-hand panel.**

The Email-to-Case information page appears. settings page appears.

**2.** **Click Continue.**

The Email-to-Case settings page appears.

**3.** **Click the Edit button and then click Enable Email-to-Case, then click Save.**

Email-to-Case settings page appears, with a new related list called Routing Addresses.

Now that Email-to-Case is enabled for your org, you should have access to the email quick action from your Case feed. For more detailed information on how to set up Email-to-Case for your organization, see *Service Cloud For Dummies*.

To email your customers from a Case, select the Feed tab and the Email subtab, and draft your email. The To, From, and Bcc and Subject fields should be prefilled for you automatically, as shown in Figure 13-4 below.

## Closing a Case

After you resolve your Case and successfully notify your customer, it's time to close the Case and move on to the next one. One of the key advantages of Salesforce is its easy-to-use reporting system (more about that in Chapter 22). Additional information is collected after you close a Case, so support executives can use the collective feedback to continuously improve the customer experience.

At the time of this writing, the Lightning Experience doesn't include the Close Case button, which is a feature in Classic. There are custom alternatives to replicating the Close Case button in Lightning, but for now, let's look at what comes out of the box.

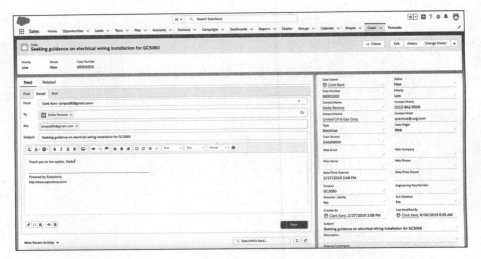

**FIGURE 13-4:**
Using the email
quick action to
email customers
from a Case.

To close a Case, follow these steps:

**1. From the Case record, double-click the Status field value and change it to Closed.**

Alternatively, if you're already on the Edit page for the Case record, just change the status value to Closed.

**2. Click Save.**

The Case status is updated to Closed and saved.

**TECHNICAL STUFF**

If you want a similar solution to the classic Close Case button, you can create a quick action to update the Case status to closed with one click directly from the feed. In this action layout, you can also select fields that will be pre-filled (such as the status field to Closed), as well as additional fields your agent should fill with additional details about the resolution or any other protocol you have for them upon Case closure. See *Salesforce Service Cloud For Dummies* for more details.

# Chapter **14**

# Diversifying Your Support Channels

C ase management is the heart of any support strategy, and Salesforce Service Cloud highlights this by giving you the tools to provide excellent customer service through a wide range of channels. In an increasingly connected social world, conventional (and more operationally expensive) service channels such as call centers can no longer be the only source of service.

Today's consumer seeks immediate service around the clock through a variety of devices and channels, without listening to hold music or repeating the issue to multiple reps. The modern customer leaves public feedback, making the customer's experience critical to your company's image and success.

No matter which channel(s) your business employs, Service Cloud gives you the tools to successfully support your multi-channel strategy to deliver consistently high-quality customer support anytime and anywhere.

In this chapter, we lay out how to prepare for your multi-channel strategy. We talk about some of the more popular support channels and show you how you can better direct your customers to self-service options. Then we take a quick look at how Communities play into your multi-channel approach in servicing your customer base.

# Preparing Your Salesforce Service Cloud Strategy

Like any new endeavor, you need to put some time and thought into a viable strategy to set you up for success. In order to prepare for some of the great Service Cloud features available to you, think about what you want to get out of this project. Are you having problems keeping your customers happy? Are you looking to reduce cost? Increase profit margins? Maybe you just want to reduce call agent attrition and make their lives easier? Identifying these reasons upfront will help you plan where you're going with your implementation.

## Planning the implementation

As a support executive, if you want to get Service Cloud working for you, you need to do some careful upfront planning. After you think through your processes, you can customize Cases either by yourself or with your Service Cloud administrator.

TIP

Here are some tips to think about before you get started:

>> **Define and prioritize your service and support objectives.**

>> **Identify and acknowledge your key challenges.** Try to identify the biggest ones first.

>> **Start with the end in mind.** The best way to customize your application is to decide what you want to measure first.

>> **Map out your key processes.** If you're a Visio whiz, use that tool. If not, grab a marker and diagram your key processes on a whiteboard or flip chart. For different types of support issues, think about the similar and different types of information that you want your reps to capture.

>> **Figure out the best approach for your business.** You have many different ways to tackle a business issue with Service Cloud — some of these approaches work better than others.

>> **Assess how much of your support efforts you and your team can share with your customers.** If your users would welcome this sort of change, you may want to set up the community.

>> **Keep it simple.** Don't sacrifice your objectives, but keep things simple. The more complexity you build, the greater the risk that people won't use the application.

**TIP**

For Cases, as with other objects, Service Cloud provides some common design elements that let you customize the record. As you consider customizing Cases, keep in mind that you should strive for ease of use, relevance, and data that can help you manage your support executive job while allowing your agents to efficiently manage theirs. (See Chapter 17 for the how-to details on adding new fields, customizing page layouts, adding record types, and other design tricks.)

## Identifying your support channels

When you've decided that you want to provide multiple channels for your customers to get the support they need, you need to do some upfront work to determine which channels you'll support, as well as how it all comes together. By offering various avenues through which your customers can get to your agents, you'll quickly learn that in doing so you are not only increasing customer (and call center employee) satisfaction, but also reducing expenses as call volumes decrease.

Which support channels do you currently have? Make a list of what you have and compare it to your desired future state. When you're ready, read on.

# Delighting Customers with Multi-Channel Support

Multi-channel support is an obvious boon to any organization with loyal customers. Offering your customers various means to reach the same end, issue resolution, has two key benefits:

>> **Increased customer satisfaction:** Customers can interact with your business the way they want to.

>> **Decreased operational cost:** Providing answers via multiple avenues keeps call volume down and your agents focused on more complex Cases.

Where in the past each channel lived in its own silo (marketing owned social data, call center managers oversaw daily call volumes, and IT departments managed web traffic), Service Cloud offers a holistic view of customer activity and real-time analytics into the utilization of each channel. Now executives and key decision-makers have visibility into channel popularity and can nimbly pivot toward more frequently used channels and divest from those left in the dust. Agents see customers' preferred method of contact and engage with them the way they like.

Let's take a look at some of the features Service Cloud has to help you connect with your customers via multiple channels.

# Web-to-Case

In addition to using the phone, your customers may want to reach you directly from your website. With the Web-to-Case feature in Salesforce, your customers fill out a brief form on your company website that automatically creates a Case in Salesforce for agents to start working. You can quickly generate a standard HTML form to put on any page; when the customer clicks Submit, the form is sent to Salesforce's servers, which converts the information to a Case. This is one of the fastest ways a customer can submit an inquiry, and one of the easiest ways to increase agent productivity and response time.

Web-to-Case is a certain choice for customer service because customers immediately navigate to a company's website when they have problems or need help. To be sure, Web-to-Case does have a few limitations and you do need to do some upfront prep work before diving in and implementing it. We go over those details in a bit. But Web-to-Case is one of the most common tools businesses use to automate Case creation directly from their site, and after setting it up, you'll see how easy it is to do in Service Cloud.

## NOTING WEB-TO-CASE LIMITATIONS

Before jumping in and discussing how Web-to-Case works and how to set it up, let's talk about a few of its limitations to keep in mind:

- **5,000 Cases per 24-hour period:** If the number of Cases entered via Web-to-Case exceeds 5,000, Salesforce sends an email to the address associated with the default Case owner containing the additional Case details. Salesforce queues these additional Cases in a pending request queue and then submits them when the 24-hour period is over. If your organization requires the ability to capture more than 5,000 Cases via web daily, submit a request to Salesforce.com customer support to increase the limit.

- **No attachments:** At this point in time, Web-to-Case does not support adding attachments.

- **No rich text:** Adding rich text area fields on Web-to-Case forms is possible, but the information captured within them is saved as plain text when the Case is created in Salesforce.

- **No spam filters:** Salesforce accepts it all and does not natively filter out spam, although you can set up validation rules and workflows to filter out Cases that appear to be spam.

## Preparing for Web-to-Case

**TIP**

Ensure the following before enabling Web-to-Case to make the setup as smooth as possible:

>> **Create an email template for the customer.** Make sure you have an available default email template that your customers receive when they submit a Case. Include a Case number or confirmation number that the customer can reference. (See Chapter 4 for more information about email templates.)

>> **Create active Case assignment rules.** Build assignment rules to assign a Case to a default user or queue. If you don't have active assignment rules or if the Case doesn't meet their criteria, the owner of a web-generated Case will default to the owner indicated in your organization's support settings. (See Chapter 5 for more on setting up assignment rules.)

>> **Customize support settings.** Use support settings to select a default Case owner that serves as a net for those Cases that do not meet your assignment rule criteria. To do this, go to Support Settings under Setup, click Edit, and in the Default Case Owner field select the desired user or queue.

Now you're ready to set up Web-to-Case for your organization.

## Enabling Web-to-Case

To set up Web-to-Case, you must first enable it for your organization. In the Setup menu, search for and click on Web-to-Case, and follow these steps:

1. **Ensure Enable Web-to-Case is selected.**

2. **Select your Default Case Origin (Web is recommended), and your Default Response Template, and click Save.**

3. **Click Web-to-Case HTML Generator in the Setup menu.**

4. **On the Capturing Cases from Your Website page, move the fields you want to display on the Web-to-Case form from the Available Fields column to the Selected column by clicking the Add arrow.**

5. **Enter the URL to which the user returns after submitting the form, and click Generate.**

   Most web forms direct users to a thank you/submitted page or a support home page.

6. **Copy and paste the provided HTML code on your website or into a page hosted on your web server, and click Finished.**

   If this step seems too technical for you, copy and paste the code into an email and send it to someone on your web services or IT team.

TIP

When the web form is up and running, test the form by filling it out, and clicking Submit, and ensuring it routes to the appropriate party in Salesforce and captures the information entered.

Your organization is now able to auto-generate Cases via a simple HTML web form that integrates directly into Service Cloud.

## Email-to-Case

Service Cloud allows agents to quickly and efficiently manage Cases through email. By sending an inquiry to an email address set up for your support team, Salesforce automatically creates a Case in Salesforce and auto-populates relevant Case fields, including any attachments the customer sends. If the sender's email address matches a Contact's email address in Salesforce, Email-to-Case will associate the new Case to that Contact record, as well as the Contact's Account record. What's more, agents can reply to the email directly from the Case, capturing the entire email thread and customer interaction in one place. For detailed information on how to set up Email-to-Case, see *Service Cloud For Dummies*.

## Computer telephony integration (CTI)

The more traditional support channel, the telephone, is not going away anytime soon. Service Cloud supports phone inquiry efficiency in call centers, which is just as important as more modern channels. CTI — technology that facilitates the interaction between or integration of telephone and computer — is commonly used in call centers. It comes in many shapes and sizes but generally reaches the same objective: enabling agents to respond to customers as quickly and effectively as possible with very little needed from the customer.

## Salesforce Chat

Another way Salesforce allows your customers to reach you without picking up the phone is through chat. Chat is a native chat application (formerly called Live Agent Chat) that is the quickest way to get in front of your customer and at the lowest cost to you. How customized you want your chat implementation to be is up to you. It can range in complexity depending on that decision.

**REMEMBER**

In order to implement the feature, you have to enable Chat, create Chat users by giving them access to it, and customize it according to your preferences and settings.

## Enabling Chat

To enable Chat for your organization, choose Setup, search Chat, and click Chat (formerly Live Agent). Then select Enable Chat and click Save.

**TIP**

If the Chat (formerly Live Agent) menu does not appear under Setup, contact Salesforce.com Support to enable this feature in your organization.

After enabling Chat for your organization, you must either create or modify pre-existing user records to provide the relevant Chat permissions necessary for them to do their jobs. There are different aspects of Chat permissions that are enabled in different places.

## Adding Chat users

In order to have individual users work as Chat agents and support your customers through chat, they need some minor adjustments to their user records. Choose Setup ⇨ Users ⇨ Users, and then follow these steps:

1. **Click Edit to the left of the user who will be a Chat user.**

   Alternatively, click the New User button and create a new user.

2. **On the user record, check the Chat User check box.**

3. **Click Save.**

**REMEMBER**

If you can't find the Chat User check box, your organization needs to buy more Live Agent feature licenses.

## Granting Chat users the right permissions

You've checked the Chat User check box on the agent's user record, but that's only half the battle. You also have to ensure that your agents have the permissions necessary to accomplish the tasks your company has set out for them. You can accomplish this in one of two ways:

>> **Profiles:** Create or enhance a specific profile to contain these specific permissions bundled within it and assign your Chat users to it.

>> **Permission sets:** Create a Chat Agent permission set that contains only Chat permissions and assign them to the relevant users.

**TIP**

How do you know which option to take? Look at the number of users. Do you have 20 Chat users or 3? If your number of Chat users is small, add a permission set. Otherwise, create a new profile for your Chat users. Just be wary of creating too many profiles — administrating an environment with a large number of profiles can quickly become difficult.

### ADMINISTRATIVE PERMISSIONS

All Chat users need to have the API Enabled permission.

### STANDARD OBJECT PERMISSIONS

The object-level permissions necessary for your Chat users depend in part on the features you're implementing. For example, if agents need to see visitor and transcript records, they'll need (at the very least) Read permissions on the Live Chat Visitors and Live Chat Transcripts objects. In order for them to create Quick Text, users need full access (Create, Read, Edit, Delete) permissions on the Quick Text object, while seeing Chat Sessions requires at least Read permissions on that object.

**REMEMBER**

Managers or supervisors may need a higher level of permissions, such as Edit, in order to modify records that agents are working on.

## Adding Skills

After setting up your Chat users, add skills if your company segments agents into different skill groupings. For example, your customers are normally routed to a first-tier customer service representative for common issues (for example, resetting passwords, making address changes, paying by phone, and so on), but more complex problems are directed to second-tier engineers (for technical assistance and troubleshooting). In this case, you would create two skill sets to segment those agents into the appropriate skill groups.

In Salesforce, you can identify and segment your agents' skills and then assign those users to the appropriate skill set so that Salesforce routes your customer requests accordingly.

To create a skill in Salesforce, under Setup, search Skills, and then follow these steps:

1. **Click the New button.**
2. **Name the new skill.**

3. **Assign users and profiles to the skill.**

   You can assign both individual users that have the skill, as well as entire profiles.

4. **Click Save.**

# DIRECTING CUSTOMERS TO SELF-SERVICE OPTIONS

You'd be surprised by how many customers would prefer to get the answers themselves (if they only knew where to go), rather than call you. One of the most obvious benefits to implementing a multi-channel approach to your customer support business is that customers can help themselves.

Whether you implement Chat to allow customers to contact your reps from your website without waiting on hold, or set up a community for customers to search frequently discussed questions or issues, you can allow your customers to solve their own issues, decreasing call volume to your call centers.

Salesforce Communities are branded online spaces for employees, customers, or partners to connect. You can choose to reveal a subset of your Salesforce data to partners, for example, so that they can help you work a deal. Alternatively, you can share files or answers to FAQs with your customers to help them help themselves.

You can also improve your agents' response times so that they don't have to constantly retype repetitive solutions, and your call center managers can track topic trends to provide feedback to product and marketing teams.

Customer service is more important than ever before to secure loyal consumers. As excellent customer service becomes an expectation and not a luxury, consumers are becoming more demanding than ever. Companies need to be proactive and can no longer afford to be reactive. One of the most effective ways to do this is by making your service about your customer.

Let your clients choose the way they want to get in touch. Provide different options for your customers to receive consistent service, regardless of where they are or what time it is. This is the essence of true customer support and is the purpose of offering a multi-channel strategy.

The skill you've just created appears on the screen, with its name and its assigned users and profiles.

Once you set up your organization and users for Chat, you also need to set up the delivery or routing of these chats to the right agents, as well as create a chat window or button for your customers' experience. To do this in Lightning Experience, you must use Omni-Channel (the Omni option for routing) as well as Embedded Service for the customer experience chat window for desktop or mobile on your website or community.

For more information on chat agent configurations, buttons, and deployments in your implementation of Chat, see *Service Cloud For Dummies*.

# 5

# Empowering Marketing to Generate Measurable Demand

# Chapter 15

# Creating Marketing Campaigns to Drive Demand

Companies want to increase revenue by spending marketing dollars intelligently to build awareness and inform an increasingly savvy business buyer. However, because many sales and marketing teams may still not have shared and measurable business objectives (though this is changing for the better), marketing managers have more pressure than ever to execute effective Campaigns that drive qualified Leads to the sales department. The dramatic increase in apps available to marketers to execute and track more online Campaigns means there is a lot more digital data to wade through to ascertain the effectiveness of those efforts. Now, more than ever, marketing departments have to prove that they're contributing quality names to the sales funnel instead of being regarded just as the "arts and crafts" department. Marketing executives have to show that their marketing spending is resulting in additional revenue. If this sounds familiar to you Campaigns in Salesforce can help you manage and track your marketing programs more effectively, helping you manage your customer acquisition costs, bring in more qualified Leads, and contribute more to sales. It's critical to associate Campaigns to Leads and Contacts so when they're associated with Opportunities, the related Campaigns will also follow.

A *Campaign* is any marketing project that you want to plan, manage, and track in Salesforce. The higher-level goal is to create something (a paid digital advertising link, a direct mail content piece, or an Event, for example) that generates demand for your product or service. Depending on your current or planned strategies, types of Campaigns cover both online and offline channels: trade shows, paid ads on search engine sites, email marketing messages, online promotions, webinars, online Events, and print advertising, although this is by no means a complete list.

In this chapter, you find out how to create and manage Campaigns, segment target lists, execute Campaigns, track responses, and analyze Campaign effectiveness.

**REMEMBER**

To administer Campaigns, you must be a system administrator or a user with permission to manage Campaigns (that is, a marketing manager type). See Chapter 21 for details on configuring your user information and profile to manage Campaigns.

*Note:* Salesforce uses common vocabulary used by marketers (like *Campaigns*), that can also have similar-but-slightly-different meanings in other vendor's applications, like marketing automation platforms (MAPs). If you're quite familiar with these definitions in other systems, review this chapter to understand where Salesforce is similar and different. If you're not familiar with other vendor's apps, realize that how Salesforce defines and uses these concepts may differ elsewhere. Thus if you aren't also managing other marketing tools, but need to work with others that do, make sure to take the time to communicate clearly and not assume you're speaking the same language even if you're using the same words (like *Campaign*, *lead*, *prospect*, *conversion*). It's key to understand Salesforce terminology for concepts associated with the Campaign object, because there may be slight differences in semantics with what another vendor may use.

## Understanding Campaigns

Available for users of Professional, Enterprise, or Unlimited Edition, the Campaign area in Salesforce is a set of tools that you use to manage, track, and measure your marketing programs. Its foundation is the Campaign record, which can be manually or automatically linked to Lead, Contact, and/or Opportunity records to provide hard evidence on how a Campaign influenced the closure of an Opportunity.

A Campaign record comes standard with a set of fields that help you manage and track your Campaigns. Here are the fields used most often to measure the effectiveness of a Campaign:

>> **Campaign Name:** This is the name of your marketing project. Choose a name that's readily obvious to sales reps and other users whose Leads or Contacts

might be included in the Campaign. Keep it organized by using a consistent naming convention, as you may have a lot of Campaign records in a short amount of time. For example, if you email monthly customer updates, you might distinguish each Campaign by year and month, as in "2020-Q3 Administrators Newsletter — Sep 14."

*Note:* For those of you in enterprise-sized marketing departments, an equivalent concept of the Campaign record is a *tactic* — that is, a specific execution of a marketing Campaign that may be a small part of an overall strategic marketing effort with many moving pieces.

>> **Type:** This drop-down list includes the types of Campaigns that you run within your marketing mix (Paid Digital, Direct Mail, Email, and so on). This list is customizable to fit the needs of your marketing efforts, and provides one dimension of what you want to ultimately report on in determining the success of your various Campaigns.

>> **Status:** This drop-down list defines the statuses of a Campaign and can serve as light project management for the various ongoing and temporary marketing Campaigns you manage. Salesforce provides a simple default drop-down list of statuses to measure a Campaign's progress, from the initial planning stages to completion.

>> **Start Date, End Date:** These date fields track when a Campaign begins and ends. Though optional to fill out, again, Salesforce provides these defaults to help you better organize, getting to the more pertinent marketing Campaigns faster.

>> **Expected Revenue:** This currency field estimates how much revenue you think the Campaign will generate. After all, the investment in the Campaign isn't due to the altruistic generosity of your CFO. It's because your managers expect to see new Leads and Opportunities that came as a result of the Campaign, and it'll be your job to prove that.

>> **Budgeted Cost, Actual Cost:** These are the amounts that you have budgeted for the marketing project, and the actual cost of it. For offline Campaigns, this provides a simple area for you to track your expenditures. For digital Campaigns, as costs might constantly be changing, using these fields can be time consuming to maintain. More and more third-party vendors are coming up with integrations with major advertising platforms and web analytics providers (like Google Analytics), so digital marketing managers and marketing operations folks spend less time trying to consolidate data across multiple apps.

>> **Expected Response:** This percentage field is your best guess of the response rate of a Campaign. For example, if your email Campaigns typically receive a two percent response rate, you might use this value to benchmark the effectiveness of the Campaign you'll be tracking in Salesforce.

» **Num Sent:** This is the amount of people targeted in the Campaign. For example, if you executed an email Campaign to 10,000 email addresses, that would be your Num Sent.

» **Active:** This check box marks whether a Campaign is active. If you don't select it, the particular Campaign doesn't appear in reports or on related lists and other Campaign drop-down lists on Lead, Contact, and Opportunity records.

» **Description:** This field allows you to describe the Campaign so that other users who want more detailed information on the Campaign can get a solid snapshot.

TIP

Over the years, marketing automation platforms have taken over a lot of the management and execution of online email Campaigns. However, they still all need to move their Leads (which some systems call *prospects*) into Salesforce at some point when a Lead becomes qualified and is ready for sales to take over. Make sure you are aligned with your peers in other marketing departments so that everyone understands the names, definitions and various marketing processes tracked in other systems, and how they can or need to be similarly configured in Salesforce. (See Chapter 17 for details on customizing Salesforce.)

If you're a marketing manager, you might be planning and managing the majority of your Campaigns in the MAP. You'll be deciding what portion of all your marketing Campaigns you want to capture in Salesforce. One consideration is around the quality of the Leads you want to maintain in Salesforce. Some companies load all "suspects" (people who are very early in their buyer journey) into Salesforce, while others let the MAP or email productivity app handle that and then only bring in Leads into Salesforce after they person has passed some sort of qualification threshold.

In this section we cover common actions you may need to do in Salesforce, even if your MAP is already integrated and up and running.

## Creating a new Campaign

To create a Campaign, log in to Salesforce and follow these steps:

1. **Use the App Launcher to go to the Marketing app.**

2. **Select + New Campaign from the drop-down list to the right of the Campaign tab on the navigation bar that runs across the top of the screen.**

   A New Campaign page appears, as shown in Figure 15-1.

3. **Fill in the fields as much as possible or as required.**

   See the preceding section for a summary of the standard entry fields. When you're done, click Save.

**FIGURE 15-1:**
Fill in the
Campaign
record.

After you save your Campaign, the newly created Campaign page appears with the information you entered, as well as additional system-generated fields that automatically update as your company makes progress on a Campaign.

**TIP**

You can associate Campaigns to a parent Campaign and see the aggregate performance statistics in one place. For example, our *Salesforce.com For Dummies, 7th Edition* Launch Event could be a parent Campaign to other Campaigns such as Email Drop, Google Adwords Free Chapter, and Dreamforce book signing. Just look for the Parent Campaign field to associate child Campaigns with a parent. See Chapter 17 for more information on page layouts if you don't see it — it may need to be added by your administrator.

## Modifying the Campaign member status

A *Campaign member* is a Lead or a Contact who's part of a specific Campaign. Think of this as the attempted marketing effort directed to a human, who's represented by the Lead or Contact record. A Lead or Contact record can be the target of multiple (and sometimes the same) marketing Campaigns, each tracked as a Campaign record that is a child record to the Lead / Contact record. The Campaign is composed of multiple Campaign Members, each represented by a Campaign Member record. The Campaign Member allows the tracking of all those marketing Campaign touches without needing to create duplicate Lead or Contact records for each attempt.

Depending on the type of Campaign you're running, you can modify the Campaign to have a unique set of Campaign member statuses to track where they are in your marketing outreach efforts. For example, the member statuses that you track for an email Campaign may have a particular set of stages (Sent, Opened, Clicked,

Downloaded Whitepaper) that are typically different from those of a VIP Event that you're sponsoring.

There may be some overlap with how you track prospect statuses in your MAP, or you may want to track the exact same statuses.

# Building Target Lists

One of the biggest challenges that marketing managers face is developing the right target lists for a Campaign. *Target lists* are the lists of people you're targeting in your Campaign. Depending on the type of Campaign that you're planning, your lists might come from different sources, such as third-party providers or existing Leads and Contacts already entered in Salesforce. If your target list is composed of the latter, you can create your target list directly from the Salesforce Reports tab and associate specific Campaigns to those Leads and Contacts, or you may add Leads and Contacts directly to specific Campaigns.

## Using external lists

With a third-party list, your options are varied. Depending on the circumstances, sometimes you don't know who's on the list because the list is controlled by the vendor. They might give you a sample extract based on a query you provide, or demonstrate in real time what information they have on you and your buying committee.Other times, you agree to limited use terms, such as one-time usage. Regardless of the methods, expect some percentage of inaccuracy jut given the nature of people changing jobs, and the databases needing to catch up with that. There has been lots of innovation at the time of this writing, in using machine learning and other automation approaches, to both increase the database size of these target lists, and to increase the accuracy of target recipient's contact information. In these circumstances, once you've selected a vendor whose data accuracy you trust, simply use the external list as the target list instead of importing the list into Salesforce. Make sure you ask the vendor how they integrate their list into your MAP, or Salesforce (or both).

## Importing new Campaign members

Even with various marketing automation systems, you may find a need to manually import a list of people to associate with a Campaign. For example, this might occur right after a tradeshow. You can import the list into Salesforce as Lead records and automatically link the records to a common Campaign.

Here, we show you how to select a list on your computer to import, mass-associate various characteristics to the list (such as the Campaign), perform the import, and verify that your settings came through.

To import a list and attribute it to a Campaign, follow these steps:

1. **On the Campaign record, under the Related subtab, locate the Campaign Member Statuses related list to verify that the member statuses are accurate.**

   If you don't see the Campaign Member Statuses related list, it will need to be added to your page layout. Check with your administrator to do so. If you need to add a new Campaign Member Status, you can do so from the related list, too.

2. **From the Campaign Members related list, select the Manage Members option.**

   You may need to click the downward-pointing triangle icon to expand additional options to see Manage Members.

   The Import Your Data into Salesforce wizard appears, with Campaign Members pre-selected as the Standard Object that you want to import records into.

   ***Note:*** As of this writing, within the Lightning Experience, selecting the Manage Members option and the Import Leads and Contacts option both take you to the Data Import wizard. The differences are what Standard Objects are pre-selected.

   Follow the instructions in the wizard to choose what type of data you want to import, edit the mapping of fields from your file to Salesforce fields, and then start the import.

3. **By default, these imported Campaign members will be assigned to the Campaign that you were on before invoking the Import wizard.**

**REMEMBER**

   (1) When preparing your import file, add and fill in a column for Member Status unless all records will use the default Campaign member status.

   (2) Add and fill in a column for Lead Owner unless you'll be the owner or you're applying Lead assignment rules.

   Because large files may take a while, you'll be emailed when your import has finished. Your new Campaign members will appear under your Campaign record, which you can access from the Campaign tab.

# Targeting existing members

Assuming that your company has already imported users' Leads and Contacts, you can build your target lists directly in Salesforce in three ways:

>> Associating existing Leads and Contacts manually or in bulk to a Campaign

>> Adding members from custom reports

>> Adding members from a List View

After you link your desired Leads or Contacts with a specific Campaign, you can begin to target them.

## Adding Campaign members from a Campaign record

You can manually associate a Lead or Contact to a Campaign record by simply clicking the Add Lead or Add Contact button from the Campaign record's Related subtab's Campaign Member related list. This allows you to quickly associate a small amount of names, as needed.

1. **The Add Leads (or Contacts) to Campaign pop-up window appears, with a list of names.**

2. **Use the + button next to each name to add them to the Campaign, or begin typing in the name into the search bar, and the auto-complete will suggest some names for you.**

3. **Once you've selected the names you want to add to the Campaign, click Next.**

   You are brought to the Add to Campaign page which will be a common step in all the options we note in this section.

4. **Select the appropriate Campaign in the Campaign field, which will auto-suggest the some recent Campaigns. You can also start typing the Campaign Name in the field to turn up other options.**

5. **Select the desired Member Status that will be applied to all selected Leads.**

   If you happen to add a Campaign member who is already associated with the Campaign, you get to choose if you want that prior status to remain, or if you want the import's status to apply.

## 6. Click Submit to complete the association.

A notification bar appears to confirm successful association of those records to the Campaign.

## Adding Campaign members from a list view

To associate existing Leads or Contacts with a Campaign you're planning, start by making sure that you can see the Leads or Contacts via a List View. See Chapter 17 for information on creating List Views. Then follow these steps:

## 1. From the specific Contact or Lead list view, select which people you want to add to the Campaign.

Do this by selecting the check box to the left of each name, on each row. To select all the names in the list, click the check box in the column header row to select all rows.

## 2. Click the Add to Campaign button on the list view page.

In this example, we add existing Leads. The Add to Campaign page appears.

## Adding Campaign members from a custom report

To add existing members directly from a Salesforce report, follow these steps:

## 1. From the Reports home page, search for and click a custom report of the Leads or Contacts that you'll be targeting. (See Chapter 23 for more information on creating custom reports.)

The report appears, as shown in Figure 15-2.

## 2. Click the Add to Campaign button.

A similar Add to Campaign page appears.

## 3. Follow the steps in the previous section to submit all Leads/Contact from the report, to be associated with the selected Campaign.

**FIGURE 15-2:** Add report members to a Campaign.

# Executing Campaigns

Depending on the type of Campaigns you're running, you might execute those Campaigns online, offline, or in combination. And, based on the complexity of the Campaign and your resources, you can use Salesforce to assist with the execution parts of your Campaign.

## Delivering an online Campaign

For email Campaigns, you can use Salesforce for elements of the execution. Those elements may include

- **Exporting an email list** from Salesforce for delivery to your marketing automation platform

- **Building a web form** to capture Leads as part of your email's or webinar Campaign's call to action (see the later section "Using Web-to-Lead forms")

- **Using standard email templates with merge fields** so that you can control the look and feel of your messaging

The latter two options are generally managed nowadays via your marketing automation platforms. If, for some reason, you're not using a MAP, rest assured that Salesforce does provide you with some basic options to get you up and running with your initial marketing Campaigns.

Salesforce can deliver and track some bulk emails, but Salesforce Sales Cloud wasn't originally designed or intended to be used for large-scale, mass email marketing.

**TIP**

With marketing automation platforms, marketing managers can more seamlessly deliver larger volumes of email Campaigns and track it in the cloud. The costs and functionality vary across the email marketing vendors, so check out the options on the AppExchange directory at www.appexchange.com. Search using the keyword.

## Executing an offline Campaign

If you execute offline Campaigns, you can also use Salesforce in a variety of ways to simplify the process. How you use Salesforce depends on the type of Campaign, but here are some suggestions:

- **If you're sponsoring a conference:** Capture information on attendees who visit your booth, usually by scanning a badge provided by the conference organizers, or have your own registration form from your booth tablets or computers.

>> **If you're sending out direct-mail pieces:** Use Salesforce to generate lists for your fulfillment vendor.

# Tracking Responses

After you launch a Campaign, you can use Salesforce to track relevant responses. You'll have your responses synchronized with your MAP, most likely. Just make sure you know at what point responses from new names enter Salesforce. Usually this occurs when the respondent has filled out a form on your landing page.

TIP

To track responses on a Campaign, you need to be able to view the Campaign-related list on Lead and Contact records. If you can't view this list, see Chapter 17 on customizing page layouts or ask your system administrator for help.

## Using Web-to-Lead forms

Whenever we help clients with using Salesforce, we take a look at their Contact Us web page. If it's filled with a bunch of text of email addresses (like info@ mycompany.com), and they're not using a MAP to host the form creation, we immediately recommend that they get Web-to-Lead up and running.

Web-to-Lead is a Salesforce feature that enables your company to easily capture Leads from your websites and automatically generate new Leads in Salesforce. With Web-to-Lead, you can collect information from your websites and generate as many as 500 new Leads daily. Say that you already have a registration or Lead form on your public website. With Salesforce, you can — in minutes — generate HTML code that your webmaster can apply to your existing form. Then, when people fill out the form on your website, the information is routed instantaneously to users in Salesforce. By using Web-to-Lead, your reps can follow up on Leads in a timely manner.

Specifically for Campaign tracking, you can also create forms for specific landing pages designed for a unique Campaign to capture information on a Campaign member who responds.

Before you can capture Leads from an external web page, though, you need to enable Web-to-Lead, add any additional custom fields to your Lead record, generate the HTML code, and add the code to a web page. Of course, involve your web team and web designers to test and review the page before it goes live.

*Note:* If you are using a MAP, most likely your forms are created and supported by that technology.

The following section is for customers who may not yet have a MAP, or are not using one as they don't have the resources to make use of the additional email and form management options that a MAP can offer.

## Enabling Web-to-Lead

All Salesforce customers can capture Leads from web forms. First, check whether you need to turn it on for your company.

Log in to Salesforce and follow these steps:

1. **Choose Setup and then type in Web-to-Lead in the Setup Search bar in the top-left of the Setup sidebar.**

   The Web-to-Lead Setup page appears. Under Web-to-Lead Settings, make sure that Web-to-Lead is enabled. If it's selected, you're good to go. If not, enable it.

2. **Fill out the other fields on the page.**

   - *Default Lead Creator:* Use the Lookup icon to select the default person to be record owner for when a Lead is generated from a web form. You usually select the user who manages marketing Campaigns for your organization, or an automation user.

   - *Default Response Template:* Select a default email response template. You don't need to have one, but it's a good practice to reply to Leads so that they know you got their request.

3. **When you're done, click Save.**

   The Web-to-Lead Setup page reappears.

## Generating HTML

You can use a tool in Salesforce that takes the guesswork out of generating HTML code for your web forms.

1. **To generate a general or Campaign-specific Web-to-Lead form, click the Create Web-to-Lead Form button on the Web-to-Lead Setup page.**

   The Web-to-Lead Setup page appears.

2. **In the Create a Web-to-Lead Form section, customize which fields you want to include on your Web-to-Lead form.**

Click a field name in the Available Fields column, as shown in Figure 15-3, and then click the Add or Remove arrows to add or remove those fields from the Available Fields column to the Selected Fields column (or vice versa).

Balance selecting enough fields so that they help you route the Lead to the right person with the patience level of the prospect filling out the form.

3. **In the Return URL field, enter a return URL (if known), whether you want a captcha or not, and then click the Generate button at the bottom of the page.**

The return URL corresponds to the landing page that appears after the Lead has submitted his information online. A captcha helps reduce the chances of spammy forms being filled out, by forcing some information to be filled out on the form that usually only humans can do. When you click the Generate button, a page appears with HTML code inserted in a box.

If you're creating a web form specific to a Campaign, create the Campaign first, and make sure that you selected the Active check box for that Campaign record. By doing this, you can select the fields for Campaign and Campaign Member Status, which enables you to track the specific Campaign.

4. **Copy and paste the HTML code into a text file and send it to your webmaster.**

5. **Click Finished when done.**

You return to the Web-to-Lead Setup page.

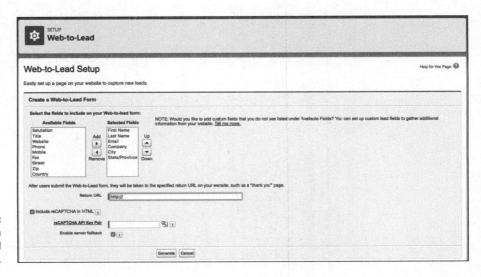

**FIGURE 15-3:**
Creating a Web-to-Lead form.

### Viewing and testing the form

You can view and test the HTML code as an actual form by using a web browser to open the HTML file and filling out the fields from there. After submitting the form, check your Leads view to confirm the new record arrived. When you look at the Lead record, check out the Campaign related list to see the appropriate Campaign is associated.

## Mass-updating Campaign member statuses

If Leads or Contacts that are part of a Campaign respond in a batch, you can do a mass update of Campaign members' statuses. For example, if you sent an email Campaign to existing Contacts and received a batch of online registrations as responses, you could perform a mass update. The following sections tell you two ways to update statuses: in a Campaign or in a report. Sometimes you'll be working directly out of a Campaign. Other times you may be running a specific report that isn't Campaign related (for example, an existing "Northern California Active Customers" report), but you may want to update the status of people who turn up in that data set.

IN THIS CHAPTER

» Using content in Salesforce

» Understanding files

» Creating libraries and managing
Salesforce Files

» Using Files with Chatter

» Understanding the different content
options

Chapter **16**

# Driving Sales Effectiveness with Salesforce Files and Content

I f you, as a sales or marketing manager, expect to get the most out of your sales reps, you have to put the best tools at their fingertips. Aside from a desk, chair, phone, and some caffeine, reps need accurate and compelling documentation: sell sheets, white papers, case studies, and so on. All too often, however, sales documents reside in multiple places: network drives, emails, laptops, and so on.

If your reps are losing business because they can't access the right documents, take advantage of Salesforce Files, which you can use to store the latest sales collateral in an easy-to-use, searchable library. And as long as your reps have an Internet connection, they can access Files, even if they're sitting in an airport in Omaha, Nebraska.

What does an easily accessible library mean? If you're a sales rep or manager, this means spending more time in front of your customers and less time chasing information. If you're in marketing or product management, you can better control the message to customers with the confidence that sales reps are providing customers with the most up-to-date information available. And regardless of your role, you can individually store documents in your own personal folder.

In this chapter, we show you how to use Salesforce Files, as well as how to search for documents so that your reps can put them to work to sell more effectively.

# Understanding Content in Salesforce

Salesforce Content is more than just the place where files are stored in Salesforce. With Salesforce, you get a full content management system that allows you to collaborate, manage, and share material anywhere on the Web.

For companies that need to organize a large amount of current documents, Salesforce allows you to search document contents, notifies you when content is updated, and tracks user feedback. All these features help to further increase your sales and marketing teams' productivity. Best of all, everything is built into Salesforce, so it's waiting for you to use as soon as you're ready.

Anyone who has ever managed a document repository can tell you that repositories need to be maintained to remain effective. If you sell a variety of products, for example, your product sheets need to be updated as specs change, deleted if you retire products, and added as you release new products.

And even though Salesforce provides easy-to-use tools to help you manage the workload of document control, keeping a large volume of material up to date can still be a daunting task.

If your company is committed to using Salesforce Content as the central repository for every department's content, you may want to consider using Salesforce Content for the following reasons: increased collaboration, document tagging, deeper search capabilities, and notification of content changes.

**TIP**

Salesforce Content is a Salesforce Classic feature that is not compatible with Lightning Experience. Salesforce Files is used to replace this functionality and can accomplish almost all of the same tasks. Before users can interact with Salesforce Content, they have to be granted permission to access that feature. From the Setup menu, find and click on Users, and then edit the users that you want to have maintaining your content management system. Make sure that the Salesforce CRM Content User check box is selected for those users.

# Learning about Files

The main purpose of Salesforce Files is to upload, store, and collaborate on files in the cloud. Using Files, you can collaborate with other users in Salesforce by posting files to your Chatter feed or within records directly.

**TIP**

The maximum size for a file in Salesforce is 2GB.

You can upload multiple files simultaneously, directly from your local drive, into Salesforce's drag-and-drop interface on the Files home page, which you can see in Figure 16-1. You can upload every type of file — from PowerPoint presentations to videos, as well as PDFs and Excel documents.

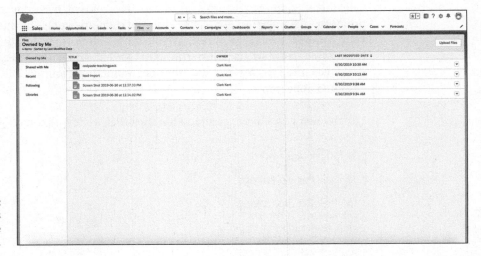

**FIGURE 16-1:**
Using the Files
home page
interface.

**TIP**

Files in the file list can come from a few places. Files uploaded to a record through the Notes & Attachments–related list will appear in your list, as will a file that was attached or posted within the Chatter feed.

# Using Files

Prior to the addition of Salesforce Files, you could store files in Salesforce on the Documents tab. Although not as robust as Files and not available in Lightning Experience, the Documents tab is still available in Classic and useful in many ways. For example, you can host images referenced in email templates, custom apps, fields, and even Force.com sites on the Documents tab. These files typically don't change often and definitely don't need to be collaborated on, so you can continue to store them by clicking the Documents tab.

You can also think of the Documents tab as a place where system administrators house files. However, if you need the ability to preview files, collaborate on them with Chatter, or store larger files, those files belong in Salesforce Files.

# Creating Libraries

If you want Salesforce to be a highly effective sales tool for your staff, you have to organize your content so that people can easily find it. By using libraries, you can sort files into logical groupings.

We've seen many different and effective approaches to organizing libraries in Salesforce. Some companies like to separate content by product family; others prefer to take a vertical approach. The only right answer is the one that works for your company, so make sure that you spend some time deciding on a naming convention for your libraries. The Libraries list under the Files homepage will grow over time, so a clean and intuitive naming convention will help prevent a cluttered appearance.

The following is a list of common libraries that work for many organizations:

>> Hardware

>> Sales presentations

>> Product data sheets

>> Case studies

>> Professional services

>> Salesforce training

To create a library, click the Files tab, select the Libraries tab on the left-hand sidebar, and follow these steps:

1. **Click the New Library button.**

   A New Library edit screen appears.

2. **Type a name and description for the library, as shown in Figure 16-2.**

3. **When you're done, click Save.**

   The new Library appears in the list, and you may begin contributing by adding new files, members or subfolders to your new library. You can return to your library at any time by clicking the Files tab and looking at the Libraries list.

New Library

**\*Name**

Superman

**Description**

A library dedicated to all the assets our super women and men work on.

**Library Image** 🛈

⬆ Upload Image

Cancel    Save

**FIGURE 16-2:**
Creating a new
library in
Salesforce.

**REMEMBER**

As you plan your content strategy, keep in mind that not all sales documents need to be in Libraries. Some may be better suited as attachments on an Account record; others you may not even want to have in Salesforce. As a general rule, files that may be reusable or have wide applicability are good for Libraries. Documents that relate to a specific record are typically more relevant as attachments on record detail pages.

# Adding Files

Adding files to a library is simple. To upload a new file, follow these steps:

1. **Click the Files tab and then click the Upload Files button.**

   A screen to select a document from your local hard drive appears.

2. **Browse your hard drive and select the file you want to upload and click the Choose button.**

   Salesforce automatically uploads the file you select.

3. **When it is finished uploading, click Done.**

   The file is uploaded and appears in the Owned by Me tab.

**TIP**

After Salesforce uploads your file, you can select the drop-down arrow to the right of the file, and select Edit File Details to give your content a descriptive title and description. We recommend following standard naming conventions within your company.

To add this file to your library, go back to the library you created by clicking the Libraries tab, and follow these steps:

1. **Select the library you created from the list.**

2. **Click the Add Files button.**

3. **Select the file you just uploaded, and click Add, as shown in Figure 16-3.**

   Alternatively, if you want to add a different file that you didn't upload, you can search for files using the search bar on top, or filter them using the tabs on the left.

**FIGURE 16-3:**
Adding files to
your library.

**TIP**

If you have some content that you want to share with two different groups, like sales and marketing, instead of creating a new library just to house their shared documentation, you can add the file to multiple libraries by following the same steps as above.

You can also look at a file's details, to see which people, records, or libraries it is shared with, or how many views it has, by selecting the drop-down arrow to the right of the file and selecting View File Details.

**TIP**

While your content is a work in progress, you can leverage the Files tab to combine the features of Chatter and Libraries. You'll be able to share with specific co-workers or groups, collaborate and get feedback, and upload revisions.

## Using Files with Chatter

Whenever you upload a photo or document to a Chatter post, it automatically creates a file record for that upload. You can attach multiple files to a Chatter post as well, by following these steps:

1. **Under Post in the Chatter Publisher, click in the Share an Update field to expand the publisher.**

    The publisher expands, and the attachment icon of a paperclip appears at the bottom-left.

2. **Click the paperclip icon to add an attachment.**

    The Select Files dialog box appears. You can search the list of files in Salesforce using the search box, filter the files using the left-hand tabs, or select Upload Files to select one from your local drive, as shown in Figure 16-4.

3. **Select your files (up to 10) and click Add when finished.**

    The post contains your selected files.

**FIGURE 16-4:**
Adding files to your Chatter post through the publisher.

## Using documents

After you create documents in Salesforce, you can use them in various ways in the course of your selling. You can search for documents from the Documents home page or browse through your document folders. You can leverage an image that was uploaded from the Documents tab in Email Templates. If you're an administrator, you can also customize the logo in the upper-left corner of Salesforce with an uploaded image, as long as it's at most 20KB and 300 pixels wide by 55 pixels high.

TECHNICAL
STUFF

Documents are not available in Lightning Experience. To upload documents, you must revert to Classic and upload Documents in the Documents tab there.

# 6

# Mastering Basic Salesforce Administration

IN THIS CHAPTER

» Customizing page, search, and compact layouts

» Managing record types

» Using dependent picklists

» Setting workflow processes

» Planning before using Process Builder

» Summarizing Actions

# Chapter **17**

# Performing Common Configurations

I f you're just beginning your implementation, Salesforce comes preconfigured with a number of common fields in simple layouts for each of the tabs. You could buy your licenses, log in, and without any customization, start using it to track your customers. So, why are no two instances of Salesforce likely to be identical?

The answer is a key ingredient to your success: The more Salesforce is customized to your business, the more likely your company will use it effectively and productively . . . as long as you lay a strong foundation (and using this book will help)!

With great (customization) power comes great responsibility. Be considerate of the customizations you make and their impact on future generations of Salesforce administrators and end users. As Salesforce enters its second decade, some companies may have been using Salesforce for a long, long time. Some end users may complain about data being inaccurate, or there being too many fields to fill out, so they don't fill out any. Those that inherit customizations from previous system administrations often find themselves trying to reverse engineer how something was designed in order to try to understand the business reason why.

Remember that these are all a result of people before you, who customized Salesforce in an attempt to capture information to (hopefully) reflect a desired business process. Maybe there were lots of changes happening and cleaning up old fields didn't occur, or their purposes weren't documented too well. Throughout this chapter we provide points of consideration so any customizations you make will make sense for future generations.

If you're an administrator or a user with permission to customize Salesforce, you have a universe of tools to design Salesforce to fit the way you do business. And you don't need to be a technical wizard to make these changes. With common sense, patience, logical thinking, and a little help from this book, you can customize Salesforce on your own in a way that will allow Salesforce to scale as your business matures. If you're an end-user, you, too, have some basic customization tools you can use to more efficiently navigate Salesforce, and see the records that matter the most to you.

**REMEMBER**

You may hear the phrase *Lightning Platform* used when talking about Salesforce's customization capabilities. That's the umbrella term used to describe everything under the Setup Home, where all the many Salesforce customization features are located. It's described as the foundational platform that makes Salesforce and its many custom applications possible.

We could write another book if we tried to address each feature. In this chapter, we show you how to perform all the core customization options, including creating fields and rearranging layouts. We discuss certain customizations that end-users should be familiar with. Then, for companies that have Enterprise or Unlimited Edition and have complex needs, we show you how to develop custom page layouts, build record types that link to custom profiles, and use the Process Builder to map your business process right into Salesforce.

# Discovering the Power of Customization

All your customization tools are conveniently accessible from the Setup Home menu. If you had system administrator privileges, access the Setup Home by clicking the gear icon in the upper-right of every Salesforce page.

In the Lightning Experience, customization tools have been re-organized from the previous way in the Classic interface. Rather than explain to you what features are under what categories, in Figure 17-1 we'll instead highlight some tools to make you get to where you need go, faster.

At the top of the left sidebar is the Quick Find, a search bar that helps you locate a customization area without you having to remember exactly how to navigate there. If you know the name of the setting you're looking for, like "Process Builder," just start typing this in the Quick Find and the link to the feature will appear in the sidebar.

Similar to viewing regular record pages, at the top of the Setup Home page is another search bar. This is the Setup Search, which allows you to search for anything that you would find within the Setup area: a feature name, a user, a profile, an app, fields, objects. You no longer have to spend multiple mouse clicks to drill down a hierarchy of menus to get to what you want. We know you system administrators are just a little busy.

To the right of the Setup Home header bar is a Create drop-down list. Salesforce knows which settings are most commonly used and gave us a shortcut to frequently-used functionality around creating new: users, objects, tabs, email templates, and workflows.

In the navigation bar, the next tab over is the Object Manager, which is another quick way for you to create a custom object, or if you just click on that tab, you'll be taken to a list of all standard and custom objects. From there you can drilldown and make specific changes to those records.

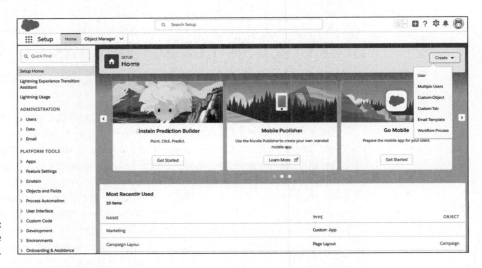

**FIGURE 17-1:**
Exploring the Setup Home.

**TIP**

If you're a configuration expert and have been using Salesforce since the Classic days, and you just want to be able to click your way from the object you care about to its specific attribute you want to configure, you can still do so from the Object Manager. When you click the Object Manager tab in the top of the Setup Home's navigation bar, you'll see a list of standard and custom objects. Clicking the name of the object gets you to customization aspects for that specific object (see Figure 17-2).

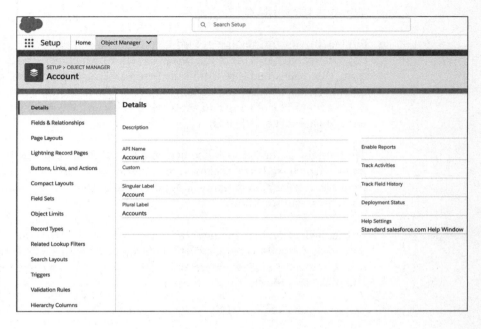

**FIGURE 17-2:**
Using the Object Manager to find Account-related settings.

## Breaking down basic elements

When diving into customization, keep in mind these basic elements of Salesforce:

>> **Records:** Records are the high-level data elements that capture information that's determined by its corresponding object (such as Accounts, Contacts, and Opportunities) that are stored in the Salesforce database. Think of records like the skin that resides on top of your skeleton, both of which are objects. Each tab in the navigation bar corresponds to a type of record. Records consist of fields that hold information specific to that particular record. If you think of the Salesforce database as a filing cabinet holding all your company's information, a record is like a type of form that you house in your filing cabinet. Alternatively, think of a driver's license as a record. There are fields and information on it that, altogether, are used to describe you.

>> **Page Layouts:** Page Layouts allow you to control how fields on a page are displayed to users. Different users (like those in marketing and sales) may need to see some common fields on a Contact record, while also focusing on

other fields relevant to just their departments (support agents may need to see some things pertinent to sales people, but not everything). Different page layouts help different teams see fields that are most relevant to them, which helps with adoption and increased usage of your CRM system.

>> **Lightning Record Pages**: These are the next generation of page layouts, which give you more customization flexibility (without having to code anything) with how you want to display various page elements. Your Classic-created page layouts will automatically display in the Lightning Experience (for the most part). With Lightning Record pages, you can change the traditional Salesforce layout and even have certain elements only show up with a certain condition is met (like a congratulatory message for a big deal that is won). Lightning Record Pages are configured using the Lightning App Builder, which allows point-and-click dragging of various Lightning components onto a Lightning page layout.

Lightning Record Pages do not support the following Classic elements, at the time of this writing: Expanded lookups, mobile cards, S-controls, tags.

>> **Search Layouts:** This feature allows you to control how search results are displayed to users. It corresponds to the organization of columns displayed on a Search Results page, and within the lookup pop-up window that appears when you hover over any link (the "lookup") to another object. In the Classic world, this also determined the column that showed up on a record home page in Salesforce. In the Lightning Experience, clicking on an object's tab takes you to a list view for those records.

>> **Compact Layouts:** This feature determines

- The fields (up to five) you see when you hover over a lookup field (and you get a preview of what that link references, prior to clicking on that field).

- The fields you see in the Highlights Panel of every object's record page (these are up to seven fields that are used to summarize a record so viewers don't have to do any scrolling to get key information).

- The fields that appear for similar use cases on the mobile app. When creating compact layouts, consider the use cases and most frequent user types, for that particular object. The more you can eliminate mouse clicks by providing supporting information when just hovering over a lookup field, the faster your user can get the info they need and return to the original record to finish their work.

>> **Related Lookup Filters:** When you're on a record and need to look up another record to populate a field, you may click a magnifying glass so that field can "lookup" some possible records for you to select. To improve efficiency and potential data quality, you can create these filters to narrow down the search results that happen when a user types in values into the

lookup field. This can help a sales rep hone in on just the Accounts she owns, for example, when trying to populate the Account Name field of a related record.

>> **Processes:** This is an option for some objects, allowing you to map various sales, marketing, and service processes in Salesforce that you want your reps to follow, depending on their profile. So an enterprise sales rep may see more Opportunity stages than what an emerging markets sales rep might see, assuming the emerging markets rep is addressing a much shorter sales cycle with a higher volume of clients. A customer support ticket may have different lifecycle stages if the issue is a product issue versus a billing inquiry.

>> **Record Types:** Record Types allow you to match certain business processes (see the previous paragraph) with their subsets of process drop-down lists to users based on their profiles. Not to be confused with a type of record (such as an Account or Contact), a record type, when used with page layouts and profiles, can make only some of the drop-down list values available to users within a profile. For example, the enterprise sales business process described in the previous paragraph would be assigned to a custom record type, that then is assigned a page layout and to certain profiles.

## Customizing for relevance

Prior to customizing Salesforce, your CRM project team should conduct a series of business process reviews with functional representatives or stakeholders of the teams that will be using Salesforce. In those meetings, not only should you map out current and desired processes, but you should also ask sets of leading questions that will impact the design of fields, records, objects, layouts, and more. Key questions should include

>> How do you define your customer?

>> What information do you want to collect on a Contact (or other object)? Why?

>> Whom do you expect to fill out this information? Is that realistic? Is this information going to need to be repeatedly captured for this customer / their next deal, ticket, etc.?

>> How do you know that you have a qualified Lead?

>> What do you want to know about an Opportunity?

Use the answers to construct a list of standard and custom fields per object that you believe should be in Salesforce. That spreadsheet should include columns for field name, field type, field values, justification, and so on, and you should review it with your project team prior to customization.

When customizing, keep it simple at the beginning. Don't add or keep a field unless you ultimately believe that you or someone else will use it. You can always build additional fields in the future, especially if you build momentum based on early user adoption success.

**WARNING**

Even if you feel you con't have the time to conduct this type of assessment, or you think you know what your users need, we strongly urge you to at least document, in chronological order, the changes you've made and the context for why you made them. Especially with Salesforce customers that are making customizations without much change management processes, experimental fields get deployed for public consumption within a company and many might get abandoned. Think of your notes as a historical file for the next time someone wants to create a similar field but finds yours already there and doesn't have any idea why it's there ("'Major Accounts'? No one know what that field was for, so let's just create "Key Accounts" now . . .).

**TIP**

When you create and modify the uses of custom fields, fill in the Help and Description fields for them, too. This is often overlooked and results in future generations of employees often scratching their heads as to a field's original intent. Custom fields get created over time and names sound familiar (but may be obvious in their differences when you create them), and this tacit knowledge rarely gets passed on. Consider the Help text as your future self, training the next new sales rep, marketing manager, service agent, and so on. Use the Description field to give a little more background to which group requested this field and to what they were trying to report with this data. If you're inheriting a field and need to alter its use, jot down the date in the Description and a brief note as to what changed and why.

# Building and Editing Fields

When it comes to customizing Salesforce fields, one word describes the experience: *easy*. The hard part is confirming why you want it, who will be realistically filling out the information that you want to capture, and whether this information will be easily reportable when hundreds or thousands of records have this data. The more relevant you make the record fields to your actual business, the better the user adoption batting average and the higher the likelihood of hitting a home run.

## Adding fields

All editions of Salesforce allow you to add fields, but some versions allow you to add significantly more fields than others. For example, if you have Group Edition, you can add 100 custom fields per object; with Enterprise Edition, you can create up to 500 per object.

To add a field, from the Setup home, click the Object Manager tab in the navigation bar to get to the list of objects. You can then use the Quick Find in the object manager to get to the object for which you want to add a field, without scrolling. When you click on the object's name, you're taken to that object's configuration page.

1. **From the left sidebar of the configuration page, click the Fields & Relationships link.**

   All fields for the object appear, sorted by field name (aka Field Label).

2. **Click the New button that's to the right of the Fields & Relationships page header, to create a new field.**

   Step 1 of the New Custom Field wizard appears. Data types with descriptions of each of them appear in a list, as shown in Figure 17-3.

3. **Select a radio button matching the type of field that you want to create and then click Next.**

   Step 2 of the wizard appears, asking you to enter details about the field you want to create. These two fields are required:

   - A *field label* is what's displayed on page layouts, in reports, and to end-users' eyes (for example, "Reimbursement Date").

   - A *field name* is auto-populated right after you click away from adding the field label. That's because it should match your field label. Field names are used as an internal reference by Salesforce and are key for integration (for example, "Reimbursement_Date").

4. **Enter the details and click Next.**

   Step 3 of the wizard appears. The details page varies based on the field type you selected. For example, the settings for a Text Area field are different than for a Currency field.

   If your company's edition is not Enterprise or Unlimited Edition, click Save and you're done. If you prefer, click Save & New to immediately save this custom field and begin creating another one.

5. **For Enterprise or Unlimited Edition, use the check boxes to select the field-level security access and edit rights per profile and then click Next.**

   Step 4 of the wizard appears.

6. **For Enterprise or Unlimited Edition, use the check boxes to select the page layouts that should include this field and then click Save.**

   The Fields page for the selected record reappears.

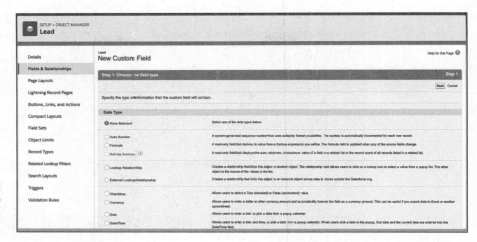

**FIGURE 17-3:**
Choosing a new
Lead custom
field's data type.

# Viewing and updating custom fields

On an ongoing basis, situations come up in which you may need to update the properties of a field. For example, management changes or adds statuses, or changes nomenclature so that field labels need to change, and so on.

To view and update your custom fields, get to the Fields & Relationships section of the object's configuration page. At the right end of a custom field's row, there's a drop-down arrow. Select that to locate the Edit picklist option. That's also where you navigate to instead choose the Delete option if you want to delete that field. From the Edit Custom Field page, you can:

>> **Update a field.** You can change the field label and even the API name (though we recommend you only do that if this is a very new field and you're 100 percent certain nothing else is referencing it, especially any code).

>> **Change the field type on a field.** Clicking the Change Field Type button at the top of the Edit page brings up Step 1 of the wizard again, and you can follow the steps in the preceding section, starting with Step 3.

**WARNING**

If data already exists in a field and you want to change its data type, you risk losing that data. Also, not all data types can be converted into a different data type. For more details, click the Help question mark icon in the upper-right corner of any Salesforce page and type **changing custom field types** in the search bar.

>> **View the field and its properties.** Hopefully someone has described the intention of this field, in the Description.

>> **Add values to a drop-down list.**

>> **Replace values in a drop-down list.**

The Replace feature is really helpful when you have existing records with old values that need to be switched to new values. Take the Lead Status field, for example: You could use the Replace feature to update Leads formerly marked as Unresponsive and replace them all instantly with a new value called Nurture. However, check to confirm that this doesn't impact any historical analysis, let alone workflows or code that other teams rely on.

>> **Reorder values in a drop-down list.**

## Replicating your key standard processes

On certain standard records in Salesforce, you use a standard drop-down list to map your business processes.

You'll probably want to put some careful thought into handling each type of record. To define your standard business processes, do the following:

**1.** **Navigate to the Fields & Relationships page for a particular object.**

The page appears with Standard Fields and Custom Fields & Relationships related lists.

**2.** **Depending on the object you chose, search for the Status or Stage field to modify the corresponding processes.**

In each circumstance, a field page appears with a Picklist Values related list, listing all the values within the process.

**3.** **In the Picklist Values related list, adjust your process, as necessary.**

You can choose to replace values, add new values, or re-order them.

## Understanding custom formula fields

A *custom formula field* is a type of custom field that automatically calculates its values based on the content of other values or fields. For example, if you charge your customers a professional services fee based on the total amount of products sold in your Opportunity, create a custom formula field called Implementation Cost that multiplies your total product amount with a predefined value.

To create a custom formula field, do the following steps:

1. **First, define the task at hand. Some questions to consider:**

   - What is it you want to calculate?

   - How often do you assume the source fields' data will change, and how might that impact whatever reporting accuracy you might be seeking?

   - Who can see this field, and modify the underlying source fields (maybe that depends on where one is in the record's lifecycle). Sales might be able to change the Opportunity amount up until the Opportunity stage is closed-won, at which point only Sales Ops can make edits as part of their data cleansing responsibilities.

   - What format do you want the result to be displayed as? A percentage, a currency, a regular number, text? For numerical results, how many decimal places should be displayed?

2. **Follow the same Edit Custom Field wizard described in the "Adding fields" section earlier in this chapter, and add a Formula field. Enter in information based on the various answers to the previous questions.**

   When you get to the part of the wizard where you must enter a formula, Salesforce displays two subtabs options — Simple Formula and Advanced Formula — to help you with creating your formula and adding your formula for Salesforce to process:

   - *Simple Formula:* Reveals a subset of merge fields to add to your formula, along with standard math operators.

   - *Advanced Formula:* Reveals all possible merge fields for your record, provides more operators, and shows you a set of Excel-like function categories that you can use to plug into your formula.

   To use either, simply move your mouse over the tab that you want to use and click it. The body of that tab appears.

3. **Click Check Syntax when complete to make sure that your formula is up to snuff; if not, Salesforce will provide you with the reason in the form of an error message, so you can fix your formula.**

**TIP**

You don't have to be a math or Excel whiz to benefit from custom formula fields, although those skills sure can help you master it faster. If you're like the rest of us and you'd rather not even figure out the tip on your dinner tab, make sure that you go to the Help section from the upper-right of any page in Salesforce and search for *examples of advanced formula fields* for a ton of suggestions on how your organization can benefit from prebuilt formulas grouped by specific topics.

# Customizing List Views

If you want special lists for the way that you manage, let's say, your Accounts, build custom list views. For example, if you're a new business sales rep who focuses solely on California manufacturing companies and always researches the prospect's website before calling, creating a custom view can help you be more effective because you can build your list of target Accounts, define columns, and use that view over and over again.

These list views are also now what you see on the tab-related page when one clicks a tab (like "Account") from the main navigation bar in the Lightning Experience.

To build a list view from scratch, using the Accounts object as an example, follow these simple steps:

**1.** **From the navigation bar, click the Accounts tab to get the Account list view page.**

The default view, or the one you "pinned," is shown.

**2.** **To create a new list view, click the gear button to the right of the list search bar and select New under the List View Controls section.**

The New List View page appears. For our fictitious California manufacturing example, you might call the view *California Manufacturing Prospects*.

**3.** **Decide whether you want others to see your custom view.**

This choice might not be available to you. If it is, select the appropriate option, depending on whether you want to share your view with others. If you choose to make it visible to certain groups of users, you can search for and select groups and roles of users who will see the view.

**4.** **After clicking Save, the new list view shows up with the filter sidebar expanded on the right.**

By default, only one filter condition is applied, where the records for the object are all owned by you. Depending on your role (maybe you are a sales manager and want to see all your team's Accounts), you might want to expand the result set. Do this by clicking on the filter criteria.

**5.** **(Optional) Add Filter criteria.**

A basic criteria query is made up of three elements:

- *Field:* Select a field on which to search. One example is the Type field.

- *Operator:* Select an operator for your filter. That sounds complicated, but it's easier than you might think. Taking our example, you'd select Equals from the drop-down list.

- *Value:* In the third field, type the value that you want in the filter. For our example, you'd type **Prospect** because, for this example, you go after only new business.

6. **When you're done, click Save.**

   The list view is updated based on your custom criteria. f you don't get all the results you anticipated, you might want to recheck and refine the search criteria. For example, if your company has a habit of using postal abbreviations (NY) or the full spelling for the State field (New York), this habit impacts results.

7. **Select the columns that you want to be displayed.**

   Although Salesforce's preset views take common fields, such as Phone and Billing State/Province, you can display any of the Account fields that you're permitted to see on your custom list page. Go to the gear icon again from the object's page, and select the Select Fields to Display option from the List View Controls section of the drop-down list.

   Notice that the gear icon's List View Controls also allow certain users with the right permissions to clone, rename, share, and delete the list view.

   By default, each filtering criteria for your l st view is joined together with AND operators. If you want to get fancy with your search criteria, click the Add Filter Logic link to use a combination of AND and OR filters.

# Working with Records

After you add records into Salesforce, you can make changes to them to reflect the natural evolution of your business and its processes. For example, Opportunities may progress, stall, or fade away. Territories change, salespeople leave, or more are brought in. In the following sections, we cover common practices you perform on records: reassigning, cloning, and editing them. We also explain what related lists are, and why they're key to your holistic view of your customer.

## Reassigning record ownership

You might find that after you set up a record in Salesforce (let's use an Opportunity record in this case), you need to give that record to the right person. In sales organizations, management may have decided to reshuffle sales territories (again). Or your sales teams might be set up in a hunter/farmer configuration, in which you reassign closed Opportunities from new business reps to Account managers after a certain time has passed.

If you want to reassign a record, open the detail subtab for that record. In this example, we use an Opportunity record. Follow these steps:

1. **To the right of the Opportunity Owner field, click the Change icon.**

   The Change Opportunity Owner page appears, as shown in Figure 17-4.

2. **Type in the name of the user to whom you're assigning the Opportunity.**

3. **(Optional) Select the Send Notification Email check box.**

   The recipient gets notified of the reassignment via email.

4. **When you're done, click Change Owner.**

   The Opportunity record reappears. The Opportunity Owner field has changed to the assigned user.

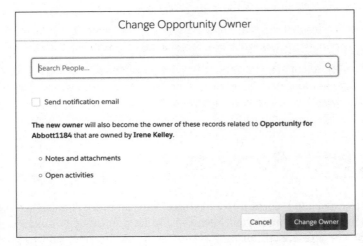

**FIGURE 17-4:** Reassigning an Opportunity.

## Cloning records

If you commonly create records that are similar to each other, use the cloning feature to reduce unnecessary retyping. For example, if you're an Account manager who creates work order Opportunities for additional purchases from the same customer, you might want to clone an existing record and change the details. The Clone button is at the top-right of the Highlights Panel section. Depending on other buttons displayed in the same row, you may need to click the drop-down arrow to show additional button options that could include Clone.

# Updating records

In the course of working with your records, you inevitably collect information that you want to save directly in that record. There are a few different ways to update your record (in this case, we'll use the Opportunity as an example):

1. **Click the Edit button on the Opportunity.**

2. **Hover your mouse pointer over the specific field on that record that you want to edit. If a pencil icon appears to the right of the field, double-click the field to edit it. (If you see a padlock icon instead, that means the field is not editable, on purpose. Move along and pick another field to update.)**

To quickly access and edit related records, locate where your related lists may be for that object. It might be under its own Related subtab, or in a sidebar. Click a drop-down icon to the right of a related list's record to see if Edit is an option.

*Note:* Pay particular attention to keeping fields such as Amount, Close Date, and Stage up to date. Nine times out of ten, you'll be editing fields that play a key role in your company's reports. By keeping your information up to date, you and other users can leverage good data when running their analyses. If your intuition is telling you that you shouldn't be updating that record (for example, if you're in sales and you're able to update your peer's closed-won Opportunity amount), you probably shouldn't have that access and will be found out at some point. Don't tempt fate. Let your system administrator know so they can adjust the permissions accordingly.

**TIP**

For the Opportunity record, you can keep track of certain critical updates to your record by using the Stage History related list. Anytime you or one of your team members who has read-write access to your record modifies the Stage field, you can quickly scan this to see who modified the record and when. Other types of objects can also track the history of changes made to specific fields that you determine. From the Help section, search for set history tracking for more information.

# Using related lists

*Related lists.* Say it three times so you don't forget the term. By designing the page with related lists, Salesforce enables you to gain 360–degree customer visibility and ensure that more detailed information is only a click away. With the Lightning Experience, Salesforce wanted to reduce the vertical scrolling that occurred within their Classic interface. They accomplished this by re–organizing related lists into its own subtab, or a sidebar area, depending on what object's record you're viewing. For example, if you open an Account's Related subtab page for one of your major customers, you can see multiple Contacts, Opportunities, Cases, and so on listed as links from organized related lists. By default, the sidebar may also show related lists for Activities. From these related lists, you can quickly open or edit the specific related list record.

# Creating Dependent Picklists

If you find your picklist values building up and affecting the user's experience, you should consider using *dependent picklists* to show values in one list based on what's selected in another list. For example, you could create a custom picklist field called Reason for your Opportunity record and offer two sets of reasons, depending on whether the Opportunity was won or lost.

Creating these lists is a two-step process. First, make sure that the interdependent fields exist (that is, create them before linking them). In our example below, we use a standard field, Stage, on the Opportunity, and the custom field mentioned above, Reason:

1. **Identify which two fields you want to use when building your dependent picklist.**

   Think about which fields will dictate the drop-down list for what other fields. The field that determines another field's values is the *controlling field* and can be a standard or custom picklist or a check box. The field that's dependent on the controlling field to determine its displayed values is the *dependent field*. We cover this step in the "Adding fields" section, earlier in this chapter.

2. **Tell Salesforce about these two fields and their roles in this relationship.**

   That's what we cover in this section.

To define field dependencies, follow these steps:

1. **Use the gear icon to get to the Setup Home. From there, click the Object Manager tab in the navigation bar to go to the object where your interdependent fields exist and then navigate to the Fields & Relationships section.**

   The Fields page appears.

2. **Click Field Dependencies.**

   The Field Dependencies page for your record appears.

3. **Click New.**

   The New Field Dependency page appears in Edit mode.

4. **Select your controlling and dependent fields; then click Continue to determine what gets filtered.**

   A field can be dependent on just one controlling field. However, that dependent field may also act as a controlling field to daisy-chain together several dependencies.

5. **At the Edit Field Dependency page, select which dependent list items are visible for which controlling field values, and then click Include Values.**

   If your controlling field has several items in its drop-down list, you might have to click the Next link to see additional columns. You can also select multiple values at once by Shift-clicking to select a range of adjacent cells or Ctrl-clicking to select cells that aren't adjacent.

6. **(Optional) Click the Preview button to see a pop-up window demo your dependent picklist.**

7. **Click Save.**

   The Field Dependencies page returns with your new dependent picklist listed.

REMEMBER

Record types allow certain people to see the same subset of picklist values every time. Dependent picklists allow a user to see different subsets of picklist values based on what they choose in the controlling field.

# Customizing Page, Search, and Compact Layouts

Wouldn't it be great if you could take the fields on a record and rearrange them like jigsaw puzzle pieces on a page until they fit just right? Sounds too good to be true, but with Salesforce, you can do just that and more.

Use page layouts to modify the position of fields, custom links, and related lists on Record detail pages and Edit pages. While you're modifying a page layout, you can also edit field properties to determine which fields should be required or read-only. You can also create sections on the layout to visually group fields together under a heading (like "Customer Success Details").

And with Enterprise and Unlimited editions, you can create multiple page layouts and assign them to profiles, record types, or a combination of both. By doing this, you can ensure that different users are viewing just the right information to do their jobs.

# Modifying a page layout

If you have permission to customize Salesforce, you can modify page layouts at any time. We typically recommend that you create some or the majority of your proposed custom fields first before rearranging them on the layout.

**TIP**

Newly created fields appear at the end of the first section of the page layout. Remembering this can save you time in locating the new fields.

To edit a page layout, follow these steps:

**1.** **Click the gear icon to get to the Setup Home.**

**2.** **Click the Object Manager tab in the navigation bar to go to the object where your interdependent fields exist. Then navigate to the Page Layouts section. From there, click Edit from the drop-down menu on the same row as any existing page layout that you want to modify.**

**3.** **Choose among the following options to edit the layout using the nifty drag-and-drop user interface:**

- *Arrange fields, buttons, custom links, related lists, and more.* By default, you see fields that go into the detail section for that record. Select other options to edit from the left sidebar of the layout editor, as shown in Figure 17-5. If you have a lot of fields to wade through, use the Quick Find search bar in the layout editor to quickly locate a field. If field name is grayed out, it means that it's already on the layout — clicking it will take you to it. If the field isn't grayed out, you can then click and drag it from the main body of the layout editor to desired locations on the sample layout.

- *Rearrange existing fields.* Hover over them in the sample layout to highlight them, and then click and drag them to the updated destination on the layout. A dark bar shows you where the field will "land" after you drop it.

- *Modify field properties.* Hover over a field on the sample layout, and then click the wrench icon to the right of the field. In the pop-up window that appears, use the check boxes to modify Read Only and Required settings and then click OK.

- *Organize the record with sections.* Hover over a section header and click its wrench icon. Alternatively, click the – Section button in the main body of the layout editor and drag it to where you want it to appear in the sample layout. In the pop-up window that appears, type a name for the section, use the drop-down lists to adjust basic settings (such as columns), and then click OK.

  For example, on an Account page layout, you might want to build a section named Strategic Account Planning to organize fields for Account planning. When you click OK, the window closes.

4. **To preview the layout, click the Preview As button in the layout editor to select which user perspective you want to view. A window appears with sample data displayed in the layout as it's currently modified. In the preview window that opens, review the layout and click Close.**

REMEMBER

The edits you make here influence the display and order of fields in both the Classic and Lightning Experiences. As of this writing, Preview As displays a layout in a Classic interface; there are commonalities that carry over to the Lightning Experience, such as the field and related list order (relative to other fields and related lists), and page sections created for the detail page.

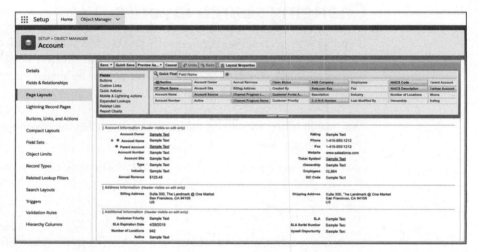

**FIGURE 17-5:**
Viewing the Page Layout editor.

## Assigning layouts to profiles

After you create custom page layouts, you can assign your layouts to profiles. By doing this, users will view detail pages based on their profile and what's pertinent for them.

To assign layouts to profiles, click the gear icon to get to the Setup Home. From there, click the Object Manager tab in the navigation bar to go to the object where your interdependent fields exist and then navigate to the Page Layouts section.

1. **Click the Page Layout Assignment button at the top-right of the Page Layouts list.**

   A Page Layout Assignment page appears with a list of current page layouts and which profiles they're assigned to.

2. **Click the Edit Assignment button.**

   The page reappears in Edit mode.

3. **In the Page Layout column, highlight one or multiple cells by clicking the links.**

   Ctrl+click or Shift+click to select multiple cells.

4. **From the Page Layout to Use drop-down list, choose the page layout that you want to assign to the selected profiles.**

5. **When you're done, click Save.**

   The Page Layout Assignment page reappears, displaying your changes.

## Changing search layouts

If you've ever seen some search results and wished that they showed a few more or different column headers, you're in for a treat. Search layouts allow you to determine which standard or custom fields appear as headers in multiple types of search features for your organization:

>> Search results from the global search bar in the top middle of every Salesforce page

>> Lookup dialog boxes that pop up a window when you click the Lookup magnifying glass next to a field

>> Recent Records lists that appear on your Home page

To change a search layout, click the gear icon to get to the Setup Home. From there, click the Object Manager tab in the navigation bar to go to the object where your interdependent fields exist and then navigate to the Search Layouts section and follow these steps:

1. **Click the drop-down arrow on any Search Layout row you want to change, and select the Edit picklist option.**

   The Edit Search Layout page for the chosen search feature appears.

2. **Move fields from the Available Fields column to the Selected Fields column using the Add and Remove arrows, as needed. Select or clear any standard or custom buttons that you'd like to have on your list view.**

3. **Click Save when finished.**

   The Search Layouts page for the selected tab reappears.

   You can also modify what buttons you see on the object's list view (the page you see right after you click the tab for that object). Just edit the List View layout to select and de-select buttons, or add new ones.

## Managing compact layouts

Remember that compact layouts influence what subset of fields you see when hovering over links to other objects, what appears in the Highlights Panel, and what fields appear when viewing record summaries via Salesforce Mobile.

Managing compact layouts is similar to that of page layouts. Key concepts to remember:

» Create the compact layout using the New button from the Compact Layouts section of the object's configuration page. Remember it's called a "compact" layout for a reason! Focus on the most essential fields for informing a certain user group.

» Compact layouts like page layouts, exists for each object.

» Where compact layouts differ from page layouts, however, is in the compact layout assignment. You can pick only one layout for a primary compact layout that all users are exposed to. As of this writing, you can't assign compact layouts to different profiles.

# Using the Lightning App Builder to Build Lightning Experience Page Layouts

Salesforce will have a default Lightning Experience page layout for your records that is compatible with your page layout from the Classic UI. But if you want to truly optimize the experience for your users who are using the Lightning Experience, or who'll be accessing Salesforce via their mobile phone, created Lightning Page Layouts using the Lightning App Builder.

Although the Lightning App Builder doesn't help you create custom fields or move specific fields around (that's what the Page Layout editor is for), it does allow you to drag and drop various pre-existing Lightning Components into regions of your Lightning page layout. The regions on a Lightning page work together to provide maximum compatibility in mobile and desktop experiences, so you don't have to get a UX or mobile app designer to help you.

This section provides a quick overview of a Lightning Record page. Get to this area from any object in your Object Manager. After selecting the object you want to build a Lightning record page for, you arrive at the object's detail page. Then, do the following steps:

1. **Click the Lightning Record Pages link on the left sidebar.**

2. **Click the New button to start the New Lightning Page wizard.**

   The App Page is selected by default. To learn more about the types of Lightning Record Pages, reach Chapter 18. Click Next to continue.

3. **Provide a name for your Lightning Record Page. Click Next.**

4. **Select the layout template for the page and click Finish.**

   This preconfigures a browser window into various regions. A sample of each option appears, showing how it will render on the desktop as well as on mobile devices.

   The left sidebar contains Standard and Custom Lightning Components. These are the items you can drag and drop into the various regions of your Lightning page template. Multiple components can be placed within one region; you'll see the page preview generate as you drag components onto the layout. If a component can be further configured, details appear on the right sidebar after you highlight the component on the layout.

5. **After you've configured the layout that is most helpful for your end users, click Save to save it.**

6. **Next, you have to activate the layout to make it available to various users.**

   This isn't immediate, to accommodate different company's needs around getting user feedback, training, and rolling out updates.

7. **When you activate a Lightning Record Page, you choose a name for the app (which could be just one page), a corresponding app icon, who will see this, which app they'll see this in, and how they'll see it in the mobile UI.**

8. **Click Save to finalize and launch your activation.**

## Using Record Types

If you're using Enterprise or Unlimited Edition, you can use record types to expose subsets of drop-down lists, which are available to specific sets of users. For example, if you have two sales teams — say, one that sells into healthcare services and another that sells into retail verticals — both teams might share common picklist fields on an Account record but with very different values. With record types, you can customize Accounts so that the same Industry field displays retail sectors for one group and healthcare services verticals for the other. When you provide record types to your users, the big benefit is that you make common drop-down lists easier to fill out and more relevant.

You can build record types to support all the major records in Salesforce, including Leads, Accounts, Opportunities, and so on. Before users can take advantage of the record type feature, though, you need to first create the record types and then assign them to profiles. The good news is that with the Salesforce Record Type wizard, you can perform both actions in a series of guided steps.

**TIP**

Before creating your record types, check that you first added all values to a master picklist field (drop-down list). (See the section "Viewing and updating fields," earlier in this chapter, for details on editing drop-down lists.)

To create a record type, click the gear icon to get to the Setup Home. From there, click the Object Manager tab in the navigation bar to go to the object where you want your record type and then navigate to the Record Types section to follow these steps:

**1. Click the New button.**

Step 1 of the New Record Type wizard appears, as shown in Figure 17-6.

**2. Complete the fields at the top of the page.**

Most are obvious, but here are three important pointers:

- *Existing Record Type:* Choose from this drop-down list to clone from another record type. The new record type will inherit all the drop-down list values from the existing record type. You can then modify it later.

**TIP**

If you choose not to clone, the record type automatically includes the master drop-down list values for both custom and standard fields. That's okay — you can edit the drop-down lists later.

- *Business process:* On a Lead, Opportunity, or Case record type, select the business process from the drop-down list. See the preceding section for details.

- *Active:* Select this check box if you want to make the record type active.

**3. Select the check boxes in the table to make the new record type available to different profiles. When you're done, click Next.**

Step 2 of the wizard appears.

4. **Use the drop-down lists to select the page layout that different profiles will see for records of this record type. When you're done, click Save.**

You can apply one layout to all profiles or assign different layouts to different profiles. Once saved, the new Record Type page appears with a section called Picklists Available for Editing, which list the drop-down lists on the record type.

5. **Click the Edit link next to a picklist to modify the values.**

A Record Type Edit page appears.

6. **Highlight values in the Available Values or Selected Values list box and use the arrow buttons to build the Selected Values list as you want it. Select a value from the Default drop-down list, if necessary, and then click Save.**

The Record Type page reappears.

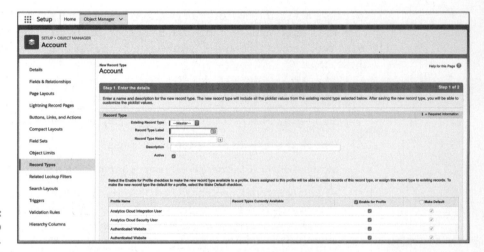

**FIGURE 17-6:**
Creating a new
record type.

**REMEMBER**

If a user will need to make use of multiple record types, remember to add the [Object Name] Record Type field manually to a page layout. For example, if a sales rep sells both generators and engines (and Opportunity record types exist for both), providing the Opportunity Record Type field on an Opportunity layout allows the rep to switch a generator Opportunity to an engine Opportunity, if needed.

# Managing Workflow and Approvals

How many times have you lost or delayed business because someone forgot to do something in your sales process? With the workflow feature in Salesforce, you can create a rule and associate it to emails, tasks, and alerts that can be assigned to different users. You can also update the value of a field on a record if a certain rule occurs. Enterprise Edition and Unlimited Edition users can use workflow to automate certain standard processes to make sure that important balls don't get dropped. For example, if your sales reps create Opportunities that sometimes require special pricing paperwork, you can use a workflow rule to automatically send email alerts and tasks to finance and sales managers, and you can set these alerts and tasks to go out a set number of hours later.

Before creating a workflow process, take a moment to understand some basic workflow concepts:

>> **Workflow rules** are the criteria you set that, when triggered, tell Salesforce to assign tasks or send emails.

>> **Workflow field updates** specify what field is updated on an object when a workflow rule is triggered.

>> **Workflow tasks** are the tasks that a workflow rule assigns to users when triggered.

>> **Workflow alerts** are the email templates that a workflow rule sends to specific recipients. (Before creating a workflow alert, make sure that you've created the email template that you'll be sending.)

>> **Workflow tasks and alerts** may be reused for different workflow rules.

To create a workflow, first make sure that you can fill in the blanks in this sentence: *When X happens, I want A, B, and C to happen.* X is your workflow rule, and A, B, and C are the field updates, tasks, and email alerts. Click the gear icon to get to the Setup Home. From the Quick Find in the Setup sidebar, type in "workflow" and click on the resulting Workflow Rules link. If this is your first time to this area, the Understanding Workflow page appears.

## Creating workflow rules

To create a workflow rule, follow these steps:

1.  **From the Workflow Rules page note all workflow rules that currently exist. Click the New Rule button.**

    Step 1 of the Workflow Rule wizard appears for your new rule.

2. **Select the type of object to which the workflow rule should apply.**

3. **Click Next to continue.**

   Step 2 of the Workflow Rule wizard appears. To configure your rule, do the following steps:

   a. *Enter a Rule Name and optional description.*

   b. *Decide when the rule will be evaluated by Salesforce. The options are Only when a new record is created; When the record is created or it's been edited and didn't previously meet the triggering criteria (listed as anytime the field is edited to subsequently meet criteria); Every time the record is created or edited.*

   c. *Use the rule criteria to determine what conditions must be met to trigger the rule. Use the Add Filter Logic link for more complex AND/OR scenarios.*

4. **Click Save & Next.**

   The Specify Workflow Actions screen appears. You've just created your rule. Now you have to describe the subsequent workflow actions that you want to occur.

5. **Identify what happens when the workflow criteria is met.**

   An action can happen immediately, or it can happen a specific number of hours or days before or after certain criteria are met. You can create new actions or use existing ones associated with immediate or time-based workflow triggers.

## Managing workflow actions

The types of workflow actions include:

>> **Assigning workflow tasks**: You can decide if a task is assigned immediately, and what due date to include (if any).

>> **Updating certain fields**: Decide what field on which object changes when the workflow rule is triggered.

>> **Sending workflow notification emails:** You must have an email template created first, to assign to the specific desired workflow action that sends out emails. You can determine who gets to receive these emails. Keep the details brief, and the subject line informative, as sometimes people may receive a lot of these.

# APPROVAL PROCESSES

Approval processes are a more advanced type of workflow that notify users when an action is triggered, require the user to review and then approve or reject the action, and then set off additional actions. For example, a discount for an Opportunity may follow one route of approvals if it's for 25 percent off list price and another process if it's for larger discount (say, 45 percent). Before setting forth with activating this feature for a certain record, make sure that you think through the following questions:

- Do all records of this type absolutely require approval, or just certain ones?

- Who's allowed to submit records for approval?

- Should a record be automatically approved or rejected in certain circumstances?

- Should any actions take place on the record as it moves through the approval chain?

- Who should be able to edit records that are in the process of being approved?

- Who should approve or reject items? Can that person delegate that privilege to someone else, in his or her absence?

- What should happen when a record has received all necessary approvals?

- What should happen when a record has been rejected?

Although it may be nice to automatically shepherd an approval process through to the right people, make sure that your business process is fairly rock solid. For example, are the bottlenecks you face today in your approval process going to disappear, be reduced, or remain if the process is automated? If a busy executive needs to approve all the expense reports but she doesn't manage her email inbox well, you'll have to carefully set expectations about what efficiency gains you'll get with automated approvals. Or if your company culturally allows a lot of exceptions without a lot of hard logical criteria behind it, your processes will only be perceived as hindering the sales cycle, not helping it.

Approval processes can also allow snowball in complexity so that multiple "if/then" business logic criteria is added to alleviate undesirable previously-built automations, without understanding the original logic behind it. Regularly evaluate the various approval logic as a whole to see if it's efficiently written out, which of course means that you should be able to articulate what the business logic is, in the first place.

# Understanding the Process Builder

Now that you've learned about workflows as a new Salesforce administrator, you'll find that you can reflect many business process steps in Salesforce with a few clicks, without having to stand in line and wait for programmers to get around to helping you out. For example, you can easily create a workflow to create a "Schedule on-boarding call" task for your success manager, three days after any Opportunity over $250,000 reaches the "Closed Won" stage.

There are times when you may have to link several business steps, and find that manually creating workflow rules can get a little tedious. In the preceding example, you may want to instead schedule the sending of an onboarding email two days after any Opportunity below $5,000 reaches the "Closed Won" stage.

In this section, we provide a high-level introduction to the Process Builder and its various steps needed so you can, well, build your first process.

## Choosing to use the Process Builder

If you find that you have more than one "If this happens, then do that" process that you want to daisy-chain together and automate in Salesforce, consider using the Process Builder. The Process Builder is a more powerful alternative to workflow rules, and is accessed via a point-and-click graphical interface. It lets you build and see all the logical "if this, then that" actions for one business process. The Process Builder is available in Enterprise and Unlimited editions.

Some more commonly requested actions that Process Builder can perform that a regular workflow can't, include the following:

>> Creating a new record

>> Updating a related record in addition to the specific one that kicked off the process

>> Posting a comment to Chatter

>> Submitting an approval

**TECHNICAL STUFF**

If you've inherited a Salesforce organization with a lot of custom code and have technical knowledge about Apex, review the details about Process Builder limits and considerations, accessed via Salesforce Help. Click the Help link at the top-right of every Salesforce page, and type **process limits and considerations** for more detailed technical reading.

# Creating processes

In this section, we continue with our high-level overview of what steps are needed to build a new process.

Before you dive into using the Process Builder, make sure you can sketch out your process as simply as possible. Streamline your process so you can explain, "If X happens, then Y. If X doesn't happen, then evaluate this other criteria and decide to do something." Identify on which object what action occurs. Note when you want the "then" part to happen — immediately? After a certain number of days or hours? Be specific.

**WARNING**

If you start hearing yourself describe umpteen subjective exceptions like "Well, sometimes we don't do ABC; instead, we do XYZ if the sales rep doesn't like to do DEF" with no consistent pattern, stop and take a step back. If you can't explain the process using words that can then be reflected in a business process diagram, the technology won't be able to understand you, either.

**REMEMBER**

The goal of automation is to streamline the execution of repetitive business processes that impact the majority of your use cases, and to accommodate common exceptions. Check that your teams aren't over-engineering a solution that is built for exceptions. Consultants and developers may willingly build you something that matches your exact specifications, but making that flexible and scalable in the future to adapt to changing business processes may be more time-consuming (or expensive) than anticipated. If you do end up having a complicated process that you want to replicate via automation, consider where you would document the whats and whys for the next you that inherits this. If you think your company's processes change too quickly to make this documentation realistic, you should also reconsider building in so much exception logic that you need to review each time any part of the business process changes.

A process starts when a record belonging to an object that you specify is created or edited. For example, a process can be built based on the Opportunity object, which you'll identify. The process can be run the first time a new record is created, or when the record has been created or edited.

# Adding process criteria

After identifying the object that will start the process, you'll want to add in your various criteria. Think of these as the "ifs" in the number of if/then conditions that you want to build. You'll add criteria based on conditions that you get to set, either via filter criteria or by writing a formula. You can also set criteria to evaluate nothing, and automatically default to being true, which then executes the actions.

If initial criteria are not met, you may create further criteria to address what happens next. If you don't create other criteria and your one criteria's condition isn't met, then nothing happens. Which sometimes is what you want to happen.

## Adding process actions

After creating your criteria that initiates the process, you need to define at least one process action that occurs if those criteria are true. Actions can happen immediately, and more than one action can happen simultaneously. Depending on certain details (for example, if actions are executed only if specific changes are made to a record), actions can be scheduled to happen a set time in the future.

## Activating and deactivating processes

After you've created your process, you'll need to activate it to make it live. If you realize that, after it's activated, you need to make edits to your process, you'll need to deactivate the process. If something is really not going right, deactivate it immediately. If you want to make a more iterative adjustment, clone the process first to make changes, then plan out a smoother deactivation of the outdated process, and an activation of the cloned-and-edited process. Even if a process is deactivated, you won't be able to edit it. This is most likely due to compliance-related reasons.

If you're up for diving into the details of building out your first process, click Help in the upper-right of any Salesforce page; then type **process builder** in the search bar that appears in the Salesforce Success Community.

# Creating Actions

In the Lightning Experience, you often see what we've been referencing as "buttons" on the upper-right area of various record and list view pages. Salesforce actually refers to these as "Actions" and, depending on what the button is meant to do, these can be re-used with different objects.

As you and your users begin to adopt Salesforce more, you can really help accelerate user adoption by helping them reduce clicks and page scrolling for their most common tasks with Actions. In this section, we provide a high-level overview of Actions, various types of Actions, and how you can create new ones for your users.

Actions (not to be confused with process actions mentioned in the previous section) can be considered shortcuts to most common repetitive behaviors performed by your users. Actions appear in the upper-right of any record page for any object for which you have enabled it. Some of the more common terms that you'll hear include the following:

>> **Default Actions:** These are canned behaviors that Salesforce has already created, which you can use to get up and running with Actions. Behaviors like logging a call or Event, or creating a new Contact, can be done from these predefined Actions. You'll have the freedom to decide which standard object records can benefit from this.

>> **Nonstandard Actions:** These are Actions that you create, because they don't already exist as default Actions. They don't require additional programming to create the Action.

>> **Object-specific Actions:** These are default or nonstandard Actions that are used for a specific object's record. This means that details from that related object can be auto-populated in that Action, to reduce manual entry and increase productivity.

>> **Global Actions:** These are Actions that can appear on any page, like the Home or Chatter page, or also on object pages. Unlike object-specific Actions, clicking a global Action creates records that have no relationship with the record from which the Action was invoked.

Knowing where to go to create Actions depends on whether you want to create an object-specific action or a global one. Object-specific actions for standard objects are created from the specific object's section which you can access from the object, which is listed in the Object Manager. From the object's configuration page, click the Button, Links, and Actions link to see all of those for that object.

Creating an action is straightforward, as shown in Figure 17-7. You tell Salesforce what type of action you want performed, what name is displayed for the action, and whether you want to accept Salesforce's default icon (which is related to how this action is displayed in the Salesforce Mobile app). For certain fields, you can assign predefined values, which helps the users reduce the clicks they have to make.

After you've created the action, Salesforce displays what default fields someone has to fill out when she invokes that action, in the Action Layout Editor. You can move fields around, remove some fields, add some fields — all using the same user interface as the Page Layout Editor, mentioned earlier in this chapter in the "Customizing Page, Search, and Compact Layouts" section.

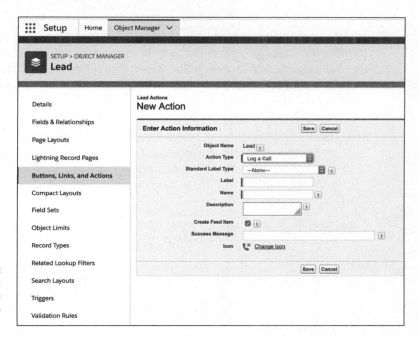

**FIGURE 17-7:**
Creating an action on the Lead object to quickly log a call.

**REMEMBER**

These are actions meant for quick creation and completion. Don't overwhelm the action layout with too many fields.

After creating your Action, you now need to add that button to the page layout for the object on which you want the Action to appear. We discuss how to access page layouts to customize earlier in this chapter in the "Customizing Page, Search, and Compact Layouts" section. The point is that you can move your Action so that it falls anywhere within the list of other action icons.

On the page layout editor, you'll see various Action layout options. *Quick Actions* are synonymous with actions we described in the previous section. They appear within a web browser page of a user's Salesforce Classic UI. The Mobile and Lightning Experience Actions section refers to what order and what Actions you want displayed on a mobile device, or within the Lightning Experience.

Chapter **18**

# Diving Deeper into Standard Object Setup

I n Chapter 17, you get an understanding of the most common configuration options available to you out of the box. If you've read that chapter, you understand what it means to build fields, work with records, use record types, and get even more comfortable with business automation. In Chapter 19, we go over how to further customize Salesforce by building objects and apps that make sense for your particular business model. This chapter, on the other hand, shows you some specific configuration options for standard objects in Salesforce.

As you already know (assuming you've read some of this book before turning to this page), Salesforce comes preconfigured with standard objects and standard fields in simple layouts for each of these standard objects. We cover these objects — such as Accounts, Contacts, Leads, Opportunities, and Cases — in earlier chapters.

In this chapter, we set out to show users common configuration tools and settings as they relate to these standard objects, and what they do for your organization. We cover sales-specific standard object settings, and then discuss settings on marketing-related objects, followed by service settings. By the end of this chapter, you'll have a good idea of which settings can be toggled for specific objects, as opposed to the more general settings that apply across all standard objects in Salesforce.

# Configuring Sales-Specific Settings

As you probably already know, Sales Cloud standard objects really center around Accounts, Contacts, and Opportunities. Of course, we can extend that to include a number of other objects. You're probably already raising your eyebrows and wondering about them. However, if we wanted to cover everything, we'd need a lot more blank pages and you'd have a lot more reading to do. Let's get into some of Salesforce's configuration settings that are specific to sales organizations.

## Using Account Settings

You use an *Account record* to collect all the critical information about the companies with which you interact. If you go to the Setup menu, you'll find some options under Feature Settings that tend to be more object or feature specific. One of those subheadings is Sales. There are various basic and advanced settings that you can find in this part of the Setup menu, but we will cover the most commonly used ones. Let's first look at Account Settings.

You can use Account Settings to indicate default Account behaviors for your organization. We'll talk about two common ones: the first toggles the organization's View Hierarchy link and the second enables News. You can read more about what the News feature is in Chapter 7.

### Showing the View Hierarchy link

In Salesforce, you can create Account parent/child relationships to distinguish between departments, subsidiaries, or locations of the same overarching entity you do business with. For example, your APAC sales team can be selling to Goldman Brothers Headquarters in Hong Kong, while your central region sales director attends meetings at the Goldman Brothers office in downtown Chicago. (See Chapter 8 for in-depth information on Account parent/child relationships in Salesforce.) The children all roll up to the parent (usually, HQ), and the tiers can be easily viewed in the form of an Account hierarchy, as shown in Figure 18-1.

To make this tiered hierarchy visible directly from the Account record, you have to enable this setting under Account Settings. To do this, choose Setup ➪ Feature Settings ➪ Sales ➪ Account Settings and if not clicked by default, check the Show View Hierarchy link on Account pages check box. Now, when you click into an Account, you see a hierarchy icon to the right of the Account Name and when you hover over it, it says View Account Hierarchy, as shown in Figure 18-2.

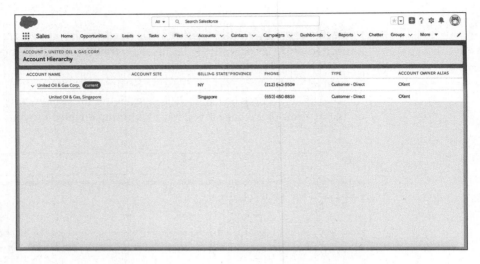

**FIGURE 18-1:**
Viewing the
Account
hierarchy.

**FIGURE 18-2:**
The View
Hierarchy link on
an Account.

This step is important to save time when navigating between large volumes of subsidiaries or locations for a single customer. It allows users to view hierarchies visually, making the tiered structure less theoretical.

**REMEMBER**

You can't enable this feature for a subset of users. When you turn it on, anyone with access to that Account can see and click the link.

## Enabling News

News uses relevant news articles from third parties to gather real and recent insights and news information about the Account in question. It helps users and salespeople stay up to date on relevant Accounts and industries they work with on a daily basis. For example, News can help a rep know that now is not the best time to reach out to his point of contact at Larry's Laundry, if news articles show that Larry's Laundry is currently under investigation for money laundering.

To enable News, choose Setup ⇨ Feature Settings ⇨ Sales ⇨ Account Settings, select the Enable News check box, and click Save. Figure 18-3 shows what News looks like on the Account detail page if you have Lightning enabled for your organization.

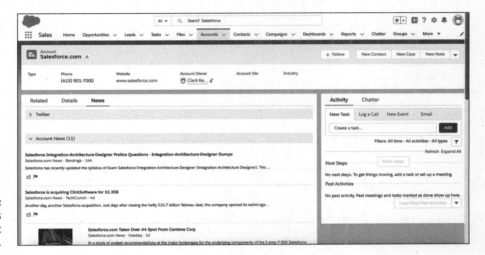

**FIGURE 18-3:**
Viewing News
on the Account
detail page.

**TIP**

You can only view News if your organization is Lightning enabled.

There are two other features in Account Settings worth noting:

>> **Enable Automated Account Fields:** This feature suggests recognizable company names as an Account name is being typed, saving time during manual data entry.

>> **Enable Account Logos:** Turn this feature on to have Salesforce automatically search and display company logos on Account records.

## Identifying Contact Roles on Opportunities

Adding Contact roles to your Opportunities is pretty easy (see Chapter 10). In case you don't remember, Contact roles are really a way to specify the role the Contact plays on this Opportunity or in your business process. In this way, the individual or team that is selling on a given Opportunity can better understand the players involved and whom to reach out to. If a business user asks for a new Contact role or wants to customize the existing Contact roles available on your Opportunities, read on.

To customize Contact roles on Opportunities, follow these steps:

1.  **Choose Setup⇨Feature Settings⇨Sales⇨Contact Roles on Opportunities.**

    The Opportunity Contact Roles picklist values appear, as shown in Figure 18-4.

2.  **Click the Edit link to the left of the role you want to edit.**

    The edit page appears for the Contact role picklist value you selected.

3.  **Rename the role in the Opportunity Contact Role field, or select the available check box to make this role the default value.**

4.  **Click Save when you're done.**

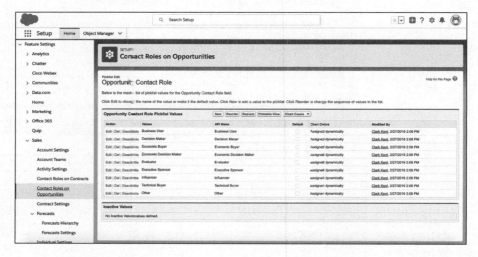

**FIGURE 18-4:**
Customizing
Contact Roles on
Opportunities.

Now that you've edited the default Contact roles for a given Opportunity, you're ready to let your sales users select them. To learn how to add them to your Opportunities, see Chapter 10.

## Tracking different sales processes

The final sales-related setting that we cover is what Salesforce calls *sales processes*. In Salesforce, a sales process determines which Opportunity stages are selectable for a given record type. (See Chapter 17 for more information about record types.)

You can create multiple sales processes if your organization has different types of deals that follow different paths to close. In other words, if selling one product line requires more effort, qualification, and stages than another, simpler product, you can use multiple sales processes to accommodate both.

To create a sales process in Salesforce, choose Setup ⇨ Feature Settings ⇨ Sales ⇨ Sales Processes, as shown in Figure 18-5.

**1.** **Click the New button.**

The New Sales Process page appears.

**2.** **Type a name for your sales process and a description to make it easier to identify later; then click Save.**

The Sales Process Opportunity Stages page appears, as shown in Figure 18-6.

**3.** **Select the Opportunity Stage values for the process by using the add and remove arrows; when you're done, click Save.**

That's it! You've created your first sales process and added the appropriate stages to it.

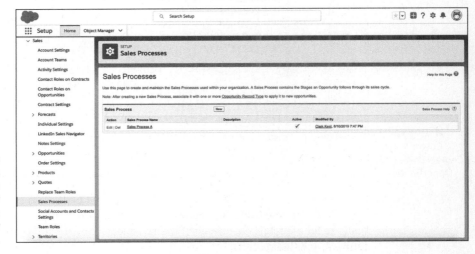

**FIGURE 18-5:**
Using the Sales Processes page to create or maintain Opportunity processes.

TIP

To use each of your processes, you'll have to associate them to your Opportunity record types. When you create or edit an Opportunity record type, you'll see a picklist value called Sales Process, where you can select the corresponding process for that Opportunity type.

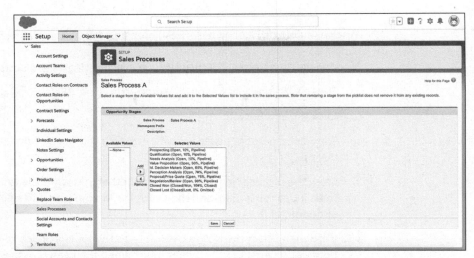

**FIGURE 18-6:**
Selecting
Opportunity
Stages for your
sales process.

# Managing Marketing-Related Settings

Now that you know about sales-specific settings and where to go to enable them, let's talk marketing.

## Assigning Leads

Nobody wants a database full of Leads if they're not assigned to the right people. When you have incoming Leads, you have to make sure they're assigned appropriately. To do this, you can set up some assignment rules to automate Lead routing, as we show you in Chapter 7. Reassigning Leads is easy — we show you how to reassign record ownership in Chapter 17. Use these out-of-the-box Salesforce tools to increase your marketing power and efficiency.

## Choosing a default Lead owner

Salesforce requires that you choose a default Lead owner, so that new Leads that come into your system don't fall through the cracks (assuming they don't meet any of your Lead assignment rule criteria). The Lead owner can be a Lead queue, an appointed data steward in your organization, or your system admin, depending on the size of your company and whether you have a governance structure implemented within it.

To select a default Lead owner, click Setup and follow these steps:

**1. Choose Customize ⇨ Feature Settings ⇨ Marketing ⇨ Lead Settings.**

The Lead Settings page appears, as shown in Figure 18-7.

**2. Click the Edit button.**

The Edit Lead Settings page appears, with the Lead Queue Settings section at the top.

**3. From the drop-down menu, choose whether you want the type of owner to be a User or Queue, and then click the lookup icon and select the user or queue.**

**4. (Optional) Select the Notify Default Lead Owner check box to send a notification email to the owner inbox when the Lead is assigned.**

**5. Click Save when you're done.**

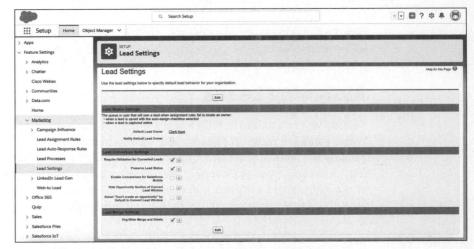

**FIGURE 18-7:** Looking at the Lead Settings page.

Great! Now you've assigned a default Lead owner, so your Leads will be auto-assigned to this user or queue when they can't be routed based on other rules and criteria you've established.

## Confirming Lead conversion settings

Lead conversion is an important process in Salesforce, and we talk a lot about it in Chapter 7. There are three default Lead conversion settings you can set up for your organization.

First, choose Setup⇨Feature Settings⇨Marketing⇨Lead Settings. You see the second section, Lead Conversion Settings, with five options, as shown in Figure 18-7:

>> **Require Validation for Converted Leads:** Use this option to enforce validation rules when converting Leads.

>> **Preserve Lead Status:** This option comes into play if your organization uses record types on the Lead object. If this check box is selected, the Lead Status doesn't automatically change to the new owner's default value during conversion. Use this option if you want to keep the Lead status as-is during conversion no matter what.

>> **Enable Conversions for Salesforce Mobile:** Use this option if you want to give users the ability to convert their Leads through the Salesforce mobile app.

>> **Hide Opportunity Section of Convert Lead Window:** This will prevent users from seeing the Opportunity section when converting Leads, effectively stopping them from creating Opportunities off of a newly converted Lead.

>> **Select Don't Create an Opportunity by Default in Convert Lead Window:** Selecting this setting makes sure the check box preventing Opportunity creation will be selected by default upon Lead conversion. It can still be toggled off, but will default to not creating Opportunities.

## Capturing Campaign influence

Campaigns and Campaign influence are two cornerstones of marketing. Any marketing department sees the value in capturing the return on investment (ROI) of their Campaigns and tying revenue back to their efforts.

Importantly, marketing just for the sake of marketing is not useful to anyone in your company. In other words, marketing just to get as high a volume of Leads as you can is not good practice because it does not always translate into dollars in the B2B world. Salesforce's Campaign influence module allows you to choose to associate influential Campaigns to Opportunities automatically or manually in order to track the efforts you put forth, where they helped and where they didn't. This in turn will give your business better visibility and actionable insights into where to invest in (and divest from) future endeavors.

Campaigns can be sending out all kinds of marketing collateral such as print ads via snail mail, promotions via email, or even webinars that help promote your business. Campaign influence is a way to track how these Campaigns affect your pipeline (ahem, Opportunities).

You can automatically associate influential Campaigns to Opportunities using Automatic Associations in Salesforce.

To enable the automatic Campaign association to Opportunities, follow these steps:

**1.** **Choose Setup➪Feature Settings➪Marketing➪Campaign Influence➪ Auto-Association Settings.**

The Campaign Influence page appears, as shown in Figure 18-8.

**2.** **Under Auto-Association, click Enabled.**

Now, if a Campaign is related to a Contact role on an Opportunity and the Opportunity hasn't closed, the Campaign will automatically be associated with that Opportunity. See more about Contact roles on Opportunities in Chapter 10 if you need a refresher. Select Disabled if you prefer to manage and associate influential Campaigns manually on a one-off basis using the Campaign Influence related list.

**3.** **(Optional) Enter a Campaign Influence Time Frame.**

This allows you to designate the maximum number of days between the date when the Campaign was first associated and the date the Opportunity was created. For example, if you enter 20 days as the time frame, and one of your Contacts becomes a member of a Campaign on August 1, the Campaign will be considered influential to any Opportunity associated with that Contact by August 20.

**4.** **(Optional) Create association rules to add additional criteria that Campaigns must meet in order to be automatically associated with an Opportunity.**

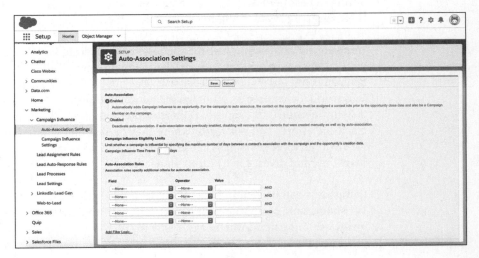

**FIGURE 18-8:**
The Campaign Influence page.

# Setting Customizations for Your Service Organizations

The service side of Salesforce also has some settings that need to be taken into account when setting up Cases and other service-oriented objects. Let's jump in and take a look at what we can configure out of the box.

## Understanding Support Settings for your Cases

Support Settings are fairly comprehensive in Salesforce, and we don't go into every one. However, we do cover the most commonly used settings, and for the rest, you can consult other resources, like *Salesforce Service Cloud For Dummies,* by Jon Paz and TJ Kelley (Wiley), to get the help you need.

To get to the Support Settings, shown in Figure 18-9, choose Setup ➪ Feature Settings ➪ Service ➪ Support Settings. Here are some common settings:

>> **Default Case Owner:** A required field that defaults to an owner for Cases when Case assignment rules fail to locate one.

>> **Automated Case User:** A required field that is listed as the actor in the Case History related list for automated Case changes, such as when escalation or assignment rules fire.

   It's usually best to have the Automate Case User be a Service Cloud admin or super user.

>> **Show Closed Statuses in Case Status Field:** Select this option if you'd rather not have users fill out information on a separate closed Case page layout and you'd prefer to let them just close out a Case quickly through the status picklist.

>> **Enable Case Feed Actions and Feed Items:** Select this option to change your Cases to the upgraded Case user interface. You'll have to also give users access to the Case Feed.

For more in-depth information about these options and others, see *Salesforce Service Cloud For Dummies.*

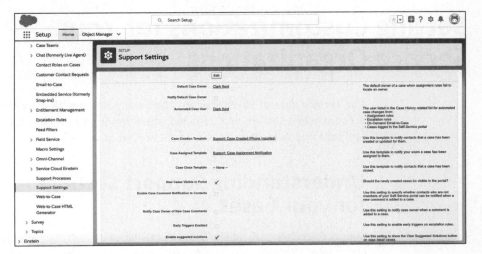

**FIGURE 18-9:**
The Support
Settings page.

# Defining escalation rules

Escalation rules are criteria and rules you define when you want Cases to be automatically escalated. For example, let's say you have three different tiers of support: Gold, Silver, and Bronze. You can create different escalation rules to say that if a Case with Gold support isn't resolved within 24 hours, it will be escalated to a support manager.

To create an escalation rule, choose Setup ⇨ Feature Settings ⇨ Service ⇨ Escalation Rules, and follow these steps:

1. **Click the New button to create a new escalation rule, enter a name for it, and click Save.**

   Don't select the Active check box until you're done with the escalation rule and you deactivate any currently active rules.

2. **Click the new escalation rule you created, and then click the New button in the Rule Entry list.**

   The Rule Entry Edit page appears, as shown in Figure 18-10.

3. **Enter the sort order in which Salesforce will run this particular rule entry.**

   This comes into play when you have multiple rules. Salesforce evaluates each entry in the order you designate and stops looking when it finds a criteria match.

4. **Select criteria for the rule entry.**

   In Figure 18-10, the rule entry indicates two criteria that, if met, will automatically escalate the Case. If the Case is (a) high priority, and (b) owned by Tier 2 (or the second highest tier of support), the Case will be escalated.

**5.** **Select the business hours criteria for the rule.**

You can choose to use the organization's business hours, use the Case-specific business hours, or ignore them altogether. Business hours help support teams so that you time-based criteria run only during your business hours.

**6.** **Select how escalation times are set, and click Save.**

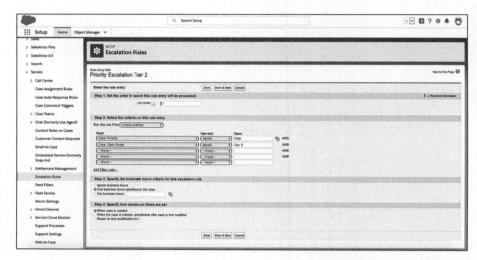

**FIGURE 18-10:**
Entering
rule entry
criteria for your
escalation rule.

Now you've created your first escalation rule! Go into a Case, set the criteria you've chosen, and test it out. But first, don't forget to go back and activate the escalation rule.

We've shown you some of the inside tips on object-specific settings in the Setup menu for Sales, Marketing, and Service. Now you have a basic foundation and understanding of where certain settings are toggled for which objects. We encourage you to go in and get your hands dirty. Explore for yourself!

Chapter **19**

# Building Custom Apps

What if you could modify your business applications in minutes to match the unique ways you manage your customer relationships? How much more productive could you be if you spent less time fighting your technology and more time with your customers?

The Lightning platform (formerly called the Force.com platform) includes several back-end "platform as a service" (PaaS) features, as well as the functionality you use to customize and create on-demand applications simply by pointing and clicking your mouse on easy-to-use web pages. In fact, with the Lightning platform, you can not only customize your existing Salesforce applications, but also build entirely new applications to fit the way you do business. If you need a little inspiration, you can also install a preexisting solution from the AppExchange directory (www.appexchange.com).

In this chapter, we demystify the Lightning platform and define some basic terms to give you a glimpse of the awesome power of creating custom apps. Then we discuss general concepts related to the AppExchange. Finally, we offer simple and critical tips for preparing your deployment game plan.

# Understanding Elements of the Lightning Platform

The Lightning platform is the Salesforce.com on-demand platform: a suite of development tools for customizing, building, integrating, and installing business applications — and you don't need to build or maintain any infrastructure yourself to use it.

The Lightning platform is both a collection of customization tools as well as the underlying infrastructure that powers the Salesforce app that you use. The cool part is that, over time, Salesforce engineers have exposed parts of their secret sauce so that you can use it, too, and they've also used these customization tools to build additional features into Salesforce.

Briefly, here are some key terms you need to know:

>> **Lightning (formerly Force.com) platform:** The engine that makes Salesforce what it is today. It's the underlying technology that enables you to customize existing applications from the Setup area, create new ones (with or without any programming experience), integrate Salesforce with other company systems, and share these snippets online with others.

>> **Lightning Experience:** This is the visual front-end that provides Salesforce users with a different look and feel than the original UI, called Salesforce Classic. The new UI provides new functionality not previously available in Classic, functionality that existed previously in Classic but is interacted with or customized in a different way, or functionality that existed before, and the customization steps haven't changed. The features that become supported in the Lightning Experience (versus just in Salesforce Classic) continue to grow, given the iterative nature of Salesforce's releases.

>> **Lightning Pages:** (Yes, they sure love to use the word "Lightning" in front of many features.) Lightning pages are page layouts built to work optimally in the Lightning Experience and on the Salesforce mobile app. You don't have to create one of these if you already have a custom page layout in Salesforce Classic, but you might not be taking advantage of more customization capabilities in Lightning. There are three types of Lightning Pages:

- Record pages (similar to page layouts in Classic

- Home pages (which are a type of page layout specifically for the Home tab)

- App pages (which are pages you design that can be used as custom home pages within a custom app, and re-used as a tab within other apps)

- » **Lightning Components:** These are the building blocks that form the blueprint of what goes where on a Lightning page, as well as in any mobile version of your customization. They come in three flavors:

  - Standard (which you can use without any coding, just clicking and dragging it onto a page)

  - Custom (which can be developed using code, which means that you can have special components built for your specific company)

  - Third-party (which can be downloaded from the AppExchange)

- » **Lightning App Builder:** This is the point-and-click user interface where you go to create and edit your Lightning Pages. Don't worry, you don't have to manually re-create every existing Classic layout; Salesforce is smart enough to have standard Classic customizations roll into the same page in the Lightning Experience. If you have built some custom pages using VisualForce in the past, you should check to see how that code is interpreted within the Lightning Experience, and consider making some modifications.

- » **Apex code:** Another subset of the Lightning (formerly Force.com) platform. The Salesforce proprietary programming language that allows users to write custom logic and create integrations between Salesforce and other systems. If you're technical, you have the ability to build new objects, create triggers and classes, change the user interface (UI) to handle custom forms and interactions, use a web services application programming interface (API), and all that techno-speak stuff

- » **Visualforce:** An additional proprietary language that Salesforce provides, built long before custom Lightning Pages were an option. You can use it to customize the actual front-end page design and components of your custom application. You're no longer limited to Salesforce's default colors, visual design, and tab layouts. Make sure your technical resources check the developer forums over at http://developer.force.com to understand when you might want to develop custom Lightning Pages or maintain Visualforce pages. The cool part is that with Lightning, you can even embed Lightning-like UI and functionality within a Visualforce page, or vice versa. It just depends on your company's resources and capacity.

- » **AppExchange:** An online directory where you can quickly browse, try, download, and install apps that can instantly run alongside your existing Salesforce applications, within your Salesforce instance.

**REMEMBER**

Salesforce frequently rebrands the names of its various offerings. The preceding terms are the most recent versions as of this book's publication. The underlying functionality, look, and feel that we discuss is still the same as we describe it.

Unless you're a developer (or a glutton for punishment), you don't need to know the technical ins and outs. What you do need to know is that the Lightning platform enables Salesforce administrators to easily customize and extend their existing on-demand applications without extensive involvement from developers. For building applications, which can take months with traditional software, you can point and click to quickly develop new applications in hours or days, completely integrated with your existing Salesforce customer relationship management (CRM) system.

To see all current custom apps, log in to Salesforce and follow these steps:

1. **From the gear icon in the upper-right of your page, choose Setup ⇨ Apps ⇨ App Manager.**

   The Lightning Experience App Manager page appears. This page highlights all apps that currently exist in your Salesforce instance. You get to see apps that were created by third-party vendors (installed via the AppExchange), as well as ones built internally to organize a set of pages together. You'll also get to see what UI the app was built in, whether it is managed or not (which means that a third party vendor owns most of the customization options), and if the app is visible in the Lightning Experience.

2. **It is from the Lightning Experience App Manager where you would create a new Lightning App, as noted by the button in the upper-right of this page.**

# Preparing Your Custom App Strategy

The Lightning Platform places so much potential at your fingertips that, just like a kid in a candy store, you may have the urge to just jump in and start building custom objects and tabs — a baptism by fire. Although that method is appetizing in theory, it's a quick way in reality to get a stomachache, especially if your business grows and more people start entering information in Salesforce. Resist that impulse until you review these simple steps for planning your strategy for on-demand applications:

1. **Define and prioritize objectives.**

   Your wish list doesn't need to be very involved, but it should spell out the who your users will be, what business goals they're trying to accomplish, when this app would be used and the desired timeline for it to debut, why there is urgency now for this app, and how you'd build it. Bucket your wish list into themes, hopefully centered around business outcomes, like increasing efficiency or data accuracy, improving adoption (and data quality), and so on.

2. **Build a plan.**

   With agreed-upon objectives, take your project down another level and lay out a plan to address the most pressing objectives, and who is going to help you with that (if anyone else). What eventually do you want to report on, with regards to this business challenge?

3. **Determine the most suitable approach.**

   You have many different ways to tackle a business issue with the Lightning Platform — some better than others.

   - *Use the discussion boards* at the Salesforce Trailblazer Community website (http://success.salesforce.com) to check your gut on existing or upcoming functionality. You may not need to build a unique solution.

   - *Browse the App Exchange* to see whether any available prebuilt applications meet your general requirements.

4. **Keep it simple.**

   Don't sacrifice your objectives at the expense of simplicity — although at the beginning, simple is often better.

5. **Start with the end in mind.**

   If a custom app seems like the right strategy, figure out what it is that you want to measure. Understand how well your solution may scale (or not).

TIP

A great way to design your application so that it takes full advantage of relationships is to simply draw it out on a piece of paper or a white board. Your design doesn't have to be fancy or complicated, but it should define the standard and custom objects you need and how they should be linked.

# Creating Custom Objects

Once you have a plan for what will go into your app, and what that app's tabs comprise, you'll have to know how to create its building blocks. In this section, we tell you how to create custom objects and relate them to each other, so they ultimately make up your custom app.

## Building your custom objects

Typically, you create a custom object to house a discrete set of information that's different from what is contained in other standard objects. For example, an

Opportunity object contains Opportunity information. A Custom Expense object contains information about expenses that's unique from the typical purpose of other standard objects.

If you want to build a home, you have to add the basic building blocks first. The same analogy applies to custom apps and objects. For example, if you want to build a recruiting application, you may decide that you could use the Contacts object for applicants and need to build custom objects for Job Postings and Interview Feedback because they're distinct blocks of data.

To set up a new object, follow these steps:

**1. Choose Setup ⇨ Objects and Fields ⇨ Object Manager.**

The Object Manager page appears. This page, your starting point for creating an object, is where all your standard and custom objects are displayed. There's a column displayed by default, called "Custom" that shows if an object is one that came standard with Salesforce or not.

**2. Click the Create button to show the drop-down list options.**

Select Custom Object. Then the New Custom Object page appears.

**3. In the Custom Object Information section, type the basic details for your object.**

You usually just need to fill out the Label and Plural Label fields. This will then automatically populate the Object Name field. Labels are what your end-users see (like "Time Off Request"). The object name is what the Lightning Platform sees (like "Time_Off_Req") in case you need to have another system (or another part of Salesforce) talk to it.

**4. Complete the Enter Record Name Label and Format fields.**

The record name appears on page layouts, related lists, lookups, and search results. This is what you use to differentiate one record of this object from another. Depending on the type of object you're creating, you may want to switch the data type from Text to Auto Number.

Here's how to tell when to use text versus auto numbers:

- *Text:* The name has some intrinsic value.

- *Auto numbers:* You're creating an object that will relate to other standard objects in a unique, fundamental way. Auto numbers are useful for sequenced business documents, such as invoices, purchase orders, IT tickets, and timecards.

**5.** **Select the custom object's optional features.**

With simple pointing and clicking on your part, the Lightning Platform allows you to select your custom object's features that are identical to many of the features found on standard objects, such as tracking activities, allowing reporting, or tracking its field history.

**6.** **Leave the Deployment Status as In Development so that only you can see it, instead of all the other Salesforce users within your company.**

TIP

We recommend making sure that you can explain the business process around using the new object *before deploying it* to help guide correct adoption. This could be as easy as an email or mention in your weekly team meeting, or it could entail a larger training effort.

Select the Deployed button if you're ready for your users to begin using it. If you wait to deploy the object, return to this screen by choosing Setup ⇨ Objects and Fields ⇨ Object Manager. Find your object from the list of standard and custom objects, click the drop-down arrow in the far right of that object's row, and select Edit to return to the custom object detail page.

After you've saved details about the new custom object, you can add custom fields to this object just like you would a standard object, as discussed in Chapter 17, "Performing Common Configurations."

TIP

If you already mapped the custom objects that will be part of your app, create all the objects first before modifying them. This action is especially helpful if you're building relationships between them.

## Modifying custom objects

Revising a Salesforce custom object can be as simple as modifying the default layout for that object or associating additional related objects in the related lists portion of that custom object's page layout. If you need to change the basic settings, simply click the downward-pointing triangle button on the same row as the object you want to edit. Then from that drop-down, select Edit, and the Edit Custom Object Details page reappears.

If you want to customize your new object, you can point and click through the customization options on the left sidebar of the Object's page.

REMEMBER

Certain Setup features — including custom profiles, multiple page layouts, record types, workflow, and field-level security — are available only in the Enterprise and Unlimited editions.

# Building relationships

One primary reason for building applications with the Lightning Platform is to create a single, integrated, one-stop business experience for your users.

The key to those linkages is building custom relationships between objects. For example, if your company wants to manage Account planning in Salesforce, you want to create a relationship between the standard Account object and a custom object for the Account Plan.

To build a relationship, follow these steps:

**1.** **Choose Setup ⇨ Object Manager from the top set of tabs.**

The Object Manager page appears.

**2.** **Click the desired custom object under the Label column.**

The Custom Object's Details page appears.

**3.** **Click the Fields & Relationships link from the left sidebar (see Figure 19-1).**

The Fields & Relationships page appears showing the fields related to the custom object. Click the New button in the upper right of this page. The New Custom Field wizard appears.

**4.** **In Step 1 of the New Custom Field wizard, choose the type of relationship with another object.**

The Lightning Platform supports two primary types of custom relationships: Master-Detail and Lookup. They're both one-to-many relationships.

REMEMBER

A Lookup relationship links one object to another. The representative custom field will be colored in blue with the text underlined, signifying that you can click it or hover your cursor over it to "look up" a value and other details from that related object. Master-Detail (also known as parent-child) relationships are a special type of association: The relationship is required for the detail. If you delete the master record, its related children are also deleted.

The two relationships look the same in the UI — text colored in blue and underlined.

But here are two big differences:

- *Master-Detail relationships cause the cascade deletion of child records to occur when the parent record is deleted.* For example, if you delete an Account, all related child records are also deleted.

- *In a Master-Detail relationship, the detail record inherits the Owner and sharing rules of the master record.* Detail objects are dependent on their masters. In Lookup relationships, however, they don't transfer sharing rules — they're completely independent.

**TIP**

When in doubt, start with the Lookup option. You can also convert it to a Master-Detail relationship later, as long as each record has that lookup field filled in.

**5.** **Click Next to continue.**

**6.** **In Step 2 of the wizard, select the other object that you want to relate your object to.**

You can create as many as 40 Lookup relationships and up to two Master-Detail relationships with a custom object.

**7.** **Click Next to continue.**

**8.** **In Step 3 of the wizard, enter the label for the lookup field.**

As a default, the Lightning Platform prefills the fields with the name of the object you selected, although you can change it. You can also configure a Lookup Filter to further narrow down the number of that related object's records you can choose from when making the lookup association.

**9.** **Click Next to continue.**

**10.** **If you have Enterprise or Unlimited Edition, set the field-level security in Step 4 of the wizard. (If you don't, skip to Step 14 because you won't be able to set field-level security.)**

This allows you to determine which types of users can see this field, and how they can interact with it. If you know this field is irrelevant to a subset of user types, best to keep their user interface clean and not bog down their record with irrelevant fields. If you chose the Master-Detail option, the security is set for you because it must be available within field-level security. If you chose the Lookup option, select the appropriate check boxes to control visibility and edit rights to the field.

**11.** **Click Next to continue.**

**12.** **If you have Enterprise or Unlimited Edition, in Step 5 of the wizard, select the page layouts in which you want to display the field.**

Suppose that you're creating an expense application. You may want the rep's layout to be different from the manager's layout.

**13.** **Click Next to continue.**

**14.** **In Step 6 of the wizard, deselect the check boxes if you don't want the custom object to appear on the related list of the selected object.**

For example, if you're linking expenses with Accounts, you may not want a long list of expenses showing up on an Account record.

**15.** **When you're done, click Save.**

The Custom Object's Fields & Relationships page reappears, and your custom relationship is displayed.

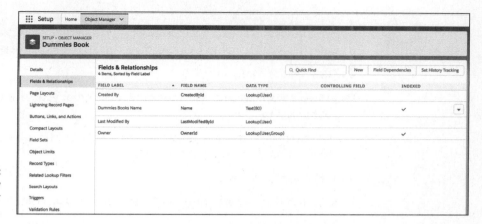

**FIGURE 19-1:**
Create a new
custom field or
relationship.

TIP

Build your relationships before loading any actual data.

Remember that between two objects, you can have only one object that allows the Master-Detail relationship, so the other object has to be a Lookup relationship. A standard object also can't be the child of a Master-Detail relationship.

TECHNICAL
STUFF

If you're drawing out your entity relationship diagram and find that you need two objects to have a many-to-many relationship with each other, build a junction object between the two. The junction object will act as a bridge between two objects, to give the impression of two Master-Detail relationships.

Here are some other ways that you can modify custom objects to fit your company's business processes:

>> **Creating fields:** With the Lightning Platform, you can quickly add fields to your custom object, much like you can with a standard object, such as an Account or a Contact. See Chapter 17 for more information on creating custom fields.

>> **Changing layouts:** After or as you build fields, feel free to start rearranging the page layout for the object record. Often, that's one of the easiest ways to get a pulse on what's missing from your record. See Chapter 17 for more information on editing page layouts.

>> **Customizing related lists:** After you add your Lookup relationships and custom fields, you're ready to start customizing your related lists. The Lightning Platform allows you to modify the columns that are displayed in a related list.

**REMEMBER**

Don't forget this step because without customizing this section, your users don't see much in a related list. When you add the right columns, though, the related list becomes a powerful tool for your users. By customizing the columns displayed in a related list, users can quickly see a summary of relevant information from a record's detail page. See Chapter 17 for more information on customizing related lists.

# Creating Custom Apps

After you sketch the basic requirements for your new application, and built the objects that you need, you're ready to begin assembling this into an app. The custom app is much like a container, into which you associate your objects and tabs.

**TIP**

To see an example of custom apps that others have created, visit the AppExchange (www.appexchange.com) and browse apps by category. Apps created by Salesforce Labs are those that came from Salesforce's own employees.

Using the Lightning Experience App Manager, you can start creating a new app with a easy configuration wizard that can empower your business faster than the status quo of traditional software solutions.

## Setting up a custom app

**REMEMBER**

To add the custom app, choose Setup ➪ Apps ➪ App Manager and then follow these steps in the Lightning Experience App Manager:

1. **Click the New Lightning App button in the upper-right of the page.**

   The New Lightning App wizard begins. Here you begin with App Details & Branding — telling Salesforce the name of the app, what color you want the app's tab to be, and if you want to associate a custom logo for the app.

2. **Click the Next button to continue to the App Options step.**

   Here you can specify if you plan for your app to just be used by users on a desktop or mobile device, or both. Remember, the Lightning Experience accommodates mobile layouts with little extra effort.

3. **Click the Next button to continue to the Utility Items step.**

   You have the option to add shortcut links to various functionality in the footer of your browser. These act as an "always present" set of links readily available with this app.

4. **Click Next to continue to the Navigation Items step. Here you select the tabs or other apps that you want this app to be able to navigate to.**

   You do this step simply by clicking an item from the Available Items box and using the arrow buttons to move that to the Selected Items selection box.

5. **Click Next to arrive at the User Profiles step.**

   Select the profiles in the Available Profiles area and use arrows to move the selected profile to the Selected Profiles box.

   REMEMBER

   You want to make sure that the right apps are available to the right people in your organization.

6. **When you're done, click Save & Finish.**

   The Lightning Experience App Manage page reappears, and your new custom app now appears in the list.

## Creating custom tabs

When creating a new custom object, you can create a custom tab to go with the object, which will allow the object to be easily reachable from top header navigation area of any Salesforce page.

REMEMBER

Don't over-tab your application if it's not necessary. Ask yourself: "Will my users need all the object's data available from a central area?" If the answer is yes, you may need a custom tab.

To build a custom tab, follow these steps:

1. **Go to User Interface ⇨ Tab to select a custom icon to associate with the new custom object.**

   From the Custom Tabs screen, click New to go to the New Custom Object Tab wizard.

2. **In Step 1 of the New Custom Object Tab wizard, select the object from the picklist, and then use the Lookup icon to choose a tab style.**

   The tab style affects both the color of the tab and the icon associated with the custom object record, that will be reflected in the Lightning Experience both on your desktop and the Salesforce Mobile app.

3. **In Step 2 of the wizard, select the desired tab visibility for your user profiles.**

   With the radio button feature, you can control which profiles see this tab by default, which don't but can show it if they want, and which just won't see it at all.

4. **In Step 3 of the wizard, select the apps to which the new custom tab will be available.**

   This step makes it simple to associate custom tabs with just the right apps for your users. Maybe it's needed for different use cases addressed by different apps, or it's specfic to a custom app that you created.

5. **When you're done, click Save.**

   The Custom Tabs page reappears with your new custom tab listed.

# Understanding the AppExchange

As customers, employees, and partners began building custom applications (or *apps*), some bright person came up with an idea: Wouldn't it be great if other customers like you could simply try, download, and install these custom apps without having to build them on their own? iTunes uses the web to distribute music, so why shouldn't enterprise applications work the same way?

Enter the AppExchange, the website owned and operated by Salesforce where you can try, download, and quickly install apps that can extend the value of Salesforce to meet your unique needs. You can even use the AppExchange to share your custom apps with everyone.

Of course, the biggest benefit beyond how much easier your life will be is the impact on your users. The AppExchange isn't just about easy sharing — it's about your employees using integrated business apps with all your information in one place.

**REMEMBER**

Customers, partners, and Salesforce personnel can all provide AppExchange with applications. Many of them, particularly the ones published by Salesforce employees (a.k.a. Salesforce Labs), are free to install and use. Others, such as the ones provided by partners, may have a fee associated with them. Some apps may be very straightforward to customize and use, other can help address complicated business processes and be fine-tuned to the specific needs of your business, but may need a more formal requirements gathering process.

Downloading music and videos from the web is something we take for granted nowadays. But downloading enterprise apps? Wow, that was like a whole 'nother animal back in the day. Salesforce's innovation here has made this a normal expectation of enterprise cloud applications.

When you get down to t, the AppExchange is still about the exchange of a package of goods from one party to another. As with many innovations, getting the most out of a new system usually amounts to understanding some basic terms and knowing your limits before jumping in.

Here are a few key terms you should know before you get started:

>> **Installation:** The process by which you download, install, and deploy a custom app from AppExchange. You can control how many profiles can have access to the app upon download.

>> **Publishing:** The process by which you package a portion of your customizations and make them available, either publicly or privately, on the AppExchange. The users that do this the most are independent software vendor (ISV) partners of Salesforce, who market, sell, and distribute their custom app here.

>> **Managed package:** An AppExchange package created and maintained by a verified third-party vendor, typically an ISV partner. Unlike unmanaged packages, whose components you can modify and customize, managed package components have limited customization capabilities. This allows vendors to provide you with an offering with some proprietary code that you can't muck around with, and a subsequent upgrade path that'll leave you successful instead of stuck in the mud because you changed something that's not supported by a newer version.

And here are a few more things to keep in mind:

>> Although anyone can visit the AppExchange to view videos, and review marketing collateral and installation guides, to install and share apps, you must have a Salesforce instance and have administrative rights to that instance. (Did we just hear a sigh of relief?)

>> You can publish many types of AppExchange components, not just custom apps, on the AppExchange. You can exchange custom links, dashboards, Lightning components, Visualforce code snippets, and more.

>> Some apps are self-contained — *native* — in Salesforce. They were built with the Lightning Platform and don't depend on other external applications. Other custom apps are *composite.* Such apps may look and feel like Salesforce apps but connect with other services not owned by Salesforce. A large network of ISV partners have created apps that have become "household names" (at least to Sales Operations teams), like DocuSign and Conga. At the same time, newer vendors continue to appear and provide solutions. Apps do go through a security and business plan review, but you should still remember *caveat emptor* (let the buyer beware). Do your research, read the reviews, and make sure to review the package's components before opting to test this out in a sandbox environment.

Familiarize yourself with the AppExchange at www.appexchange.com, and then try out some apps before you decide whether you want to use them.

If you want to install a custom prebuilt app, you can do it with a few simple clicks. This process amounts to downloading the package, installing the app into your instance of Salesforce, and deploying it to all or a portion of your users.

REMEMBER

A *package* refers to all the components that make up the custom app. A package may include custom tabs and objects, code, custom links, custom profiles, reports, dashboards, documents, and more.

To install a custom app, follow these steps:

**1. Click the Get It Now button on the app's detail page in AppExchange (at www.appexchange.com).**

**2. Click the Log In button to log in using your Salesforce credentials.**

This identifies who you are. If you've already got Salesforce open in another tab in your browser, you'll move to the next step. Make sure you enter the information that reflects which org you want to install the app into.

**3. Choose whether you want to continue the installation of the app in your production or sandbox.**

Larger organizations may have customizations that need to be tested with this package. A sandbox that is practically an exact copy of what you have in your live system is a good place to kick the tires without the potential of impacting your business if something goes wrong.

TIP

If you don't have access to a sandbox, make sure you have some more information on the vendor and what exactly the app will do. If you trust the vendor and package, install the app in your production environment, but make sure you make it visible just to system administrators first until they've thoroughly tested the installation.

**4. Review the installation details that appear, which confirms what you'll be installing and what information will be provided to the publisher.**

Salesforce makes this as transparent an installation as possible.

**5. Check the box to confirm that you've read the terms and conditions, and then click the Confirm and Install button to continue.**

**6. Enter your Salesforce login and password again for the org in which you want to install the app.**

The Package Installation Details page appears in Salesforce.

**TIP**

If you're experimenting with the AppExchange for the first time, you may want to consider using the Sandbox Edition or a free Developer Edition instance to install, customize, and test the custom app.

**7.** **Examine the details of what's getting installed by clicking the View Components link.**

This page pops up to summarize the custom app's details, including objects, code, fields, tabs, reports, and dashboards.

Make sure that you examine the contents of a package thoroughly before proceeding. Understand the package's API access to various objects, including details of what permissions the package will have on what objects.

**8.** **Select a radio button to choose the audience that you'll be installing this package for: admins only, all users, or certain profiles.**

We recommend that you start with first testing this out to admins only. Then you can think about who has access to edit and view the contents of the app before you're ready to deploy it live. If you want to install the app for select profiles, the Select Specific Profiles details appear on the same page.

**9.** **Click the Install button.**

A progress page appears as installation begins. If the installation is taking a while, a notification will appear that Salesforce will notify you when the installation is complete. In the meantime, you'll be directed to the Installed Packages page to monitor the status of the package.

**REMEMBER**

After you install the app, you can use the Lightning Platform to modify its tabs, objects, and other customizations, just as though you had built the custom app yourself. Even though you've installed the app as we recommended above, it's not available to non-administrators until it's deployed.

IN THIS CHAPTER

» Managing users over time

» Planning your sharing model

» Building profiles to determine access

» Defining your role hierarchy

» Delegating administrative duties

Chapter **20**

# Accessing the Right Data with User Permissions

How can Salesforce be customized for your company so each user sees only pertinent information? You've come to the right chapter.

For administrators or members of your customer relationship management (CRM) project team with the right privileges, Salesforce allows you to easily configure your system so that users can access and share information according to your goals. With Salesforce, you have a variety of ways to control access and sharing of data, from system-wide sharing rules to assigning profiles. And, if you have Enterprise or Unlimited Edition, you have industrial-strength flexibility, even to the point of field-level security.

In this chapter, we show you all the steps you can take (or should consider) for configuring Salesforce to ensure that users see only what they need to see. We discuss concepts around creating the role hierarchy, assigning profiles, determining field-level security, creating users, and setting up your sharing rules.

# Understanding User Administration

When Salesforce.com supplies user licenses for your organization, administrators can add users into Salesforce. You don't have to create the roles and profiles before you add users, but we recommend doing so because Role and Profile are important fields when you're creating a user record. In this section, we discuss various ways of creating users and managing them.

**TIP**

Not sure what roles and profiles are, but want to get started quickly? At least review the "Defining the Role Hierarchy" and "Reviewing the standard profiles" sections later in this chapter, so you understand what the out-of-the-box permissions allow.

## Creating a new user

To add users, click the Setup link and follow these steps:

**1. In the sidebar under Administration, click Users to expand the submenu and then click the Users link.**

A users list page appears.

**2. (Optional) Use the View drop-down list if you want to select from standard or custom list views of your users.**

Salesforce presets your views with three standard options: All Users, Active Users, and Admin Users.

**3. Click the New User button to add users one at a time.**

A New User page appears in Edit mode.

**TIP**

To enter a list of users that need to be created (instead of one at a time), click the Add Multiple Users button instead.

**4. Complete the fields, paying close attention to selecting appropriate Role and Profile values.**

Select the Generate New Password and Notify User Immediately check box at the bottom of the New User page if you want the user to immediately receive an email with her username and temporary password. If you're in the midst of an implementation, we recommend deselecting this check box and doling out passwords when you're good and ready.

**WARNING**

If your company is just starting out with Salesforce, be cautious and don't give all your new users the System Administrator profile. Future generations of users at your company will thank you for taking a prudent approach to configuring things in Salesforce, as opposed to allowing too many cooks into the Salesforce kitchen.

5. **Click Save.**

   The User detail page appears.

## Activating and deactivating users

After you've created a new user, you can activate or deactivate him. Activation means the user is able to log in to Salesforce and start using it. Deactivation means, well, the opposite. There is no concept of deleting a user, which helps with compliance and auditing purposes, as well as avoiding a lot of complications when it comes to historical records owned by and actions performed by that user.

To activate or deactivate a user, click the Setup link and follow these steps:

1. **Click the Users link under the Administration ⇨ Users heading on the sidebar.**

   A users list page appears.

2. **Click the Edit link to the left of a user's name.**

   The User Edit detail page appears for that user.

3. **Check the Active box, depending on what you want to do.**

   If you see a checkmark, that means the user is active. Removing the checkmark means that user is deactivated.

4. **Click Save to save your action.**

   You're returned to the user list page.

## Freezing users

What if the user you're trying to deactivate is associated with some special settings in Salesforce (like being a default Lead or queue owner)? This may take some time as you confirm with business users who the replacement assignee should be. In the meantime, the clock is ticking and you still need to prevent this user from accessing Salesforce. That's when you can freeze a user's record, which disables that user's ability to access Salesforce while you perform related system administrator duties.

To freeze a user, click the Setup link and follow these steps:

1. **Click the Users link under the Administration ⇨ Users heading on the sidebar.**

   A users list page appears.

2. **Click the name of the user you want to freeze.**

   The user's detail page appears.

3. **Click the Freeze button.**

   You're returned to the user detail page, and the button name changes to Unfreeze. To unfreeze that user record, click the Unfreeze button.

# Establishing Data Access Concepts

Before jumping into the guts of system design, take a minute to review five basic configuration elements. These will help as you begin to think about who in your company should see and edit what in Salesforce.

» **Users:** These are the specific people who use your Salesforce system.

» **Sharing model:** Defines the baseline, general access that users have to each other's data. Also known as organization-wide defaults, org-wide defaults, or simply, OWDs. If you already know that certain groups should not be seeing other groups' information, you want to start with the most restrictive sharing model and use things like the role hierarchy and sharing rules to open access to information. It's easier to provide more access than it is to selectively restrict it.

» **Roles and role hierarchy:** Define who reports to whom in your organization, for the purposes of seeing and editing information owned by others, which aids in running reports. Think of roles as a way to provide *vertical access* to data (that is, up and down a hierarchy). People higher up in the hierarchy are able to report on those below them in the hierarchy. For example, if you're a manager of a team of sales reps, you'll have a role above your team and be able to see all the Account, Contact, and Opportunity data owned by your team. Individual sales reps, however, may not be able to see Opportunity information owned by their peers. This doesn't always have to mimic your company's org chart exactly, however. Another example is that a sales operations analyst may not have any direct reports, but must run reports on the entire sales team. This person could share a role with the head of sales, only because of her reporting needs. Each user should have an assigned role within your defined role hierarchy.

# PLANNING USER ACCESS TO ACHIEVE SUCCESS

Put the major stakeholders of your Salesforce solution in a room and ask them one question: "How do you envision people sharing information in Salesforce?" More often than not, you'll get blank stares.

Discuss sharing issues with your CRM project team after you hear about their current CRM processes. Current business processes, explained without any Salesforce jargon from the team, can often help you formulate an opinion based on what you believe would be best for your company. Take into consideration the culture, size, and type of sales organization at your company. Use this opinion to guide the specific nature of your questions.

Now, you *should* ask that question, but we suggest following it up with scenarios. Here are a few ideas to get you started:

- Should a sales development rep be able to see what the CEO sees?

- Should a sales rep be able to view data from other reps? Should one sales rep be allowed to edit another's Lead record?

- Do certain groups need wider access than others? For example, does a call center team that supports all customers need more or less access than a team of sales reps? What about a professional services team member who helps during the sales cycle, as well as during the implementation, and answers any postlaunch questions for up to a certain number of days?

- Do you have marketing operations or sales operations staff? How will they be interacting with Salesforce? Should they be able to see everything that VPs of their organizations see, especially because they'll probably be doing all the legwork for them?

- Does a manager require different permissions than a rep, to change information that the rep can't?

- Do multiple people commonly work on the same Account or Opportunity?

- Do you have any compliance or audit concerns with a fully open or completely private sharing model?

Use these types of questions and their answers to guide your configuration.

>> **Profiles:** Control a user's capability to see and access different fields within a record in Salesforce. For example, service reps will find some fields on an Account record more relevant than other fields that may be very important to a marketing operations analyst. To make the service reps' view of the Account record more pertinent and less confusing, you could hide certain irrelevant fields from their view by assigning them a custom profile. You must assign a profile to each user.

>> **Sharing rules:** Opens up access to data for specific users or groups of users. Think of this as opening lateral or horizontal access to your data, by giving certain peer groups or individuals this exception.

You use these five elements as the primary levers to deliver the proper level of access and control for your company in Salesforce.

# Defining Your Sharing Model

As an administrator or member of your CRM project team, one of your biggest decisions in Salesforce is how users will share information. A *sharing model* controls the level of access that users have across an organization's information, not just up and down the chain. You can use the sharing model with the role hierarchy, public groups, personal groups, and the default access for each role to get pretty specific about what you want people to view or change. You use the organization-wide sharing model and, if necessary, public groups and expanded sharing rules in Salesforce to configure your sharing model.

**TIP**

For smaller, younger organizations, start with an open, collaborative sharing model, as opposed to a secretive sharing model in which no one knows what anyone else is doing. (A secretive sharing model sounds like any oxymoron, right? Well, it can be because if you don't carefully think about ramifications, you could be back to where you started with giant heaps of information.) If collaboration is one of your goals, a more-restrictive sharing model can have a greater potential negative impact on end-user adoption. You can always change the sharing model in the future if people scream loudly enough. But nine times out of ten, the value of collaboration overcomes the initial concerns with users viewing other users' data.

## Setting organization-wide defaults

The organization-wide defaults (OWDs) set the default sharing access that users have to each other's data. Sharing access determines how data created by users in a certain role or public group is viewed by users within another role or public group. For example, you many want your sales operations team to see the dollar value of won Opportunities so that they can verify what was booked versus what's listed on the signed contract, but you probably don't want them editing the amount of that won Opportunity. If any role or public group possesses data that at least one other role or group shouldn't see, your sharing model must be private; all other levels of openness must be granted as an exception via groups (more on that later).

**REMEMBER**

No matter which defaults you set to the sharing model, users will still have access to all data owned by or shared with users below them in the role hierarchy.

To configure the organization-wide defaults, click the Setup link and follow these steps:

**1.** **Choose Settings ⇨ Security ⇨ Sharing Settings.**

The Sharing Settings page appears, showing org-wide defaults for several objects, as well as specific sharing rules for those objects.

**2.** **Click the Edit button in the Organization Wide Defaults list.**

The Organization Sharing Edit page appears.

**3.** **Select the desired settings.**

Click some picklists to see the different options. The options are typically Private, Public Read Only, and Public Read/Write. Some objects may have options specific to that object's functionality, like the Calendar object, and the ability you have to set how much information people can see on others' calendars. For example, if you want the most restrictive model, choose the following as your defaults: Private for the major records and Hide Details for Calendar. Some standard objects, like the Lead and Case objects, have extra-special powers and have an additional option, Public Read/Write/Transfer. This assumes that someone working heavily in Leads or Cases will often need to transfer a Lead or Case record that isn't owned by him to someone else.

**REMEMBER**

Remember what we said about role hierarchy providing "vertical access" to data? A Private sharing setting on an object still assumes that people with a role above yours in the role hierarchy can see and report on those records. Salesforce always, by default, respects the hierarchy structure — sharing settings determine only how peers and those outside your typical chain of command see your data. For more complex sharing scenarios, you can have the option to deselect the ability to grant access to records based on role hierarchy, but, you may want to consult with Salesforce support or a Salesforce Partner before making such a complex change.

4. **Click Save.**

The Sharing Settings page reappears with your settings listed under the Organization Wide Defaults list.

## Granting greater access with sharing rules

By using public groups, roles, or roles and subordinates, you can create sharing rules to extend access above and beyond the organization-wide defaults. For example, if your default sharing model is read-only but you want a group of call center agents to have edit privileges on Account records, you could do this with a custom sharing rule.

To add a sharing rule and apply it to your data, click the Setup link and follow these steps:

1. **Click the Sharing Settings link under the Settings ⇨ Security heading on the sidebar.**

   The Sharing Settings page appears.

2. **Scroll down and click the New button next to any of the standard or custom object Sharing Rules lists, as shown in Figure 20-1.**

   All lists operate much the same but relate to different records. A Sharing Rule setup page appears for your selected record.

3. **Use the drop-down lists to define the data you want to share and the related roles or groups that you want to share that data with, as shown in Figure 20-2.**

   For example, you may want to grant your customer support team read/write privileges to Account data owned by all internal users. You can apply the sharing rule based on types of users who own the record, or create other filter criteria.

4. **Click Save.**

   The Sharing Settings page reappears with your new rule listed under the appropriate related list.

**TIP**

When you add a new sharing rule, Salesforce automatically reevaluates the sharing rules to apply the changes to all your records. If your modifications are substantial, you'll be warned with a dialog box that the operation could take significant time, and Salesforce will email you when complete. When you click OK, the dialog box closes, and the Sharing Settings page reappears. Use the Recalculate button in the appropriate related list to manually apply the changes when you've made modifications to groups, roles, or territories.

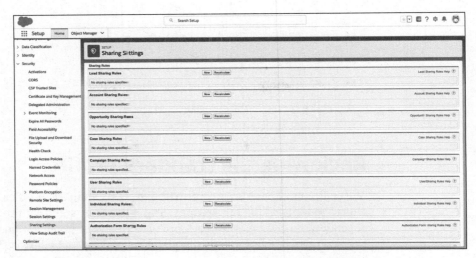

**FIGURE 20-1:**
Adding a new sharing rule.

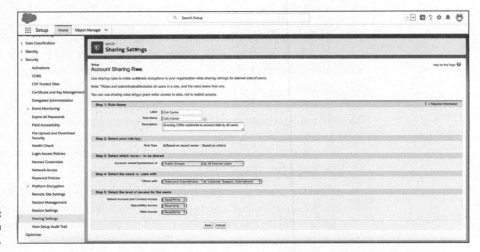

**FIGURE 20-2:**
Showing a sharing rule.

# Setting Up Profiles

In Enterprise and Unlimited editions of Salesforce, you can use profiles to control a user's permission to view and perform many functions. Roles and sharing rules determine which objects a person sees, and whether she can make changes to that object. A profile determines what details a person sees on that object. Depending on which edition you're using, you can use profiles to

>> Define which page layouts a user will see

>> Control field-level access

>> Determine the apps viewed by a user

>> Alter the tabs displayed to users

>> Make record types available to certain users

>> Secure certain login settings

## Reviewing the standard profiles

Most editions of Salesforce come with five or six standard profiles, which can't be altered except for the tab settings. The number of standard profiles may differ depending on the types of Salesforce licenses your organization has purchased. Newer organizations can stick to standard profiles and address their company's basic requirements related to user access. If you have Essentials or Professional Edition, you can't actually view the settings on the standard profiles.

If you have Enterprise or Unlimited Edition, choose Setup➪Administrations➪Users➪Profiles to see your profiles. Otherwise, here's a brief explanation of the more common standard profiles for Salesforce license types and how they're typically applied:

>> **System administrators** have full permissions and access across all Salesforce functions that don't require a separate license. You'd typically grant this level of control only to users administering the system or who play a critical part in configuring and customizing Salesforce.

>> **Standard users** can create and edit most record types, run reports, and view but not modify many areas of the administration setup. If you can't create custom profiles, you'd probably choose to assign sales reps to the standard user profile.

>> **Solution managers** have all the rights of standard users and can review and publish solutions.

>> **Marketing users** have all the rights of standard users and can perform a variety of marketing-related functions, including importing Leads and managing public documents and email templates. If your Salesforce edition has campaigns, marketing users can also administer campaigns.

>> **Contract managers** can add, edit, approve, and activate contracts. They can also delete nonactivated contracts.

>> **Read only** is just what its name implies  Users assigned to this profile can view data and export reports but can't edit anything.

**REMEMBER**

Profiles never conflict with your organization's sharing model or role hierarchy. For example, a Standard User profile allows a user to create, edit, or delete Leads, but if your sharing model is read-only for Leads, the Standard User won't be able to delete Leads owned by others.

**TIP**

Over the years, Salesforce.com has expanded the types of licenses you can buy, to better accommodate your organization's users and how often and what they need to access in Salesforce. To get the latest comprehensive list with definitions, click the Help link from within any Salesforce page and type **license types** into the search bar.

## Creating custom profiles

If you have Enterprise or Unlimited Edition, you can build custom profiles that provide you greater flexibility than the standard permissions granted to users and the layouts that they see. For example, you may want to create a custom profile for your finance team so that only users with that profile can edit check boxes on the Opportunity that track whether certain signed forms have been submitted when you close a deal. See Chapter 17 for details on creating custom layouts and record types.

To create a custom profile, you can start from scratch, but we suggest cloning and modifying an existing profile by following these steps:

1. **Choose Setup⇨Administration⇨Users⇨Profiles.**

   The User Profiles page appears. You can see which profiles are standard or custom ones based on which ones have the Custom box checked.

2. **Click the Standard User link in the Profile Name list.**

   The Profile: Standard User page appears. In practice, you can clone from any of the profiles, but by starting from the Standard User profile, you can simply add or remove permissions.

3. **Click the Clone button.**

   The Clone Profile page appears.

4. **Type a title in the Profile Name field and then click Save.**

   The Profile page for your new profile appears.

5. **Click the Edit button to modify the permissions, as shown in Figure 20-3.**

   The Profile Edit page appears.

**TIP**

Salesforce packs a plethora of possible permissions into a profile page. Some of those permissions aren't obvious; others are dependent on your selecting other permissions. If you have questions as you're working through the Profile Edit page, click the Help for This Page link in the upper-right corner of the page to go directly to the relevant Help documentation. If you place your cursor over the *i* icon, located next to certain Administrative Permissions on the Profile Edit page, rollover text appears with tips on other required settings.

6. **Under the Custom App Setting section, determine which standard and custom apps are visible for a profile and which one is the default.**

   This determines the content of the Force.com app drop-down list.

7. **Under the Tab Settings section, use the drop-down lists to determine the tab settings for your new profile.**

   Choose from the three possible options:

   - *Default On:* You want a tab to be displayed.

   - *Default Off:* You want a tab not to appear while still allowing a user assigned to the profile the choice to turn the tab back on. For example, if you created a profile for sales reps and you want to hide the Contracts tab but give the rep the option to display it, select Default Off on the Contracts field.

   - *Tab Hidden:* You want the tab to be hidden without an option for the user to turn the tab back on. For example, if your company isn't going to use Cases, you may decide to hide the tab.

**REMEMBER**

Making a tab hidden in a user's profile doesn't prevent the user from accessing those records (in reports, for example). To prevent a user from accessing a particular type of record altogether, remove the Read permission on that type of data from the Object Permissions sections of the page.

8. **(Optional) Select the Overwrite Users' Personal Tab Customizations check box if you want to overwrite the user's current personal customization settings with the settings for the new profile that you're applying.**

9. **Under the Administrative Permissions header, select or deselect check boxes to modify administrative permissions from the profile.**

   Most of these settings are designed for administrators, but some of these may be important, depending on your goals for a custom profile. For example, if you want to build a manager's profile, you may want to retain permissions such as Manage Public Reports and Manage Public List Views so that managers can create public reports and list views for their teams.

10. **Under the General User Permissions header, select or deselect check boxes to modify common user permissions from the profile.**

   For example, if you don't want sales reps to be able to export customer data to a file, you could create a custom profile for reps and remove the Export Reports setting.

11. **Under the Standard Object and Custom Object Permissions headers, select or deselect check boxes to modify standard or custom object permissions from the profile.**

   For example, if you don't want support reps to be able to modify Opportunities, you could create a custom profile for support reps and select only the Read check box in the row for Opportunities.

12. **Click Save.**

   The Profile page reappears for your new profile. Your new profile will now appear the next time you follow the instructions in Step 1.

13. **Click the View Users button if you want to assign users to the profile.**

   A Custom: *Custom Profile Name* list page appears in which you can view, add, or reset passwords for users in the profile.

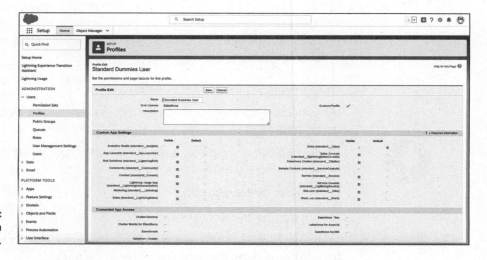

**FIGURE 20-3:**
Previewing a
Profile Edit page.

# Defining the Role Hierarchy

Think of a *role hierarchy* as the Salesforce system's data-access trickle-down org chart: If you're assigned to the role at the top of the chart, you have full access to your own data, and that privilege trickles down to the data of everyone below you in the hierarchy — and life is good.

TIP

When you're constructing your hierarchy, don't confuse your actual company org chart with the role hierarchy. Role hierarchy is all about access to data to perform your duties in Salesforce and how you want to organize certain sales-related reports. As such, hierarchies often have fewer layers than a typical org chart. For example, if your executive team will be users, you might simply create a role called Executive Team, assuming that many of those users will have similar trickle-down viewing and editing privileges.

You can use the role hierarchy in Salesforce as a primary method to control a user's visibility and access to other users' data. After you assign a role to a user, that user has ownerlike access to all records owned by or shared with subordinate users in the hierarchy. For example, if you set up a hierarchy with a Sales Rep role subordinate to a Sales Manager role, users assigned to Sales Manager would have read and write access to records owned by or shared with users in the Sales Rep role.

To set up your company's role hierarchy, click the Setup link in the upper-right corner and follow these steps:

**1.** **Choose Administration⇨Users⇨Roles.**

The Understanding Roles page appears, and you see a sample hierarchy, as shown in Figure 20-4.

TIP

To select a different sample hierarchy, make a selection from the View Other Sample Role Hierarchies drop-down list.

**2.** **Click the Set Up Roles button.**

The Creating the Role Hierarchy page appears.

**3.** **(Optional) To select a different view of the hierarchy, make a selection from the drop-down list on the right side of the page.**

Salesforce provides three standard views for displaying the role hierarchy: tree, list, and sorted list. For this example, we're opting for the default, Tree view.

**4.** **In Tree view, click the Add Role button at the place in the hierarchy where you'd like your new role to appear.**

A Role Edit page appears for the new role.

**5.** **Complete the fields.**

The fields are pretty obvious, but here are some tips:

- *This Role Reports To:* Use this lookup field to define the role's place in the hierarchy. Because the lookup field is based on roles you already created, add roles by starting at the top of your hierarchy and then working your way down, as shown in Figure 20-5.

- *Contact, Opportunity, and Case Access:* Select these options that fit your company's objectives. (You may not see these fields if you have a very public sharing model — more on that in the following section.) You can provide an Account owner with read-write access to related Opportunities or Cases that she doesn't own, has view-only access to, or has no access to. This flexibility comes in handy in heavily regulated industries, in which you might have to prevent an account executive from knowing about certain deals or issues going on with her Account.

**6.** **Click the Save button or the Save & New button.**

- *Save:* The Role: *Role Name* page appears, displaying the detail information you just entered and listing any users in this role. From the users in the *Role Name* Role detail list, you may also assign existing users to this role or create new users with this role. (Check out the section "Creating a new user," earlier in this chapter.)

- *Save & New:* A New Role page appears, and you can continue building the hierarchy. Repeat Steps 2–6 until your hierarchy is done.

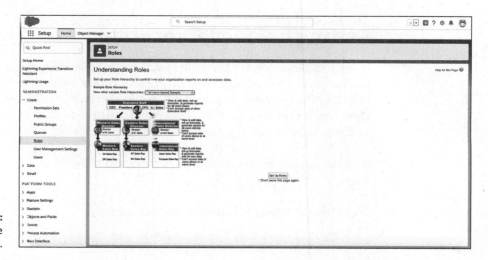

**FIGURE 20-4:**
Seeing a sample role hierarchy.

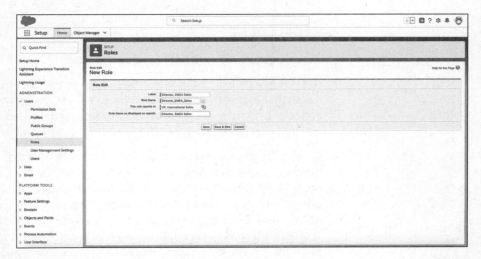

**FIGURE 20-5:**
Creating a new
role in the
hierarchy.

# Using Other Security Controls

Beyond the major configuration settings (such as roles, profiles, and sharing model), as an administrator, you have other settings for managing the use and security of your data in Salesforce. You can find these features by choosing Setup ⇨ Settings ⇨ Security ⇨ Field Accessibility.

In the following sections, we discuss how to manage field-level access and delegate a subset of administration to others.

## Setting field-level security

If you have Enterprise or Unlimited Edition, you have three primary ways to control access to and editing of specific fields: profiles (which we discuss earlier in this chapter), page layouts (Chapter 17 covers these), and field-level settings (stay right here for the details). With field-level security, you can further restrict users' access to fields by setting whether those fields are visible, editable, or read-only.

To view and administer field-level security, click the Setup link and follow these steps:

**1.** **Choose Settings ⇨ Security ⇨ Field Accessibility.**

The Field Accessibility page appears, listing all objects.

**2.** **Click the link for the type of record for which you want to view and manage field-level security.**

A Field Accessibility page for the selected record type appears, as shown in Figure 20-6. For example, click the Account link if you want to review the security settings on Account fields.

**3.** **Under the Choose Your View header, click the View by Fields link.**

The Field Accessibility page appears with a Field drop-down list. If you want to see a different view of this information — in which you get to see one profile and the security levels for all the fields for the selected data type — click the View by Profiles link.

**4.** **Select a field from the Field drop-down list.**

The page reappears with a table displaying your company's profiles and the profiles' accessibility to the selected field.

**5.** **In the Field Accessibility table, click a link in a cell in the Field Access column to edit the profile's field access for a specific record type.**

An Access Settings page for the selected profile and selected field appears, as shown in Figure 20-7. If you want to modify access for all profiles associated with the page layout assigned to this profile, you can also adjust that here.

**6.** **Select the check boxes to modify the field-level settings, and then click Save.**

The Field Accessibility page for the selected record type reappears.

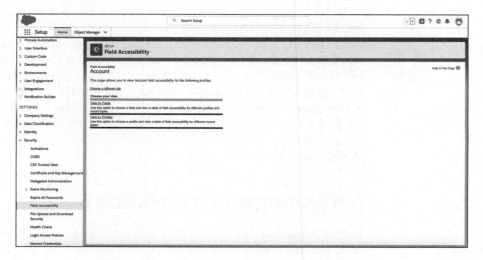

**FIGURE 20-6:**
Preparing to view field accessibility.

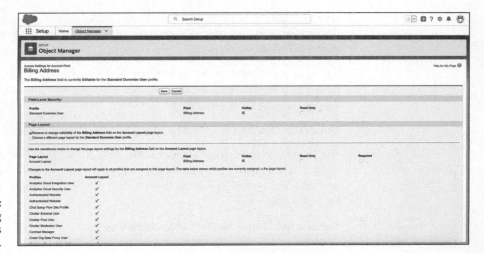

**FIGURE 20-7:**
Modifying
field-level access
on a profile.

**REMEMBER**

If you modify a field-level security setting for a profile by deselecting the Visible check box, this means that the record related to that field is still searchable. The field will never be viewable to a person with that profile, so that person won't be able to create reports or search using it, but he can use reports created by others that leverage that field. So, if an Account — say, ABC Corp. — had its Employees field filled out with the number 1001, but that field was not visible to Watson, who has the Standard User profile, Watson could still run a report created by Holmes, who, with a different profile, was able to customize a report looking for all Accounts where the Employees field was greater than 1000. In that report, ABC Corp. would be listed and Watson would see ABC Corp., but he would not see the Employees field in the output. Watson would also not be able to customize a report using the Employees field because he can't see it to modify the query.

**TIP**

If you need to provide someone with similar access to records as an existing user, with the exception of visibility to a few fields, we recommend that you do this via field-level security on a new custom profile, versus removing the field from the page layout. It may not be visible on a page, but that field is still visible elsewhere in Salesforce — like when creating and running reports and list views. Even if you're not strict about a group of people not seeing a field, field-level security can help reduce end-users seeing an overwhelming number of fields that they have to wade through when creating reports.

## Delegating administration

As an administrator for your growing world of Salesforce users within your company, you hold the key to who accesses your Salesforce instance. You shouldn't try to cut corners by making everyone system administrators just because you're annoyed each time people bug you to add a new user, or because they get impatient about your asking "Why?" in response to their requests.

Salesforce allows you to delegate some administrative duties to nonadministrators. Delegated administrators can help you create and edit users in roles you specify, reset passwords for those users, assign users to certain profiles, and manage certain custom objects. For example, if your marketing department is growing quickly, you may want to allow a manager in the Marketing Manager role to add new marketing users to Salesforce who need the Marketing User profile.

**REMEMBER**

With more users and different groups that need access to the same object, be cautious in granting delegated administration permissions to users for specific custom objects. Usually this will result in changes being made that benefit one group at the expense of another, and you're left to diplomatically mend strained relationships. It's your responsibility as a system administrator to have a holistic understanding of how system changes will affect all your users.

To delegate administration, you must first define the groups of users to whom you want to delegate these new privileges. Then you have to specify what you want those newly delegated administrators to do. To define delegated administrators, follow these steps:

1. **Choose Setup ⇨ Settings ⇨ Security ⇨ Delegated Administration.**

   The Manage Delegated Groups page appears.

2. **Click New.**

   The Edit Delegated Group page for the new delegated group appears.

3. **Enter the Delegated Group Name.**

   In our example, we selected Sales Operations.

4. **Click Save.**

   The Delegated Group page for your new group appears.

5. **Click the Add button in the Delegated Administrators related list to specify which users will belong in this group.**

   The Delegated Administrators page appears.

6. **Use the Lookup icons to find and add users to this group.**

7. **Click Save.**

   The Delegated Group page for your group reappears.

8. **To specify which roles and subordinate roles a delegated administrator can manage, click the Add button in the User Administration related list.**

   The Roles and Subordinates page appears.

9. **Use the Lookup icons to find and add roles that your delegated group may manage.**

**10.** Click Save.

The Delegated Group page for your group reappears.

**11.** Click Add in the Assignable Profiles related list to specify which profiles these delegated administrators may assign to users.

The Assignable Profiles page appears.

**12.** Use the Lookup icons to find and add profiles that your delegated group may assign.

**13.** Click Save.

The Delegated Group page for your group reappears.

**14.** Click Add in the Custom Object Administration related list to specify which custom objects and related tabs a delegated administrator may manage.

The Custom Object Administration page appears.

**15.** Use the Lookup icons to find and add custom objects that your delegated group may assign.

**16.** Click Save.

The Delegated Group page for your group reappears.

IN THIS CHAPTER

» **Understanding your migration options**

» **Executing your migration plan**

» **Organizing your data**

» **Using the right tools to migrate data**

» **Getting help**

Chapter **21**

# Managing Data

I f you're a system administrator, often your greatest headache isn't configuring or customizing the system but getting your data in and maintaining it so that it's useful. Nothing hurts a rollout more than complaints from users that their data isn't in Salesforce, that information is duplicated in several records, or even worse, that the information is wrong. Your end-user adoption suffers if you don't maintain your records after the rollout. The data upkeep sins of preceding generations compound in your Salesforce instance to result in a poor user experience for the current wave of users. Salesforce has been around a long time. Users today who are just starting with Salesforce instances may not know that those instances have been around for many years . . . Then they think Salesforce is a bad product (due to poor data quality, or a clunky user experience), even though their poor impression is caused by humans before them.

End-users love to complain about poor data quality, but they're often not initially motivated to be diligent about putting clean data in there, or they're in too much of a rush to determine sources of truth with other business groups, forgetting that garbage in equals garbage out. If you're not diligent, you can find yourself in the same mess that drove you to Salesforce in the first place.

If data maintenance is giving you nightmares, use the data management tools in Salesforce to easily import new Leads, Accounts, and Contacts, or to update data for existing ones. If you have in-house expertise or engage a Salesforce partner, you can migrate other critical data that may require a little more nuance to get in just the way you want it (such as Opportunities, Cases, and Activities) by using

Salesforce's Data Loader tool, or other third-party options. When your data is stored in Salesforce, you can rely on a variety of tools to help you manage and maintain the accuracy of your database.

In this chapter, we first discuss basic options for data import. Then we show you how to use Salesforce tools to manage your data (including mass-transferring, deleting, and reassigning data). Finally, we touch on options for advanced needs, such as mass-updating interdependent data. Complex data migration and updates of data between your data sources and Salesforce are beyond the scope of this book, but we make sure to point you in the right direction.

# Understanding Your Options for Data Migration

Salesforce has an easy-to-use wizard that steps you through importing your Campaign Member updates, Leads, Accounts, Contacts, and custom objects. If you're a system administrator or you have the right profile permissions, you can perform these tasks for your users. For other objects' legacy data (such as Opportunities, Cases, and Activities) that you want to have in Salesforce, you have to enter information manually or use the Data Loader, which is a data import and export tool that comes with Enterprise and Unlimited editions to automatically migrate data into Salesforce.

## Using the Data Import wizard

The Data Import wizard for importing Leads, Accounts, Contacts, Solutions, and custom objects is conveniently located under the Integrations heading in the Lightning Experience Setup. It has a user-friendly interface, showing in Figure 21-1, that walks you through importing or updating records.

If you're an administrator, you also see an Import button in the upper-right section of tab home pages. For example, if you want to import your company's Leads, click the Leads tab, and then click the Import button, which is to the right of the page's displayed list view title. Steps and tips for using the import wizard for different objects' records are detailed in relevant chapters of this book, as follows:

>> **Import Leads:** Only a user with the Import Leads permission can perform this operation. See Chapter 7.

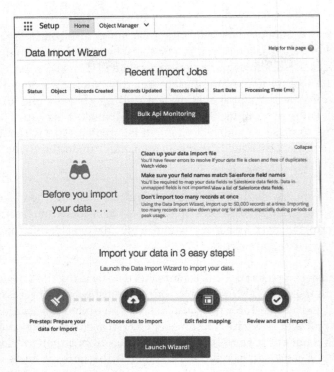

**FIGURE 21-1:**
Launching the
Data Import
wizard.

>> **Import Contacts and Accounts:** Salesforce uses the same wizard that can take you through importing Contacts and/or Accounts. Individual users also have the ability to import their personal Contacts and Accounts. See Chapters 8 and 9.

>> **Import new campaign members or update them when linked to a campaign:** Salesforce uses the same Data Import wizard, but this time exposes just the Campaign Member object to update marketing statuses for Leads and Contacts. See Chapter 15.

## Investigating the Data Loader

Data migration is a tricky matter. The Data Loader is a small client application that helps bulk-import or bulk-export data in comma-separated value (.csv) format. You access this tool by choosing Integrations ⇨ Data Loader. With this tool, you can move data into and out of any type of record in Salesforce, including Opportunities and custom objects. The Data Loader supports inserting, updating, deleting, and exporting Salesforce records.

**WARNING**

As someone famous once said, with great power also comes great responsibility. Only use Data Loader if you're comfortable with understanding how objects, records, and workflows and/or triggers relate to each other. Data Loader is a very powerful tool for nontechnical users. You can export data, import data, accidentally overwrite and delete a lot of data, and set off a domino effect of workflow rules if you're not careful. Always make sure to make a backup of the data if you're planning to make an update. You might be problem-free without a backup until that one time a mistake is made and you can't undo the 1000s of fields you've overwritten.

Several vendors also provide proven extract, transform, load tools (ETLs) that enable you to migrate records to (or from) Salesforce, automatically scrub and transform the data based on custom logic that you define, and append those records where appropriate.

**TECHNICAL STUFF**

Without getting too technical, experts link data by using the Salesforce application program interface (API) to enable your technical people to access data programmatically. The Salesforce platform (http://developer.salesforce.com) is used to customize or integrate Salesforce to do even snazzier things than what you can do with it out of the box. And before you suffer from jargon overload, a *platform* is basically a collection of rules and commands that programmers can use to tell a program — Salesforce, in this case — to do certain things. To access the Salesforce API, though, you must have Enterprise or Unlimited Edition.

# Migrating Your Legacy Data

During the preparation phase of your implementation, you need a well-thought-out and well-documented plan for your data migration strategy. That plan needs to include details on objectives, resources, contingencies, and timelines based on the different steps in your plan. In the following sections, we discuss some of the steps that you should consider.

## Determining your data sources

The companies we've worked with typically have some type of existing contact management tool, a variety of spreadsheets with other customer data, and often, contact information living in users' email inboxes and productivity applications (not to mention Word documents and sticky notes).

**TIP**

As you go through your preparation, assess what and how much information needs to be in Salesforce. Here are some tips for this step:

- **Garbage in, garbage out.** When you move to a new home, you usually look through your old home's closets and decide what to haul with you and what to throw away. Moving data requires the same type of evaluation.

- **Make a list.** Catalog the different data sources, including what types of records, what range, and how many.

- **Design a storage plan.** Work with your customer relationship management (CRM) project team to determine where different information should go — and why.

- **Think about the timing and the sequence of the import.** For example, many companies create user records first, then import Accounts and Contacts, and finally, migrate and append Opportunities.

- **Keep it simple, if possible.** The more complicated you make the migration, the greater the impact on your timeline. Assess the level of effort versus the potential value of the effort.

## Preparing your data

Clean it now, or clean it later. Some project teams like to "scrub" data before importing it into Salesforce. Identifying and merging duplicates makes finding the right record easier. Fixing inconsistencies in your data, such as ensuring that all State/Province fields hold two-character abbreviations, makes reports more accurate.

If your legacy system doesn't make cleanup easy, you might prefer to bring all the records into Salesforce first and then use the Salesforce data management tools to clean data later. The risk is that people with the best intentions may still succumb to human nature and not want to focus on the cleanup effort once the data is already in the new system.

**TIP**

Regardless of when you do it, cleaning data is not glamorous work, but it's gotta be done, and should be done on a regular basis. Here are a few tips as you prepare your data:

- **Export to a simple format.** Oftentimes, it's easiest to export data to applications like Microsoft Access or Excel, with which you can delete columns, sort rows, and make global changes.

- **Strive to use standard naming conventions.** If different data sources refer to Accounts by different names (for example, IBM versus International Business Machines), now is a good time to standardize naming. This can help avoid duplicate record creation.

>> **Edit or add fields in Salesforce to support the migration.** For example, if your pipeline reports track margin per Opportunity, you need to build a custom Opportunity field to support margin data. Read more about creating custom fields in Chapter 17.

>> **If your existing data source has unique record IDs, migrate those IDs to a custom read-only field.** You can always delete or hide the field at a later stage. Not only can this help you verify the accuracy of your migration, but those IDs might also come in handy for integration (especially if you don't plan to shut down the other data source).

>> **Map your data columns to field names in Salesforce.** For example, the Company field in Microsoft Outlook typically maps to the Account field in Salesforce. Some system administrators even rename the column headers in migration files so that they exactly match field names in Salesforce. Doing this minimizes the migration madness.

>> **Conform your data to fit Salesforce standards** (or the other way around). Each field in Salesforce has certain properties that may include size limitations, decimal points, date formats, and so on.

>> **Add a Data Source column to your import file and map it to a custom field in Salesforce.** By doing this, you can defend where data came from.

>> **Assign the correct owners to records wherever possible.** If you don't have all records assigned, the owner defaults to whichever administrator is executing the migration.

>> **Gain acceptance from stakeholders of the files you've prepared.** At least if you offer them the chance to review, you avoid surprises.

## Testing the import

TIP

Test before you execute the final migration. Often, you discover things that you missed or could improve. For example, fields can be mapped incorrectly, or you may just need to create some extra ones. Here are a couple of tips:

>> **Select a small sample of significant records.** The higher profile the records, the better — especially when reviewed by a stakeholder.

>> **Remember to turn off workflows.** You don't want to annoy other users by unnecessarily alerting them when test data flows through the workflow rules. Some of you may think that it's helpful to keep certain workflow rules on especially if they were built to prevent bad data from coming in. This is not true. Do the work ahead of time and prepare the data well, before importing.

>> **Review page layout.** Consider adjusting the page layouts to make validating the data import easier. Put fields in Salesforce in similar screen locations to those of your legacy systems.

## Analyzing the test data results

TIP

When your test data is in Salesforce, compare it carefully with your test file to ensure accuracy and completeness. Here are a few tips on how to productively analyze the test data results:

>> Build a custom report that allows you to look at the record data collectively.

>> Open a record, if necessary, and compare it against the import file. Confirm that the record's fields show what you think they should show.

>> Build a custom view from a relevant tab's home page to see your imported data laid out in columns on a list page. Users could go to a report, but a view keeps them focused.

>> Validate the data with selected stakeholders to get their feedback and support that the test data results look correct. It's not enough that you think the test import was accurate. Your end-users are the ultimate test.

>> Adjust your process or make changes to the import file or Salesforce based on the results of the test import. For example, maybe you forgot to map a field or the data didn't import correctly because of a field's properties.

## Migrating your final data

After you successfully analyze the test data results, you're ready to import your file(s). Yes, that's a simplification of what could be a complicated set of tasks, but the overall process is tried and true.

TIP

Here are a few suggestions for this step:

>> **Communicate expectations with your users.** If you're moving from one system to another, you might have a lapse in which data must be updated prior to going live.

>> **Do it during down time.** If you have significant data, consider running the migration during nonworking hours. Especially if the system is live for some groups of users already, this may avoid confusion.

>> **Save the log files of records that didn't successfully import.** The error messages are fairly intuitive, and you can usually see common rejection reasons for why certain records didn't get imported. Make sure to spend time determining whether the rejection is caused by a data-formatting or quality issue as opposed to a pesky workflow rule that you didn't intend to fire.

>> **Build yourself some cushion for error.** Don't try to execute the migration the day before sales training. Something unanticipated could happen that prevents successful completion.

## Validating and augmenting your data

Similar to analyzing results of the test data (see the section "Analyzing the test data results," earlier in this chapter), when the data has been loaded, run reports to validate a cross-sampling of records to ensure accuracy and completeness. If you can, compare screens in Salesforce with those of your legacy system. Make sure that data is stored in the correct fields and that values make sense. If you see an address in a phone field, you need to clean your data or fix your field mapping. Strive for perfectly imported data — but expect less than that, too.

Prior to rolling out Salesforce, take the extra step of manually or automatically updating some records to wow users and drive more success. When giving a demonstration or training, show users these fully entered examples and let them know the potential for Salesforce.

# Managing Your Salesforce Database

After you implement Salesforce, you need to make sure that you create processes for periodically updating and backing up your data. If you don't, human error can lead to frustration and heartache. Duplicate records, dead Leads, records that need to be transferred when a user leaves the company — these are just a few examples of data that needs to be updated. Work with the relevant operations or IT team that is in charge of maintaining the overall health of your Salesforce instance. If folks feel there isn't time or resources to figure out ongoing data quality responsibilities, rest assured that the value that end users get out of Salesforce will diminish.

Most of the data maintenance tools are accessible from the Data heading within the Lightning Experience Setup. (See Chapter 7 for details on deduplication options.)

# Backing up your data

If you have Unlimited, Enterprise, or Professional Edition, Salesforce offers a weekly export service of all your data that you can use to create a backup. Other editions have access to a monthly export, with similar behavior.

To export and back up your data, follow these steps:

1. **From the Lightning Experience Setup home page, type in "Data Export" into the Quick Search toolbar and click the Data Export link.**

   The Data Export Setup page appears.

2. **Click the Export Now button.**

3. **Select the appropriate export file encoding from the Export File Encoding drop-down list and select the appropriate check boxes for how you want to handle exporting of various images, attachments, documents, Salesforce Files and Content versions, and if you want to replace carriage (hard) returns with spaces.**

   If you live in the United States or Western Europe, you don't have to change the Export File Encoding selection.

4. **Specify which Salesforce objects you want to export, or just leave the default Include All Data check box selected.**

5. **When you're done, click the Start Export button.**

   The Export Service: Export Requested page appears. You'll receive an email from Salesforce with a link to a page where you can retrieve zipped .csv files of all your data. You have 48 hours to download your data, after which time the data files are deleted.

6. **Click the link in the email and log in to Salesforce, if required.**

   The Export Service page appears.

   You can also access the Export Service page by going to the Lightning Experience Setup ➪ Data ➪ Data Export.

7. **Click the Download link.**

   A dialog box appears, allowing you to open or save your zip file to a location accessible from your computer.

Although not required, we recommend that you schedule a routine data export of your data by clicking the Schedule Export button on the Export Service page. This option follows the same steps as an immediate backup, but it also allows you to select when you want your backup to automatically occur.

# Mass-transferring records

A sales rep leaves. Sales territories get readjusted. You imported a file but forgot to assign records to the right owners in advance. These are just a few examples of when you might have to transfer records. Salesforce allows you to mass-transfer Lead, Account, and custom object records — and the processes for all three types are very similar.

When transferring Leads or Accounts, Salesforce automatically transfers certain linked records on the detail page.

>> **For both Leads and Accounts:** All open activities owned by the current owner transfer to the new owner.

>> **For Accounts:** All notes, Contacts, and open Opportunities owned by the existing owner transfer to the new owner.

>> **For custom object records:** No linked records are transferred.

To mass-transfer records, follow these steps:

1. **Go to the Lightning Experience Setup ⇨ Data ⇨ Mass Transfer Records.**

   A Mass Transfer Records page appears.

2. **Click the Transfer link for the appropriate type of record, depending on your needs.**

   A Mass Transfer page appears with a set of filtering options to help you search for records. You can use the filters to specify the set of data that you want to transfer — for example, all Accounts with San Francisco in the Billing City field.

3. **In the Transfer From and Transfer To fields, use the Lookup icons to find the appropriate users.**

   With Leads, you can also transfer to or from queues. See Chapter 7 for details on Lead queues.

4. **If you're mass-transferring Accounts, select the check boxes to specify whether you want to transfer certain types of Opportunities, Cases, and teams.**

5. **Define additional criteria to filter your search by using the drop-down lists and fields provided.**

   You do this by selecting a field from the first drop-down list, selecting an operator from the second drop-down list, and then typing a value in the field.

For example, if you want to transfer all of one sales rep's New York City Accounts to a new rep, your criteria would be

- *Field:* City

- *Operator:* Equals

- *Value:* New York

6. **When you're satisfied with your settings and filters, click the Find button.**

   The Mass Transfer page reappears with a list of results.

7. **Use the check boxes to select the records that you want to transfer.**

8. **When you're done, click the Transfer button.**

   The Mass Transfer page reappears when the transfer is complete.

## Mass-deleting records

If you're the administrator, you may want or need to mass-delete records. A couple of typical examples include deleting dead Leads and eliminating Accounts that haven't had any activity. Salesforce allows you to mass-delete Leads, Accounts, Contacts, Activities, Cases, Solutions, and Products — and the processes are very similar.

To mass-delete records, follow these steps:

1. **From the Lightning Experience Setup, go to Data ⇨ Mass Delete Records.**

   The Mass Delete Records page appears.

2. **Click one of the Mass Delete links, depending on the type of standard record that you want to mass-delete.**

   The Mass Delete Records page appears with a three- to five-step wizard for mass-deleting. The five-step wizard for Accounts is shown in Figure 21-2. The Mass Delete Accounts page has two extra steps based on Opportunities that are closed/won or that aren't owned by you. The Mass Delete Products page has one extra step to archive products with line items on Opportunities.

3. **Review the impacts of mass deleting records in Step 1 of the wizard.**

   Consider what other related records would be deleted and the consequences of that action. For example, deleting an Account impacts the associated Contacts, and provides an option to delete its related Opportunities. If this includes closed-won deals, this will impact any historical trend reporting covering that time frame.

4. **Back up relevant data by generating a report and exporting it to Excel as part of Step 2 of the wizard.**

   See Chapter 22 for details on building and exporting reports.

5. **Use the filters in Step 3 of the wizard to define criteria for the search.**

   You do this by selecting a field from the first drop-down list, selecting an operator from the second drop-down list, and typing a value in the field.

   You can see an example of this in the preceding section.

6. **Click the Search button.**

   The Mass Delete page reappears with a list of possible records at the bottom of the page. Do the following:

   - *If you're mass-deleting Accounts,* you can select the check box in Step 4 of the wizard if you want to delete Accounts that have Closed/Won Opportunities and/or select the check box to delete Accounts with another owner's Opportunities.

   - *If you're mass-deleting Products,* select the check box if you want to archive products with line items on Opportunities.

   - *If you're mass-deleting another object,* proceed to Step 7.

7. **Use the Action column to select records to be deleted (that's the column whose column header is represented by a check box).**

8. **When you're satisfied, click the Delete button.**

   The Mass Delete page reappears, minus the records that you deleted.

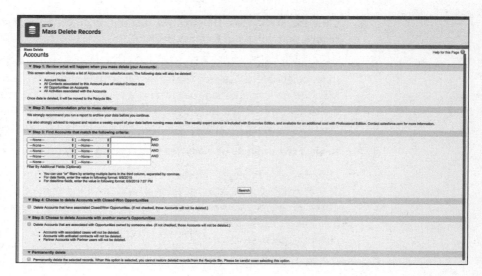

**FIGURE 21-2:**
Selecting records
for mass deletion.

# Finding and merging duplicates

Salesforce can merge existing duplicate records. The hard part is less about the technology and more about your coming up with some foundational and consistent business guidelines to determine whether data in a field is accurate. Some companies rely on data that is synced with a specific third-party service, like Dun & Bradstreet or LinkedIn. Whatever you choose, you need to establish a tie-breaking source of truth, because salespeople often find differing data from other sources that they may reference to justify moving that account into their territories. When you've established the guidelines, you can use Salesforce's standard Duplicate Management feature (see Chapter 7) to identify potential duplicates as part of a regular sales process.

For example, an inbound sales development rep may have to wade through dozens of inbound Lead records a day from users who sign up for product trials. One of the data quality steps that should be ingrained in a rep's day is reviewing the Potential Duplicates section on a Lead record to see if the person already exists. (If you don't see this section on your Lead record, you may need to add that Lightning Component to your Lead layout. See Chapter 18 for more details.)

The Potential Duplicates section displays the result of the Duplicate Management feature. On a Lead record, for example, the section identifies the number of potential duplicates found and the user can click a link to see more details about the potential duplicates. From the detailed view of potential duplicates, users can select and merge duplicate records that they own. You can select which data from a given record should survive in the merger; this is where pre-established business rules from your operations team can expedite any decision making.

**WARNING**

Even if a user can see a number of potential duplicates from the existing record, it may be too late (how many sales people do you know who are diligent with Lead and Contact housekeeping?!). With Duplicate Management, Salesforce is intelligent enough to warn someone about a potential duplicate, while in the middle of creating a new Lead, as shown in Figure 21-3. You get to decide which common fields must be reviewed to determine a match, and this is based on the general quality of the data that comes into your Salesforce instance, and your business rules.

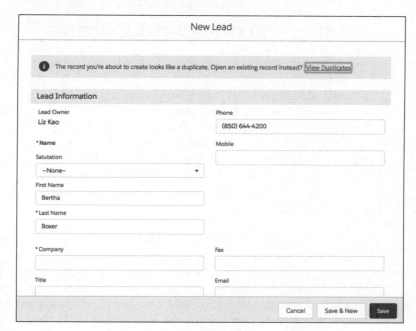

New Lead

> The record you're about to create looks like a duplicate. Open an existing record instead? [View Duplicates]

**Lead Information**

Lead Owner
Liz Kao

Phone
(850) 644-4200

* Name

Mobile

Salutation
--None--

First Name
Bertha

* Last Name
Boxer

* Company

Fax

Title

Email

Cancel    Save & New    Save

**FIGURE 21-3:**
Identifying
potential
duplicates during
Lead creation.

# Getting Help with Complex Data Tasks

TIP

This chapter shows you some of the basic operations that you can perform to import and manage your data in Salesforce. For many companies that have more complex data needs (either in terms of volume or historical interaction between records and objects), this may be an oversimplification. If you need help with your data, here are some resources you can turn to:

>> **Talk with your customer success manager or account executive.** These folks can help define your needs and point you to the appropriate solution or resource.

>> **Go outside.** If you're open to looking for outside help, contact a Salesforce systems implementation consulting partner. Your customer success manager or account executive can put you in touch.

>> **Check out offerings by ISV partners on the AppExchange.** Go to www.appexchange.com and search using the phrase *data cleansing* in the search bar.

>> **Talk to developers.** On the Salesforce Developers site (http://developer.salesforce.com), click the Community tab to talk to a forum of developers who have wrestled or are familiar with your data challenges. These forums are of a technical nature, but if this is what you're looking for, you might find it here.

# 7

# Measuring Overall Business Performance

# Chapter **22**

# Analyzing Data with Reports

How much time do you waste every week trying to prepare reports for your manager, your team, or yourself? You have to chase down the information, get it into a useful format, and then make sense of the data. By the time you do all of that, the information is probably already out of date, despite your best efforts. Have you ever felt less than confident of the details or the totals?

If this sounds like a familiar problem, you can use reports in Salesforce to generate up-to-the-moment data analysis to help you measure your business. As long as you and your teams regularly use Salesforce to manage your Accounts, Opportunities, and other customer-related information, you don't have to waste time wondering where to find the data and how to consolidate it. Instead, let Salesforce do that work for you.

And unlike other applications in which the business users often have to spend precious time relying on more-technical people to build their custom reports, you can do this all by yourself in minutes, with no geeky programming. With an easy-to-use reporting wizard, you can customize existing reports or build them from scratch.

This chapter includes an overview of the standard reports provided by Salesforce, building reports from scratch, and modifying existing reports to make them your own. Within a report, we take you through the different ways you can filter the report to get just the information that's necessary for creating a clearer picture of your business. Finally, be sure to check out our suggestions on how to keep your reports organized in easy-to-find folders as your universe of reports expands.

# Discovering Reports

With reports, you can present your data in different formats, select a seemingly infinite number of columns, filter your data, subtotal information, use color to highlight when certain conditions are met, and embed formulas, just to name a few features. And like other pages in Salesforce, you can quickly find the details. So, for example, you can go from the Reports home page to a lead report to a Lead record simply by clicking links.

## Navigating the Reports home page

When you click the Reports tab, as shown in Figure 22-1, you'll see a search bar, a set of links in the left panel of your browser, and a list of recently run reports. Salesforce has functionality on the Reports home page to help you more easily navigate through a large set of reports and dashboards. Salesforce comes standard with a set of predefined reports and folders that are commonly used for measuring sales, marketing, support, and other functions. If you've never used Salesforce reports, you can use these sample reports for inspiration, or further customization as you learn. For example, the Opportunity 4-Week Pipeline Trend report that shows how Opportunity Amounts for particular deals changed over time.

**FIGURE 22-1:**
The Reports
home page.

TIP

If you're an administrator, consider creating custom folders by clicking the New Folder button on the upper-right of the Reports main page, as shown in Figure 22-2. Organize this according to your important functional areas. Folders can also be nested as subfolders, so you extra-organized folks can minimize a potentially overwhelming number of reports for better findability.

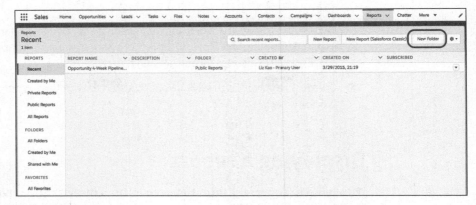

**FIGURE 22-2:**
Creating a new report folder.

From the Reports home page, you can do the following:

» **Find reports.** Type keywords into the Search All [Filter Category] search bar, and while you're typing, Salesforce will return matching reports. What the search bar searches for depends on which type of reports you're filtering on in the left sidebar. For example, if you've clicked the "Created by Me" link, the search bar will change to reflect "Search reports created by me . . ."

» **Search a folder.** Similarly, if the left sidebar is searching for a set of report folders, the search bar will also conditionally change to match searching for whatever is selected on the left sidebar. For example, if you click the All Folders view, the search bar updates to show Search All Folders.

» **Create a folder.** If you're an administrator, click the New Folder button as mentioned in the previous tip to create new report folders to house custom reports. Depending on where you click this button, your folder could be nested below another folder.

» **Select a folder.** When you click a folder in a Folder view, the contents of that report folder will appear in the main panel. To backtrack, click the All Reports option at the top of the Folders navigation tree in the Folders pane.

» **View recent reports.** The default Reports view is the Recent option from the left sidebar. You can also click and drag column headings to rearrange them or remove them.

» **Edit the list view on the Reports home page.** Maybe there's a specific custom field you'd prefer users to see, to help make their searching more efficient. If you want to see other columns than what's shown by default, rearrange column headings, or re-adjust the columns' width, click the gear icon in the upper-right to see your options.

» **Display the report.** Click a report title.

» **Edit, delete, or export data to Excel.** From any list view of reports, click the downward-pointing triangle button to the right of whatever report row you're interested in. Several options appear including Edit, Delete, Add to Dashboard, Export, Subscribe, and Move. We talk more about exporting your reports in the "Exporting Reports" section, later in this chapter.

>> **Create a report.** Click the New Report button to start the Lightning Report Builder wizard.

## Displaying a report

When you click a report title or run a report from the wizard, a report page appears based on the criteria that was set. For example, under the Public Reports folder, click the Opportunity 4-Week Pipeline Trend link. The report appears, as shown in Figure 22-3.

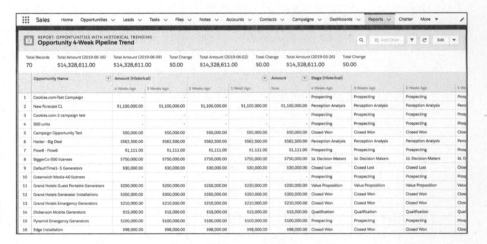

**FIGURE 22-3:**
Displaying
a report.

A basic report page in Salesforce has a few common elements across the upper-right of the results page:

>> **Search:** Click the magnifying glass icon to have a search bar show up, from where you can type in any particular words or numbers. As you type in this information, Salesforce will highlight matching cells in your report. This helps your eyes quickly find some pertinent information, especially when your report may contain hundreds of rows.

>> **Filters:** Clicking the filter icon from the report expands a right sidebar area that shows what existing report filters are in place that resulted in the rows that comprise the report. If you click on any of the filter criteria from this sidebar, you'll have the opportunity to adjust the filter criteria for that particular field, so you can get possibly different results in your report. You

can do all that without having to save the underlying report. Seeing the filter criteria for a report here saves you time from having to spend extra clicks getting to the Edit view of the report. Especially when a report title might sound very similar to other reports, the details of the filter criteria can help you quickly assess why, for example, two Opportunity Pipeline reports show different total Opportunity Amounts — perhaps one is filtered by an Opportunity Close Date of this year, whereas the other is based on an Opportunity Close Date for this quarter.

>> **Show / hide chart:** When building your report, if you've created a chart to go with it, viewers can choose to view your report with or without that chart by clicking the chart icon (which looks like a little pie chart). Sometimes people just want to get to a specific row and want to bypass the visualization. If the report wasn't built with a chart, instead of the chart icon you'll instead see a grayed-out *Add Chart*.

>> **Report Options:** This is where you click Edit to customize the underlying report, or you can click the downward-pointing triangle to reveal additional picklist options that let you Save or Save As the report (which creates a copy that you can further edit if you know you shouldn't be changing this one).

TIP

In the generated report section, which may sometimes be called the "run report" area, you can click the downward-pointing triangle to the right of each column heading to quickly re-sort or group your report by the selected column, or remove a particular column altogether. More information on specific options in the "Sorting and summarizing report results" section later in this chapter.

# Creating Your Own Reports

Salesforce comes with a huge menu of useful reports, and yet they may not be exactly what you're looking for. For example, if your company has added custom fields on the Account record that are unique to your customer, a standard New Accounts report doesn't show you all the information you want to see on recent Accounts.

The next time you need a custom report, don't pester the IT geeks. Instead, use the Lightning Report Builder to build a new report or customize an existing one.

## Building a report from scratch

You don't have to be a technical guru to create a report in Salesforce. Just make sure that you can articulate a question that you're trying to answer. If you haven't been able to find an existing report that you can copy (using the Save As functionality mentioned in the previous section), then Lightning Report Builder will guide you through the steps for creating a custom report that will help you answer the question.

To create a report from scratch, click the Reports tab and follow these steps:

1. **Click the New Report button.**

   The Choose Report Type page appears, as shown in Figure 22-4.

2. **Select the report type that you want to report on, and then click Create.**

   You do this by first selecting the basic category of object from the Choose Report Type panel, which displays a list of individual objects or object pairs based on how these objects have been set up to relate to each other. You can also type in the name of the object in the Search Report Types search bar. After you've selected a report type, click the Continue button.

   The Lightning Report Builder interface appears.

3. **Customize your report using the following Lightning Report Builder features in the left sidebar:**

   - *Adjust your filters to determine your view and time frame.* Do you want the report to show just records that you own, ones that you and your underlings own, or all records that your role is able to see? What time range do you want the report to cover? Click the Filter icon in the left sidebar to see the various pre-set filters that determine what subset of records you're seeing. Click the filter options "Show Me" to determine if you see just your owned records or more. Other filter options should exist to narrow your results by timeframe.

   - *Adjust additional filters.* To help further narrow your result set, and depending on what report type you chose, you may have other options you can adjust. Just click on the filter and a related filter box will pop up. To add a filter that isn't already listed, use the handy Add Filter search box at the top of the set of filters to type in the field name that you want to filter with. For example, you can create a custom filter to show only results where the Opportunity amount is greater than $10,000.

   - *Add and remove fields.* Click the Outline subtab of the left sidebar to find fields that may be additional columns that you want to have in your report. In the Columns section of the left sidebar (under the Outline subtab) use the "Add column . . ." search bar to find the field you want to add. The Lightning Report Builder will automatically add that column to the last spot of your report. You can then click and drag that field name to rest between other column names. You can also click the "x" next to any column name to remove it. The Preview section of the Lightning Report Builder dynamically updates as you place that new column among your other headers.

- *Group rows.* Formerly known as a "Summary Report" in Salesforce Classic, you can now use the Groups section of the Outline sidebar to create groupings up to three groups deep. Just type in the name of the field you want to group by, into the Add Group field, and Lightning Report Builder takes care of the rest. You can also drag a column from the Columns section and move it to the Groups section.

- *Add a chart.* Click the Add Chart button in the upper-right area of the Lightning Report Builder to add a graphical summary of your results. Click the gear icon from within the Lightning Chart Editor to choose how you want the report to be visually displayed, determine what data to represent, and what title or axis descriptions you want to provide. The functionality of the chart properties should look very similar to those used when creating a dashboard component (which we discuss in Chapter 23).

4. **When you're done creating your report, click the Save button.**

   Confirm the report name, and the folder in which you want it saved. The report saves, and some sample report output appears in the Lightning Report Builder Preview pane.

**REMEMBER**

Sometimes the preview pane outputs accurate-looking sample data, other times not, and other times some cells may look accurate while others are not. Always remember to run the report to get true results. The preview pane is just for determining formatting and how the types of fields you're choosing will be displayed.

**TIP**

You can get pretty advanced with filtering options. As long as you can explain to yourself in plain English what criteria you're looking for, you should be able to build a report for it using options under the Filters subtab in the left sidebar, as shown in Figure 22-5. For example, if you define strategic Accounts as companies that *either* did more than $1 billion in annual revenue *or* had more than 500 employees plus $500 million in annual revenue, you can generate this report. To do this, add your field filters from the Filters subtab and then click the downward-pointing triangle picker to the right of the Filters column name. Depending on the filters in place, you can choose the Filter Logic option where you can order each filter you have and associate it using AND or OR logic. You can also add a cross filter, which helps you include or exclude results based related objects and their fields.

## Customizing existing reports

A fast and easy way to generate reports is to customize an existing report and save it as a new one. For example, if you like the standard Opportunity 4-Week Pipeline Report but you want to modify the columns, you can simply work from the existing report.

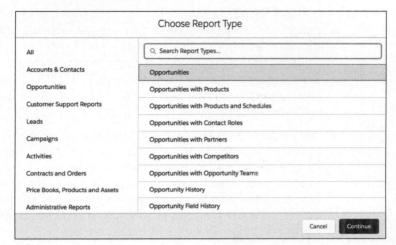

**FIGURE 22-4:**
Defining the objects for the report.

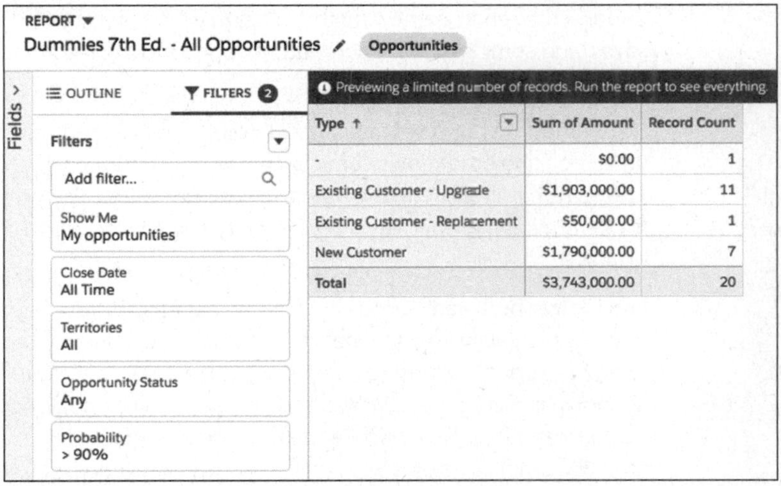

**FIGURE 22-5:**
Adding filter logic to the report.

To customize an existing report, find and select the report you want to modify and follow these steps:

1. **Click the Edit button.**

   Using the Edit button, the Lightning Report Builder page appears. You can then drag and drop interface fields into columns for that report (as discussed in the previous section). A preview of the report appears while you're customizing it.

2. **Continue customizing your report until you're satisfied, and then click the Run Report button.**

   The report appears modified based on your settings from the wizard.

## CREATING CUSTOM REPORT TYPES

The Lightning Report Builder is pretty darn thorough. At the same time, your company's quant jocks may want to perform even more advanced reporting than what's offered in the standard interface. Or you may want to simplify the number of fields that your report users see when they go through the wizard. Professional Edition, Enterprise Edition, and Unlimited Edition administrators can create custom report types (CRTs) to address both of these needs.

For more advanced reporting capabilities, in techno-speak, CRTs let you determine or change the joins on the table. So, if you have a Projects object and want to report on all Accounts with projects and project team members, you can create a CRT and determine which fields show up in your left sidebar, to drag into your preview pane. For more information on setting up CRTs, go to Salesforce Help and search for *create a custom report type*.

**3.** **When you're done, click the downward-pointing triangle to the right of the Edit button and choose Save or Save As.**

The Save button replaces the prior custom report. The Save As button saves the new report as a new one. In either case, a page appears to save the report. Make sure you know you have permission to save a customization over the existing report, as there isn't a way to automatically undo your changes!

# Filtering Reports Efficiently

Over time, you'll develop core reports that have the columns that you want in a format that makes sense to you. One of the huge benefits of reporting in Salesforce is that you can use existing reports on the fly and apply report options to filter or reorder the report results.

All those options and more are possible in seconds without having to use the Edit button. In the following sections, we show you how to filter your reports with tools and enhanced drill-down and breakout options.

## Hiding and showing report results

You can further customize how your report details are displayed by using the following Lightning Report Builder features in the lower section of the preview pane. These are all toggles to show or hide common report results.

## Detail rows

To see a collapsed or expanded view of your report data, click the Hide/Show Details toggle in the bottom of the preview pane. Hiding the details of low-level rows can make the report more readable, especially for grouped and matrix reports. This can help get to the point of whatever insights you're trying to share with this report. Sometimes you may want all the details revealed, other times, not.

## Row counts

When looking at a grouped report, sometimes you want to know the record count that comprises certain groups. Other times, displaying this may just lead to more confusion for viewers because it involves an extra cell with data to comprehend. If you toggle the Row Counts slider at the bottom of the preview pane, the Record Count column can disappear.

## Subtotals and the grand total

Salesforce will, by default, summarize information for you for each grouping, as well as provide a grand total calculation. You can optionally hide these if you think it will make your report more readable.

# Sorting and summarizing report results

You also can choose how you want your report to be ordered, along with other information that can be summarized per numerical column. The following Lightning Report Builder features are accessed from each column name within the preview pane — just look for the downward-facing triangle to the right of each column header. Clicking that shows you several additional options depending on the type of report you've created. We summarize key ones here:

These options can be selected from a view of the report, without even having to edit the report. This gives users some real-time slicing and dicing capabilities without having to rely on IT. And if it's just a temporary view of the information, there's no need to save the report; the underlying formatting is remembered for the next time you run the report.

>> **Sort in ascending or descending order:** You can choose the sort orders for each column. If there is no grouping of the rows, then you can only sort the order by one column. If there are grouped rows, the group can be sorted, and then one detail column can, too.

>> **Group columns or rows by a certain field, and removing a grouping:** If you have a lot of rows in your report's results, grouping them makes for better

readability. You can select a field for grouping by rows — this creates the old "Summary" report format in Salesforce Classic. Then you can choose another field to group by columns, which creates the Salesforce Classic "Matrix" report equivalent. If you change your mind on the grouping, you can also select an option to remove the group.

These options must be performed after clicking the Edit button for the report:

» **Summarize a numerical column:** Salesforce can find the sum, average, minimum value, and maximum value for a column. This saves you time from having to create a custom Excel-like formula for every single situation where this is needed. And if you have rows grouped, these summaries will also show per grouping as well as for the entire column. As mentioned in an earlier section, you can toggle the information to not appear at the subtotal or grand total area.

» **Bucketing fields:** This option lets you select a column in a report, define ranges for data in that field, and group them into "buckets" under a new column, with grouping names that you get to define. For example, the value captured in an Amount field could be updated into three categories: Small, Medium, and Large. You can define what amount ranges fall under the Small bucket, what range falls under the Medium bucket, and so on. You can identify columns in reports that are bucket fields by the little bucket icon to the left of the column name. To see an example of how a bucket field is created, refer to Figure 22-6.

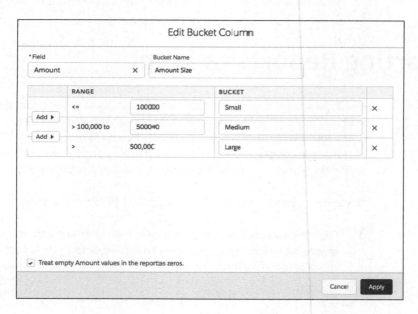

FIGURE 22-6:
Building bucket
field ranges.

## Changing or clearing filters

If you have reports using filters, you can easily view and clear or modify the filters to expand the results. For example, if you created and saved the test report in the preceding section, you may want to clear the filter on the selected rep(s) to see all closed opportunities by close month for all reps. The filters, if any, are shown when you click the filter icon, and expand the filter sidebar from the right side of the browser's window.

To clear a filter, follow these steps:

**1.** **Click the link for a report to which you applied filters. Click the filter icon to display the filters.**

**2.** **Under the Filters section, click any of the filter categories, like the "Show Me" option which determines which records you see based on the record's owner.**

The Show Me filter options page appears. If you have selected options from the Filter by Role section, clicking the Clear Selection button will remove those options. Doing that won't reset any other options. Make sure to click Done when you've finished filtering that particular filter.

Clicking any other filter options will also reveal additional filtering details. Make changes as applicable and click Apply when done to see changes appear real-time in your report.

**3.** **Be sure to click the downward-facing triangle and choose the Save or Save As option from the drop-down menu if you want to save this report.**

# Exporting Reports to Excel

Ideally, you want to run your reports right out of the application, getting rid of that mad scramble of collecting data before your next big meeting. However, sometimes you'll want to generate a report and then export it to Excel. Maybe you need to run some complex spreadsheet calculations, or you need to plug numbers into an existing macro template. No problem. You can do that with the click of a button.

To export a report, click the Reports tab and follow these steps:

**1.** **Click the downward-facing triangle in the rightmost column of the row belonging to the report you want to export. Select the Export option from the drop-down menu.**

The Export window appears.

2. **Select the export view you want, and then click Export.**

The Formatted Report option preserves the format that you see on-screen, which can be suitable if that file will be augmented but viewed by business users. The Details Only option provides the raw data in Excel or .CSV format, and is often used for feeding into other systems, or if data updates need to be made.

**TIP**

Some companies get nervous about certain users having the ability to export company data. If this is a concern, and you have the Enterprise or Unlimited Edition, you can take one precaution by using custom profiles to eliminate the ability of some users to export to Excel. See Chapter 20 for more details on creating custom profiles.

# Organizing Reports

**TIP**

A word to the wise: Reports start multiplying like rabbits as you become addicted to reporting in Salesforce. Do yourself a favor: Organize them from day one and lay out a process for maintaining and deleting reports.

## Creating new folders

Nothing is worse than seeing a gazillion reports under the very non-descript Public Reports folder. You start wasting a ridiculous amount of time just identifying which report is the one you want. If you have permission to manage public folders, avoid the headache by creating new report folders. In the Lightning Experience, you can even nest sub-folders below other folders, to your organizational heart's content.

To create a new report folder, click the Reports tab and follow these steps:

1. **Click the New Folder button to the right of the Search Public Reports search bar.**

A Create Folder page appears.

2. **Type a name for the folder in the Folder Label field.**

For example, if you want a folder for operational reports, you might name it Sales Ops Reports.

3. **From the Reports tab, select the All Folders view from the left sidebar to locate your newly created folder. Click the downward-facing triangle icon for that folder's row and select the Share option.**

The Share folder page appears.

4. **Select the various Users or grouping of people or teams to share this folder with. For each group or user, you can determine if they have view, edit, or manage permissions.**

   Once selected, click the Share button to move that user or grouping to the "Who Can Access" area that summarizes all folks, well, with access.

5. **When you're done, click Done.**

   The Reports home page reappears.

## Determining folder access

One of the great features of Salesforce reporting is the ability to determine who gets to access which reports easily and intuitively. Access to reports (and dashboards) is controlled via the settings on the folder in which they're stored.

When you've created some report folders, you can use them to determine who gets access to which folders. For example, if you don't want anyone to see a report you've created (or you're not ready to share it yet), just keep it in a personal folder that only you have access to. By default, any folder you create is only accessible to you and administrators until you decide to share it with others.

Salesforce has three different types of access levels to report folders:

>> **View:** The viewer of a folder can view a report, refresh it, and run it. A user with this access level can't customize or save the report, unless he clones it into a new report.

>> **Edit:** An editor of a folder can view, refresh, and run a report, as well as edit, move, save, or delete it.

>> **Manage:** The manager of a folder can do everything a viewer and editor can do, plus she can share the report with others and rename it.

## Maintaining your report library

TIP

Actually, what's worse than a gazillion reports under Public Reports is a universe of reports, some of which are valuable, others of which are useless. Creating public report folders is a good first step, but you may want to apply some of these additional hints on a periodic basis:

>> **Accurately name your reports.** You and your users can't know what's behind a report link unless you name it clearly and precisely.

- » **Consider using report numbers within your report names.** For instance, use standard file-naming conventions like 1.1 North America Pipeline. This way, managers can refer to report numbers so that everyone's looking at the same report.

- » **Delete unnecessary reports.** If multiple people in your company have permission to manage public reports, you may want to survey them before accidentally deleting a report. Unnecessary or redundant reports just make it harder for everyone to find what he or she wants. And in case you mistakenly delete a report (you'll find out soon enough), you have up to 15 days to rescue it from the Recycle Bin, which only exists in Salesforce Classic.

- » **Update existing reports as needs arise.** For example, if you created an Opportunity Product Report and used a filter such as Product Family equals Software, make sure that you manually update the report if the product family name changes. Otherwise, your reports will be off.

- » **Use clear report questions.** For example, you might use the Report Question field to summarize certain filters to your report.

# Mastering Reports

As Salesforce has matured over the years and more business users have come to rely on it to house the bulk of their customer-touching information, users' reporting needs have also matured. Salesforce has done a great job of making potentially very complicated database queries still accessible to the business user.

In this section, we talk briefly about some of the more advanced functionality, in case you're feeling stuck about how to get information in your reports in a certain way. Most likely, you have a way to get you what you want, but you may need to dig a little deeper into Salesforce.

## Building custom summary formulas

Salesforce provides prebuilt functionality that calculates the sum, average, highest value, and lowest value of certain fields that you select for your reports. However, you may need additional summary information based on calculations unique to your business. For example, your business may want to see win-rate percentages or coverage ratios in your reports. Salesforce allows the addition of custom formula calculations for your reports. This means that you can take summary information from other fields and lump them together to come up with a new calculation and corresponding result. It doesn't matter whether you know old math or new math, Salesforce can derive these values for you using Excel-like commands.

If you loved using custom summary formula fields in Salesforce Classic, you can use them in Lightning reports too. When customizing a report and you need to create a custom summary formula field, look to the left sidebar. There's no obvious place to create that type of field! Don't worry, it's there, just a little hidden. To the left of the left sidebar is another sidebar, which by default is collapsed. Look for the "Fields" label below a little right-pointing toggle symbol. Click that to expand that sidebar that shows all fields that you can add to this report, grouped by the object on which the field lives. Above those objects, you see a folder called "Summary Formulas." Nested below that, click the "+ Create Formula" link to get the Edit Summary-Level Formula Column pop-up to appear, which lets you create your formulas and reference Salesforce functions.

To create a new custom summary formula, after clicking the "+ Create Formula" link, follow these steps:

1. **Complete the details in the Edit Summary-Level Formula Column pop-up window, as required:**

   - *Enter a column name* as it will appear on the report in the Label field. Optionally, type a description. Ideally, this field helps explain the math formula in layman's terms.

   - *Select the type of format output* that you want your results to be in from the Format Output Type drop-down list. For example, if you want to calculate the revenue per item of all your products in the pipeline this year, you'll want your result to be Currency.

   - *Select the number of decimal points to display* for your selected data type from the Decimal Points drop-down list.

2. **Build your formula in the General section, as shown in Figure 22-7:**

   a. *Select one of the fields listed in the Fields list from the left sidebar, and then choose the kind of summary type to use in your formula.*

      This field's value, and how it will be summarized, are automatically added into your formula. In our example, we select Amount and Average.

   b. *Click the appropriate operator icons from the formula window.*

      In our example, we select the / (Divide) option.

c. *Repeat these steps, as needed, to build your formula.*

   If you need to know what functions to use for a particular operation, click the Functions subtab located in the left sidebar area. When you select a function, Salesforce will provide some help text to give you an idea of how those functions should be formatted.

3. **Choose where you want the summary calculations to be displayed in the report.** Click the Display subtab to determine if you want the output to appear at all summary levels or just specific ones.

4. **Click the Validate button below the formula window to check the syntax of your formula.**

   Syntax that contains errors is automatically highlighted.

5. **Click Apply when you're finished.**

   The pop-up window closes, and you're back at the Report wizard. You should see the new column showing sample data in the Preview section.

**REMEMBER**

   The custom summary formula isn't saved until you save the report. Clicking Apply just includes it in this step of the Lightning Report Builder. Make sure that you save the report.

6. **Click Run to run the report and see the new column showing real data.**

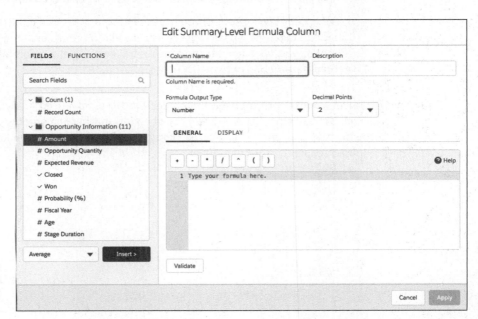

**FIGURE 22-7:**
Building your custom formula for your report.

# Understanding additional reporting options

You can do a lot more fun things with reports. Even many long-term users of Salesforce reports may not know about all these additional analytics capabilities. Here is a brief summary to get data detectives more excited about it:

>> **Conditional highlighting:** You can apply conditional highlighting to reports with groupings to help you easily highlight values that may deserve more of your attention. You can use this with custom summary formulas to highlight high or low percentages, averages, and ratios. You see a lot of syllables in this feature, but conditional highlighting translates into setting thresholds for certain key numerical values and color-coding them to show whether a threshold has been surpassed. In an Opportunity Pipeline by Rep report, you can quickly get an understanding of how people are doing when each rep's total won opportunities are highlighted in red, green, or yellow.

>> **Joined reports:** This is a powerful tool that allows you to create one report that consists of report "blocks," each of which is a separate report that may or may not be reporting off the same objects. So, if you were trying to run a report that showed both your closed won Opportunities as well as the Opportunity win rate, you could join two reports. One block would show the total of all your closed won Opportunities for a time range, while a second block could be based off of all Opportunities so that you can calculate that win ratio. Just make sure that both blocks have some field in common.

>> **Scheduled report runs:** If you have the fun job of providing the powers that be with the same type of report every Monday morning, or at the end of every month, you can automate the running and emailing of a report after you've customized it and made it just right for everyone.

For more in-depth information on each of these advanced analytics capabilities, click the Salesforce Help (that's the question mark icon) on any page and search using the appropriate keywords (conditional highlighting, bucketed fields, and joined reports) in the search bar.

# Chapter 23

# Seeing the Big Picture with Dashboards

D ashboards are visual representations of custom reports that you create in Salesforce. For example, you can see data in a chart, a graph, or a gauge. You can use dashboards to illustrate key performance indicators (KPIs) and other metrics important to your business. A *metric* is simply something you want to measure (for example, sales by rep, Leads by source, Opportunities by partner, Cases by agent, and so on).

What does this mean for you? If you're a sales or service rep, you can track your daily progress against attainment of goals. If you're a manager, you can easily see how reps stack up against each other and where you need to get involved to hit your numbers. And if you're on the executive team, you have dashboards with actionable charts and graphs for strategic decision making to improve the business.

In this chapter, we share tips on planning your metric reporting strategy. Then we show you how to create dashboards. We walk you through updating dashboard properties and components. We also explain how to organize dashboards and their related reports so that you know you're looking at the right information.

# Figuring Out Dashboards

Dashboards are pages in Salesforce comprising tables and charts designed to help you understand important aspects of your business, such as Opportunities per territory and Leads by source. Dashboards are critical to being able to assess the health of your business and spot trends early. The following sections show you some basic concepts so that you can consider your strategies before you start unleashing them on your organization.

## Breaking down basic elements

You can build a dashboard comprised of individual charts, tables, metrics, gauges, or custom components; each item is a *dashboard component*. Similar to building charts with the Report wizard (see Chapter 22), components are based on *source reports* that you create. In fact, you can click a component on a dashboard to make the underlying report appear. Here's a quick summary of the components that are available to you:

>> **Horizontal bar or vertical column charts** (see Figure 23-1) are great when you want to depict a simple measurement with an *x*-axis and a *y*-axis. For example, use bar charts if you want to create a component that displays pipeline by Opportunity type.

>> **Horizontal bar or vertical column grouped charts** work well when you want to compare groups of bars with each other. For example, use grouped bar charts if you want to create a chart that displays pipeline by stage broken out for each month.

>> **Horizontal bar or vertical column stacked charts** work well when you want grouping within a bar. For example, use stacked column charts if you want to create a chart that shows Cases by status and then by type (such as problems versus feature requests).

>> **Horizontal bar or vertical column stacked-to-100% charts** are excellent when you're more interested in percentages than amounts. If you're comparing new versus existing business, stacked-to-100% charts can help you understand what percentage of each stage was new business versus existing business.

>> **Donut charts** (see Figure 23-2) show data broken into segments of a ring (the donut), with the total for the whole chart displayed in the center. (Goes great with coffee and morning meetings.)

>> **Funnel charts** add an additional visual element to the mix by changing the height of each grouping based on its proportion. For example, use a funnel chart if you want to easily see how much each stage in your pipeline is worth.

» **Line charts** are helpful if you're trying to express trends, particularly when time is part of the measurement. For example, use a line chart if you want to analyze the number of newly created Opportunities by month for your entire company.

» **Grouped line charts** add a layer of complexity. For example, a line group chart could help you express the number of newly created Opportunities by month broken out by region or unit.

» **Cumulative line charts** allow you to track the progress of a single metric over time. For example, a line cumulative chart could help you see the number of closed cases by day over the course of an entire month.

» **Grouped cumulative line charts** allow you to track progress over multiple metrics over time. For example, a line grouped cumulative chart could help you see the number of closed cases grouped by agent per day over the course of an entire month.

» **Tables** create simple but powerful four-column tables. For example, use tables if you want your dashboard to show the top ten forecasted deals in the quarter in descending value.

**TIP**

You can create tables and gauges in dashboards but not in the charting tool of the Report wizard.

» **Metrics** insert the grand total of a report at the end of a dashboard label that you customize. Metrics are compelling when you want to tell a story that might require a bit more explanation. Metrics tend to work well in concert with other components. For example, if you use a pie chart to summarize Opportunity by stage, you could add a metric to summarize total pipeline.

» **Gauges** are useful when you have a specific measurable objective and you want to track your progress. A gauge applies the grand total of a report as a point on a scale that you define. For example, use a gauge if you want to measure actual quarterly new bookings against a quota that you define.

» **Scatter charts** aid in showing correlation between one to two groupings of data. For example, you can look at all closed-won Opportunities last quarter, and group those by Account owner. On your x-axis, you can measure the total amount of those closed-won deals (still grouped by the Opportunity owner), and your y-axis can show the annual revenue for each Account (which is a standard field on that Account record). Do your salespeople tend to close a higher value of deals when the customer itself generates more revenue? Let your scatter chart tell you.

» **Visualforce Pages** allow you to create your own custom dashboard components (or download other people's). Even if you're just interested in a snazzier graphic element, go to www.appexchange.com and click the Components category to see what others have created.

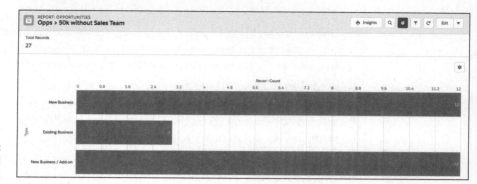

**FIGURE 23-1:**
A vertical column chart.

**FIGURE 23-2:**
A donut chart.

If you're an administrator or a user with permission to manage dashboards, you can create, edit, and organize them. And even if you don't have such permissions, you can still view them by clicking the Dashboards tab on the home page.

## Planning useful dashboards

We always say that the best way to build a system is to envision what you want to ultimately measure. Who is going to be looking at this dashboard, and what information will they be trying to derive? Do you want to know who your top sales reps are? Would you like to understand what your best Accounts are buying from you and how much? Do you wonder how long it takes to close a case? This method of starting with the business questions you want to answer applies to your building of reports and is true of dashboards. Knowing the dashboard's audience will also help you decide how much detail you want represented in the dashboard components.

**TIP**

If you're an administrator or part of the team responsible for deploying Salesforce, consider these tips as you develop your dashboards:

>> **Focus on your end-users.** Meet with sales, marketing, and support management and have them define their KPIs for their teams and business. Knowing this helps you customize Salesforce and construct useful dashboards.

>> **Sketch out a basic draft of what the dashboard should look like.** You should have an idea of what sort of charts or tables can work together to address the questions the viewers want answered. You can also visualize the sequence of how the information should be displayed to those viewing the dashboard, and determine if the order makes logical sense in telling a story.

>> **Create a common set of components to reflect a universal way to look at business health.** Once you've mocked up what you think should go into your dashboard, start building the common components. This is especially true if your company has multiple sales teams. For example, after you determine the key sales metrics for your company's overall dashboard, you can replicate the dashboard and then customize other dashboards for each sales team. By doing this, everyone in the company is speaking a common language.

# Building Dashboards

To build a dashboard, you need to create your custom reports first. You also need to create public folders for your dashboard reports if you want dashboards to be viewable for other users. See Chapter 22 for all the details on creating custom reports and organizing them in folders.

**REMEMBER**

Only system administrators and users with permission to manage dashboards can add, edit, and delete dashboards. See Chapter 20 for details on how to grant permissions.

In the following sections, we show you how to install a prebuilt dashboard and how to create a copy of a dashboard. Then we cover the steps to build a dashboard from scratch.

## Installing sample dashboards and reports

One of the best ways to get your feet wet with dashboards is to install sample dashboards from the AppExchange. Salesforce not only creates the dashboard for you but also builds the underlying sample reports to generate the components.

To install sample dashboards, follow these steps:

1. **In your web browser go to** www.appexchange.com.

   The AppExchange home page appears.

2. **Type** Dashboards **in the Search bar at the top and click the Magnifying Glass button.**

   A page full of AppExchange apps appears. The apps with the Salesforce or Salesforce Labs logos are made and provided for free by salesforce.com.

3. **Click an app's listing to see more information about it.**

   The App Overview page appears with a description and images. If you find a set of dashboards that you'd like to download and install, check out Chapter 19 for more information on installing apps from the AppExchange.

REMEMBER

If you're having trouble accessing dashboards, or installing them from the AppExchange, you may not have the proper permissions. In this circumstance, consult with your administrator.

## Copying a dashboard

To save time or repurpose useful features, you can generate a dashboard by saving a copy of an existing one and then modifying it. For example, if you envision creating multiple dashboards for different sales units with common components, you can use this method and then modify the associated reports.

REMEMBER

When you copy a dashboard, you don't copy another set of identical reports. Instead, the newly saved dashboard *references* the same custom reports that the original dashboard references. If you want the new dashboard to refer to different reports, see the "Developing a dashboard from scratch" section, later in this chapter.

To copy a dashboard, follow these steps:

1. **Click the Dashboards tab.**

   The list of recently viewed dashboards appears.

2. **Type the name of a dashboard in the Search Recent Dashboards search bar, or select an option from the list of recently viewed dashboards.**

3. **Click the name of the dashboard.**

   The dashboard appears.

4. **To the right of the page, inline with the dashboard name, select the Save As option (you may need to first click the downward facing triangle to display this and other selection options).**

   The Save As pop-up page appears.

5. **Update the dashboard name and destination folder as you see fit.**

6. **Click Create to leave the Save As screen.**

   The duplicated Dashboard appears.

7. **Click the Edit button to the right of the Dashboard name to make changes to the title of the dashboard.**

   *Note:* Click the gear icon to edit additional properties of the Dashboard, including:

   - *Folder:* Type the folder name in which to store this dashboard.

   - *View Dashboard As:* Similar to the *running user* in Salesforce Classic, this is the user whose security settings will apply to the dashboard. So, any user who can view the dashboard will be able to view the information based on this setting.

   - *Dashboard Grid Size:* You have more flexibility with your component sizes if you choose the 12-column format.

   - *Dashboard Themes & Palettes:* Depending on how your dashboard will be viewed, you can play around with having the default light background or having the data displayed in front of a dark background. There are also various color palettes to use in displaying the various charts and tables.

**REMEMBER**

If the running user for a dashboard ever leaves the company or is made inactive for another reason, the dashboard won't show data. The same goes for any reports the dashboard references if that report is moved into a folder that the running user doesn't have access to.

8. **Click Save to close the Properties page and view your new dashboard.**

## Developing a dashboard from scratch

Now that you know the basics of dashboards, let's find out how to develop a dashboard from scratch.

To create a new dashboard, follow these steps:

1. **Click the Reports tab.**

   The Reports page appears, defaulted to the most recent ones viewed.

You need to build your custom reports before you can develop a dashing new dashboard.

2. **Build your custom reports and save them to a public folder.**

   See Chapter 22 to find out how to build custom reports.

   Dashboards that you want others to see can't use source reports in your My Personal Reports folder. For purposes of this running example, we'll use a sample Sales Reports folder (which would be located in the left sidebar of the Reports⇨All Folders section of the Reports home page) and click the following reports that show up in that folder:

   - *Sales by Rep:* The report should summarize information by Opportunity Owner and then Stage. The modified copy of the report should be saved as "Pipeline by Rep and Stage" to a public folder.

   - *Sales by Account:* The report should summarize sales information by Account Name. The modified copy of the report should then be saved as "Top Revenue Customers" to a public folder.

   You must be an administrator or a user with permission to manage public reports if you want to add report folders.

3. **Click the Dashboards tab.**

   The Dashboards home page appears.

4. **Click the New Dashboard button in the upper-right area of the page.**

   The New Dashboard page appears. Similar to some of the steps from the "Copying a Dashboard" section previously, type in the name of the new dashboard and select which dashboard folder you want to save it in, and then click Create to enter the Dashboard Builder.

5. **Click the + Component button on the upper-right side of the Dashboard Builder.**

   A Select Report window appears, for you to select the source report that this dashboard component will be based off of. When you've selected a row, make sure you click the Select button.

6. **Choose which chart to display this report, and add further customizations as needed.**

   Depending on the structure of the source report, you may have several or few chart options to select from. You may be able to group your report, add or remove columns to display, and decide if certain columns are summarized. You can also enter the desired title, subtitle, and footer for your component.

   In our running example, name the title **Pipeline by Rep and Stage**. You could also add a footer at the stage, but don't bother for this example.

7. **Click Add to add the component onto your dashboard.**

   You're returned to your dashboard in its Edit mode. The component has been placed by default. You can click the component to re-size it to more or less columns or rows.

8. **Click Save to save your changes. Click Done to see what your dashboard will look like to others (when it's not in the Edit mode).**

## Modifying dashboard properties

Over time, you may have to make changes to your dashboards, whether for cosmetic reasons or to make substantive updates. We can come up with a dozen common edits, but the good news is that updating is easy.

If you need to change the basic settings of a dashboard — such as the title, folder, or running user — you need to edit the dashboard properties. To edit the properties, follow these steps:

1. **Click the Dashboards tab.**

   Find your dashboard in the Recent list, or type in its name in the Search Recent Dashboards search bar.

   The dashboard you're trying to locate appears.

**TIP**

   When you start typing a portion of the name of one of your dashboards into the Search Recent Dashboards search bar, you'll be presented with a list of matching dashboards.

2. **Click the Edit button at the top-right of the dashboard page.**

   The Dashboard Builder appears.

3. **Click the gear button to modify any properties.**

   Modify the settings, as needed, and then click Save.

   When you click Save, the Dashboard Builder reappears, and your setting changes are applied.

## Customizing components

You may want to add or edit an existing component. To edit a component, follow these steps:

1. **Go to a dashboard and click the Edit button.**

   The Dashboard Builder appears.

2. **Click the pencil icon in the upper-right section of a specific component that you want to modify.**

   For example, you may want to change the chart type or display units.

   The Edit Component dialog box appears, as shown in Figure 23-3.

3. **Understand the various types of options available to customize your component (depending on the underlying source report):**

   - *Use chart settings from report*: Sometimes the source report will have its own chart. To be more efficient, you can select this option so you don't have to re-invent what's already been set. And sometimes, like with a joined report that has a chart, the only display option you have is to use the same chart as what's in the report. In that case, you'll get notification messages that prevent you from saving the component.

   - *Display As:* These are the chart, metric, and table options available to you, based on your source report. Which visualization you choose determines additional customization options you can make. We cover some of the more common ones next.

   - *X-Axis, Y-Axis, Cumulative*: Depending on the source report, you can select picklist options that correspond to the source report's groupings of data. Sometimes you only have one option for each axis, other times there may be more (in the case of stacked bar charts, for example). If you're working with a line chart, you can choose if what is displayed are cumulative values (where the next value along the x-axis is additive to the previous value), or not (and the actual value is plotted).

   - *Value, Sliced By*: For donut charts, the "Value" option will determine what numbers are displayed in the center of the donut and along the segments. The "Sliced By" option determines what is being segmented.

   - *Display Units, Show Values, Show Percentages, Combine Small Groups into "Others," Show Total*: The first attributes lets you choose how yo want to display the numbers (if at all) on your chart. Especially when it comes to monetary amounts, and the size of your deals, these numbers can get very large. You can choose to abbreviate the numbers a variety of ways. And the values in charts aren't shown by default, because if you have a lot of data points to cover, the values could look cluttered. With a donut chart, showing the percentages of each segment gives additional perspective to what the values represent. And if you have a lot of small "long tail" segments, it's also possible to group all those into an "Others" segment.

   - *Sort By*: Salesforce dashboards are smart enough to sort calendar date groupings (like when a specific year and month are needed on the x-axis) in logical calendar order. There may be times where you're sorting on something other than time, and you can choose which grouping to sort by, and in ascending or descending order (use the little up or down-pointing arrow icon to the right of the Sort By option).

- *Title, Subtitle, Footer*: One tip in using the additional space in a subtitle and footer is to provide additional annotation on what the dashboard is actually trying to convey, which may not always be obvious in the component's title. For example, use the footer space to act as a definition, or ask a question that the component's graph answers.

- *Segment Ranges*: Ranges let you replicate the equivalent of conditional highlighting with numbers, in charts like the gauge or metric. You set the range and give each band of the range a color designation (typically red, yellow, green). The individual number is then represented in the color corresponding to the range (for a metric), or the segment is highlighted in a color associated with the corresponding range (for a gauge). This serves to provide additional context to whether the number displayed is "good" or not.

- *Table chart settings*: If you want a component that displays like a table, you can customize what is displayed to be different than the table in the source report. You can change up the groupings and add or hide additional columns. The configurations here should look very similar to options you have when editing a report.

4. **Once the component is modified, click Update to add the changes.**

   You're returned to the Dashboard Builder. Continue modifying other components until you're done with all modifications. Then click Save from the Dashboard Builder to save all changes. Click Done to return to the end-user's view of the dashboard.

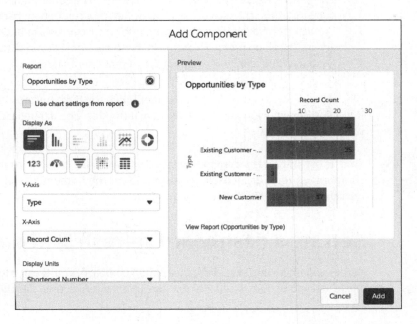

**FIGURE 23-3:**
Modifying component data.

# Changing the layout

If you need to modify the dashboard layout, you can also perform this while in the Dashboard Builder.

Go to a dashboard, click the Edit button, and alter the layout. You can

>> **Modify a component's size.** When you click anywhere in a component, the component becomes outlined with a dotted line, with select anchor points around the middle of each side, and at each corner. Click and hold down your mouse on any of those anchor points to drag that edge of the component to any new part of the Dashboard Builder's grid. With the Lightning Experience you're no longer limited to similarly sized columns and components. Some components can be extra wide (like for bar charts that span a lot of time), and some can be extra long (like a leaderboard of your reps who've closed deals totaling over a certain amount this year).

>> **Rearrange components.** Drag and drop components in your dashboard to arrange them exactly as you see fit. The additional components do need to have some sort of adjacency to other components. That is, you can't have one component in one corner of your Dashboard and a large white space before another component appears in the lower opposite corner.

>> **Add a component.** Click the + Component button and follow the steps in the section "Developing a dashboard from scratch," earlier in this chapter.

>> **Delete a component.** Click the X button located at the upper-right corner of a component, next to the pencil icon. You won't get a confirmation before this happens! If you change your mind and want that component back, click the Undo button (which looks like a counter-clockwise arrow), to undo your last action. The Undo button is located in the upper-right section of the Dashboard Builder, to the right of the + Component button.

When you're satisfied with your changes, click the Save button. Then clicking the Done button exits you out of the Dashboad Builder. The dashboard reappears with your modifications.

TIP

Your most important components should comprise the top row. The top row's components for a dashboard are displayed on the home pages of users who have chosen that dashboard as the one to view.

# Setting a dashboard refresh schedule

Before you make decisions based on your dashboard, you'll want to make sure that those decisions are based on the latest data. Click any dashboard from your dashboard list. In the upper-left just below the dashboard's title is a timestamp starting with *As Of*. You can use this to find out the last time your dashboard data was updated.

When you want to manually update your dashboard data, simply click the Refresh button at the top-right of the dashboard page. The components reappear one by one. When the refresh is completed, a new timestamp appears.

Enterprise and Unlimited Edition customers can subscribe to their dashboards to get the latest refreshed dashboard data emailed to them on a daily, weekly, or monthly basis. Just use the Subscribe button next to the Edit button in a dashboard. You can then choose the frequency of receiving the email, day of the week, and recipients.

**TIP**

If you have regularly scheduled meetings, you can automatically email your dashboard to the meeting attendees prior to the meeting to give them a sneak peak of what will be discussed.

# Organizing Your Dashboards

If you have the permissions necessary to manage dashboards, manage public reports, and view all data, you can organize your company's dashboards in folders and define the proper security access for users. By organizing dashboards, you can make sure that the right people are focusing on the right metrics to manage their business.

## Viewing dashboard lists

As with most other tabs in Salesforce in the Lightning Experience, clicking the Dashboard tab takes you to its home page, defaulting to a list of recent dashboards viewed.

**REMEMBER**

From this list page, users with the permissions mentioned in the preceding section can perform a variety of functions:

>> **Re-sort:** Click a column header to re-sort a dashboard list.

>> **View:** Click a title name to view a dashboard.

>> **Modify, Delete:** Click the downward-pointing triangle in the rightmost column of the row that matches the dashboard you want to edit or delete. A drop-down list appears with those options.

>> **Build:** Click the New Dashboard that appears to the right of the Search Recent Dashboards seach bar.

## Building dashboard folders

From the Dashboards tab, which takes you to the Dashboards home page, you can also create and edit dashboard folders. Editing a dashboard folder is easy when you understand how to create one. Just remember that it's separate from a report folder.

To create a folder, follow these steps:

1. **On the Dashboard page, click the New Folder button to the right of the Search Recent Dashboards search bar.**

   A Create folder page appears. Note that in the Lightning Experience you can nest dashboard folders, if that fits your company's organizational style.

2. **Type an intuitive name for the folder and click Save.**

   You are then shown the folder (which has nothing in it yet).

3. **Click the downward pointing triangle in the upper-right, next to the New Folder button. Select the Share option to determine who has access to the folder and their read versus read/write privileges.**

   You can choose to share the folder with individual users, specific roles (and optionally, their subordinates), public groups, territories, and other options.

TIP

When naming folders, dashboards, and dashboard reports, consider using a standard numbering convention. For example, you could name the senior management folder 1.0 Executive Dashboards. Then the executive sales subordinate dashboard might be 1.1 and the executive marketing dashboard 1.2. By using a standard numbering methodology, you can more efficiently create, clone, and organize dashboards and dashboard reports.

# 8

The Part of Tens

# Chapter 24

# Ten Ways to Drive More Productivity

Salesforce.com drives much of its feature updates based on its existing road map and requests from customers just like you. A few times a year, Salesforce.com comes out with a new release of its award-winning service. That's the benefit of these cloud-based business applications, because the infrastructure isn't maintained by you. Unlike traditional software upgrades, these releases are immediately available to all customers, and most features can be activated or deactivated when you're ready to make the change.

Keeping track of all the cool new updates that Salesforce.com releases can get a little overwhelming. The speed with which it's able to roll out releases is often faster than our ability to write all about it and get it in your hands! On the flip side, perhaps you do keep track of the newest features but you've been struggling with an apparent feature limitation or you'd like more advice on how to best implement a particular feature.

Fortunately for us, both Salesforce.com and its community of users strongly believe in helping each other out to make every customer successful. Through a variety of channels, the Salesforce.com community shares best practices and offers suggestions and workarounds for even the toughest head-scratcher questions.

In this chapter, we introduce you to ten resources and tools that will help you get the most out of Salesforce. The first five sections cover essential resources that every user in your organization should know about. The last five sections fill you in on great productivity tools that you may have overlooked.

## Salesforce Trailhead

If you haven't already, bookmark Salesforce Trailhead (https://trailhead.salesforce.com) *now*. Whether you're an administrator or end-user, here you'll find entire interactive training modules with real scenarios that help you learn various aspects of Salesforce. As you complete modules in various tracks, you'll earn badges that you can proudly share online. Salesforce has also moved its certification maintenance to this site, so you will have to get familiar with Trailhead if you plan on becoming Salesforce certified.

## Dreamforce Conference

Dreamforce (www.salesforce.com/dreamforce) is Salesforce.com's annual product conference that brings together developers, system administrators, and end-user business folks to learn from, network with, and party alongside product experts from Salesforce.com, as well as the ecosystem at large. Make the trek to San Francisco, and get inspired with all the great things Salesforce can do for your company.

## Salesforce Trailblazer Community

Online within the Salesforce Trailblazer Community (http://success.salesforce.com), you can post or vote for new product ideas, see what other users are requesting, and ask and answer questions related to configuration or code. Not only do you get to see what the masses are clamoring for, but you also get to see Salesforce.com employees, partners, and customers joining together to provide feedback and assistance.

## Salesforce.com Local User Groups

One of the best ways to regularly find out about upcoming features, hear about third-party vendor integrations, network with your peers, and provide product feedback is to join a local user group. You'll get to learn from and share tips with fellow customers in your vicinity. Search for your city in Trailblazer Community Groups by going here (`https://trailblazercommunitygroups.com`).

You can also go here (`https://success.salesforce.com/featuredGroups`), and click the Community Groups by Region category in the left sidebar. If you don't see your city, think about starting your own group.

# Salesforce Trailhead Academy

One of the best ways to become an expert and have an opportunity to ask an expert about your company's particular use of Salesforce is to be trained by Salesforce. com. Then you can be your company's expert and spearhead further ideas of using Salesforce to make your business processes run smoother. You find classes for every user role, and for every budget. If you'll be configuring and customizing Salesforce, you can find a series of certifications so that you can tell others just how special you are, and can choose to do so virtually or in person. Visit Salesforce's Trailhead Academy (`https://trailhead.salesforce.com/academy`) and look for options that meet your budget and learning style, then register!

# Salesforce Colored Favicons

This browser extension is a small one but the impact is huge. If you are an admin, developer, or even a Salesforce power user, you know what it's like to work in multiple orgs and keep track of multiple tabs. Salesforce Colored Favicons overrides the standard Salesforce favicon (or cloud icon on your browser tab) with a different color, based on the org. Additionally, if you have a sandbox open, it will display an 'S' so that you save time and don't get confused or make updates in the wrong place.

# Field Trip

Fields in Salesforce remind us of barnacles on a boat. Over time, custom fields get created, some get abandoned, and they grow and grow over time. On a regular basis, you should slough off those unused fields, just like barnacles are scraped off a boat. Abandoned fields can clutter up your instance with redundant-sounding fields that also clog up the report-building experience, and make onboarding new hires tedious when people can't remember when a field is used or not.

Field Trip (available on the AppExchange) is an oldie but a goodie. It is a free app that does some analysis on fields in an object, and lets you know what percentage of those object records have data in that field. Of course, you need a sense as to what percentage an often-used field might have, so you can compare that to a less-used field. This tool gives you an initial start when it comes to cleaning up abandoned fields.

# ORGanizer

ORGanizer is another nifty little browser extension that lets users forget about their usernames and passwords to the multiple orgs and instances of Salesforce they have to access on a regular basis. You can even use ORGanizer in incognito mode if you are an admin who needs to login as other users in a different tab! This little feature will save loads of time if you are an admin or developer with hands on the keyboard.

# Perm Comparator

If you work with sales teams, and multiple teams in general, you'll inevitably have different profiles and permissions for your disparate groups. Especially if you work for a large multinational company, these permissions can get massive and unwieldy. Perm Comparator is built on Heroku and has an easy to use interface that allows you to select different users and see exactly which permissions are not shared between them. Comparing permissions among different users is a huge timesaver in many sticky situations and allows you to get rid of the guesswork and long menial hours of work at the click of a button.

# Gmail Sidebar in Salesforce

Another browser extension is called Salesforce and allows you to add a Salesforce sidebar directly within your Gmail application. Using this you can search and view records in Salesforce without switching tabs or browser windows. You can also create emails using Salesforce templates, log emails in Salesforce, and even create new records all from within the sidebar widget.

# Chapter 25

# Ten Keys to a Successful Migration to Lightning

I f your company's instance of Salesforce is just a few years old and the Lightning Experience is enabled by default, congratulations! You have a fairly young instance of Salesforce, and hopefully the guidance we've given you in this book can ensure your Salesforce customizations use best practices that will scale for the future.

If you're like the rest of us, you could be instead inheriting an older Salesforce instance, still in the Classic UI, with a lot of ambiguous fields and customizations that no one really recalls the reasons for why the customization was done in the first place.

You could just focus on using your awesome Salesforce (Classic) administration skills to improve the customization debt that has piled up, since there are so many helpful and also cool improvements you could apply. But wait . . . new features keep getting released and many times the enhancements don't apply to your Classic UI. And your developers are also feeling a little constrained too because some technical improvements also require living in the Lightning Experience.

You really want to take advantage of the more modern interface, and the various enhancements that are available only in the Lightning Experience, but you know that your hordes of users have learned how to navigate around your particular instance and the technical resources always seem to be playing catch-up with day-to-day emergencies, let alone helping you with the transition. What's a Salesforce administrator to do?

In this section, we discuss ten steps to help you successfully navigate a transition to the Lightning Experience. With this information, the journey should become less daunting as you get a better idea of what to anticipate, taken from lessons learned from those who have come before you.

# Understanding Why the Transition Needs to Happen Now

Yes, the Lightning Experience looks so much cooler and more current than that Classic interface. Yes, all the demos and videos you see about new features always show the world through Lightning Experience lenses. But before you decide to venture on the journey to transition to this new UI, you should really understand what you get (and sometimes, don't get) with the Lightning Experience.

In building out this new UI, Salesforce prioritized key user personas and use cases in a very intentional order. As the majority of its users are in Sales, they focused on transitioning core Sales Cloud features, and over the years have iterated on additional processes within Sales Cloud, while also rolling out the experience for Service Cloud users.

Make sure you understand both the new features you get with the Lightning Experience that don't exist in the Classic world, and the ones that aren't yet supported. In this book, we have done our best to highlight any major areas (at the time of this writing), that might not yet have a Lightning Experience equivalent. However you should keep checking as Salesforce has multiple releases a year that continue to narrow the gap between UIs.

The following are page names (at the time of this writing) and related URLs in Salesforce's own Help documentation that can summarize this for you. These change often so go here for the latest information:

>> New features only in the Lightning Experience: https://help.salesforce.com/articleView?id=lex_intro.htm&type=5

>> Comparing Lightning Experience and Salesforce Classic: https://help.salesforce.com/articleView?id=lex_aloha_comparison.htm&type=5

Note the new Lightning-only features you think could benefit your company, and why. Then explain why this transition matters, now. This helps identify both the importance and urgency of getting this project on the roadmap. Tie it to business outcomes: can it help your sales teams get to creating or closing more Opportunities, faster? Can it reduce a lot of time (and thus, money) and headache shouldered by your IT or Sales Operations team? Also note any missing features and try to categorize this by teams that might be impacted by this, and by how much. That is, maybe Sales can benefit from Lightning, but the Marketing team working in Campaigns all day who also need to look at Opportunities might not have the full feature experience in the former area (for now).

# Identifying Your Executive Sponsor

Proposing a transition to the Lightning Experience is a big deal. For some managers and reps, this initiative can cause concerns for a variety of reasons: People get set in their ways, they assume that it's going to take a lot of their time, and they think there are more urgent business or technical matters to address first, and so on. When other top priorities at work begin creeping in, it's easy for the importance of the Lightning transition to fall along the wayside.

Every initiative needs a champion to help drive the Lightning migration in your company. That person is there to rally support, break logjams, and ensure that your team has the resources to get things done. Identify who that person will be, and how they and their teams will most benefit from the Lightning Experience in such a way that they realize the urgency of the transition. What are some of their current pain points that you think LEX can address? None of the cool LEX features will matter to your company until you can highlight the ones that help address business outcomes, and until you can spell out which groups will benefit (and ideally, by how much).

We recommend that you identify an executive sponsor once you've thought about who would benefit the most. Work with her to get buy-in, so that she can communicate what's in it for the implementation team and set expectations for what's needed from all participants. This will go a long way toward calming fears, gaining support and commitment, and nudging the team toward your North Star when the team members are at an impasse.

# Building Your Project Team

The transition to the Lightning Experience is less about technology and more about people, human processes, and your business. In fancy business-speak, what was just described is "change management." For your company to get the most out of LEX and the journey to enable it, you need to develop a team made up of critical stakeholders, Salesforce experts, and a cross section of end-users. If your instance is used just by sales and marketing, that might mean that the team includes managers from marketing, sales operations, and IT, some respected sales reps, and hopefully a member of your executive team. This team doesn't have to be huge, nor should members expect to be involved in this project full-time. But you must have people who can speak for the business teams, and you must have the resources you need to get the job done. Get every stakeholder to understand the team's objectives and to buy in from the first meeting.

# Evaluating Your Current Customizations

Review each business process that is reflected in your Salesforce instance, and understand how it may change in the new UI. The "it" can be anything from the number of clicks, where something is clicked, where someone has to go to initiate and complete the process, and what back-end technical work needs to be done to get the same behavior (if at all).

If you're not sure you've identified all the groups that may be using Salesforce to track something, it's best that you also check with your project team. Chances are someone may remember a team whose business process you weren't familiar with. Add that to the list.

Once you have a high level list of key stakeholder groups and the business processes they perform in Salesforce, work with your technical team members to compare notes on functionality as they should also be understanding technical improvements and workarounds that may be needed for any potential modifications to custom code.

At this point, or in parallel, a Salesforce administrator should go into Salesforce (Classic) and run the Readiness Report from **Setup ⇨ Lightning Experience**. This is an automatic report that is generated with specific analysis of your org's customizations, and permissions given to your user profiles. This is another key step in making the ambiguous daunting unknown of migrating to Lightning less intimidating and more tangible. Review this information with your technical team. If you have an old org, there may be a lot of unused (or, at least, unrecognized) customizations that come up. Make a note of these are you try to reverse engineer what business process this customization supports, which business users it impacts (if any). Try to translate what some customizations do into business-speak and work with your stakeholders to see if anyone has any historical context. Make note of which processes are old and can be deprecated for sure (at least, from a business's point of view), which ones no one knows about, and which ones are critical to keep.

*Note:* The Lightning Experience Readiness Report also iterates regularly, so make sure to routinely run this to see if any enhancements have occurred that may change any part of your last assessment.

*Note:* The Lightning Experience Readiness Report does its best to assess the majority of your org's customizations and the impact of LEX on your user profiles. Make sure to round out this report with your own education on what is and isn't yet supported in the Lightning Experience, as mentioned in the "Understanding Why the Transition Needs to Happen Now" section earlier in this chapter.

Confirm business processes as a key element to your "state of our org" assessment. Understand the level of technical effort needed for each process to live in the new UI. By doing this, you gain further understanding to drive agreement on prioritization of which business processes to replicate and when to roll them out in Lightning (if at all). Ideally you will know enough of Lightning features that you can assess if a new "standard in Lightning" feature can replace a custom less-efficient process in the current org; be sure to call out that as reducing the reliance on custom code (and internal teams that are already stretched thin). Ensure that you're creating a plan that addresses existing or desired processes of managers and their teams.

# Planning Your Change Management Strategy

Once you've fine-tuned your value proposition, spelled out the potential ROI (return on investment) that can be gained with the change, have an idea of which features will behave a certain way, confirmed the technical effort level needed, and taken inventory of the business groups that will be impacted, you need to solidify your change management strategy. That's a fancy way of saying that the more you can manage expectations, remind people of why they're undergoing this, and ensure them that it's all worth, the more you can plan for a successful transition.

To demonstrate to decision makers that you've really thought this out, make your objectives measurable by applying specific success metrics to an objective. (A *success metric* is a numerical goal that you want to achieve, ideally within a specified time frame.) For example, it's one thing to say that you want to reduce contract negotiation time, and it's quite another to define that you want to reduce response time and mouse clicks by 20 percent as a result of the Lightning transition.

Salesforce has taken its immense set of learnings and community tips and provided change management templates and guidance so you don't have to feel like you're starting from step 0 without a lifeline. These templates will help you articulate the benefits and secure buy-in from various stakeholders to address the "why are we doing this?" and "why are we doing this now?" questions.

You can find more in-depth discussion about change management recommendations at Salesforce's "Change Management for a Successful Transition to Lightning Experience" page at `https://lightning-readiness-check.salesforce.com/change`.

# Defining Your Scope and Prioritizing Initiatives

You can do a lot with Salesforce, and if you're working with an older Salesforce instance, many customizations have probably happened to it; some will be complex, some will be simple-but-convoluted (why did they build so many workflows chained together?), and sometimes the odd process in Salesforce is just reflecting odd inefficiencies in your business process that no one has bothered to optimize because "that's how we've always done it," or "that's the only way we could do it in Salesforce X years ago."

As you evaluate these customizations, the more complex ones could increase the time to fully transition to the Lightning Experience, as more teams (often technical ones) have to get involved. As you assess the various business processes, prioritize initiatives and determine what's in scope and out of scope for the initial implementation. Consider keeping the transition limited by focusing on the major priorities, but only if you can determine a fair and painless workaround for teams and processes not in the first phase.

Also evaluate which existing business processes could be dramatically improved and simplified in Lightning (whether that's counted in mouse clicks, or transitions or notifications to different business teams). This transition could be the kick in the pants that some teams need to improve previously inefficient processes (since who wants to transition a known crappy process into a new world?). You'll need to balance the ability to improve broken processes in the new UI, against the time it may take to get all the buy-in and do the standard transition work to make the behavior change. Be prepared to propose potential new behavior to key stakeholders so they understand the benefits. Manage expectations as to the effort level needed for any retraining. (You know that old adage about old dogs learning new tricks? You don't have to be physically old to be established in your ways around how you work in Salesforce . . .) Be ready to socialize this with key approvers who might be managers that may not be in the tactical weeds every day, so you can gain their support if there are behavioral issues where you need their help to unblock stubborn situations.

# Confirming the Lightning Experience for Your Business

After you evaluate your company's business processes, understand which ones are supported and not-yet supported in Salesforce, the effort level needed on the business and technical sides to make this transition, and what sort of rollout approach you're going to take, you're going to want to start prototyping the new world to ensure it can still be modeled to reflect your business.

There may be times where the location of a Lightning button may change, or the need for an existing button goes away due to standard functionality in Lightning. At this point you should be able to tell if there are any core business processes that totally won't work in the new UI, will work with retraining, or will work as before.

However, we realize that you're probably new to the Lightning Experience too, or at least a transition, and may have some questions to confirm your assessment. Work closely with your Salesforce Customer Success Manager and technical team to validate your findings, to ensure questions can be addressed sooner rather than later. If you still have questions, make sure to ask your peers on the community forums as well.

# Customizing for User Relevance

When designing Lightning records and layouts, keeping it simple isn't always appropriate. Some businesses do have complex needs. Some may just have a lot of custom field buildup that they haven't ever prioritized the time to clean up. In the old Classic UI, when a record got too long and bloated with a ton of fields, people would create page layouts to hide fields that no one used but no one wanted to spend the time to determine if they should be deleted or not.

Use this transition as yet another housekeeping milestone. If you could scrub your page layouts yet again, what additional fields would you hide? Which are the handful of fields in a record that all users swear by? It'll be helpful to know this as you build Lightning page layouts, as fields are surfaced in a new look and feel, and can be highlighted in new ways. When folks hover over a lookup field, is the information they're seeing, sufficient? Use this as a time to make low-effort small adjustments to search result layouts too, to improve relevancy and adoption while people learn a new interface.

Regardless of UI adopted, it's just good practice to focus your customization on relevancy to your users. Standardize information as often as possible, using picklists rather than free text fields, which will help with more accurate reporting. For fields that have to be text fields (such as the Opportunity Name), use this time to determine a simple standard naming convention.

As you accomplish major milestones (such as customization of different records or layouts), validate and socialize your work with a representative of your end-users. By doing this, you can make sure at key points that you're building a solution that works for your internal customer, while also giving them an advance preview of the Lightning Experience, which should make the transition more tangible and less daunting.

# Building a Comprehensive Training Plan

As early as you can in the transition process, start building a training plan. (A change management plan is different in that training is a part of change management, but also encompasses a lot of other elements around socialization, alignment building, and expectation setting.) Don't assume that users will know what to do their first day in the Lightning Experience. Just because the look appears and feels more modern, user's brains still have to undo (sometimes) years of learning how to navigate within Salesforce Classic. Those who think they can just brute-force learn this on their own will miss out on a lot of nuances and productivity improvements, even if they do learn a few small processes very well.

While Salesforce has a ton of online videos, documentation, and Trailhead self-paced learnings, you should still prepare training materials relevant enough to your customization. Take parts of the online materials and weave it into your own company's custom training efforts. Make sure you preview materials — there may be some features you're not implementing, and you may be asked why or why not.

Blend prerequisite classes, custom sales training, and reinforcement training in your plan. The key is to make sure that enough relevant training is provided so that people effectively and correctly know how to use Salesforce in the Lightning Experience on the day they transition, or feel they remember enough of the training to unblock themselves if they get stuck. Your new customization may look awesome, but if a user feels helpless (or worse, stupid) in a new UI that they previously thought they were very proficient in, you will have a much harder adoption journey. If you don't have the time or resources to deliver the training part, consider reaching out to Salesforce for help with some custom training made for your business. Also, be sure that your end-users have personal copies of this book — just in case.

## Connecting with Peers

As you evaluate the transition to the Lightning Experience, and after your teams are up and running in it, you should constantly gather feedback and track how adoption is faring. Also, get out there and meet your peers — others who have rolled out Lightning and have advice and stories to share. Through online community discussion boards, local user group meetings, and Dreamforce (Salesforce's annual user conference), you have several channels where you can ask questions, seek guidance, and share information that can ensure a smooth transition to the Lightning Experience.

# Index

business, measuring, 11
buttons, using in record page, 57–58

# C

Calendar (Google), 32
calendars
    managing, 31–32
    syncing, 65
campaign members
    adding, 212–213
    importing, 210–211
    mass-updating status of, 218
    modifying status of, 209–210
    targeting, 212–213
Campaign Name field, 206–207
campaigns, marketing
    about, 205–208
    building target lists, 210–213
    capturing influence, 269–270
    creating, 208–209
    executing, 214–215
    modifying campaign member status, 209–210
    tracking responses, 215–218
Campaigns tab, 33
capturing campaign influence, 269–270
cards, 60
Case feed, 185
Case Number field, 185
Case Origin field, 185
Case Reason field, 185
Case record, 184–186
cases
    about, 183
    closing, 190–191
    communicating about, 190–191
    creating, 186–188
    emailing customers from, 190
    entering new, 187–188
    managing, 189
    managing customer interactions with, 18
    roles and responsibilities of service agents, 184
    Support Settings for, 271–272
    tracking support life cycle with, 183–191
    viewing, 125–126

Cases tab, 34
CC field, 72
change management strategy, planning, 369–370
changing
    activation on Price Books, 169
    campaign member statuses, 209–210
    custom objects, 281
    dashboard properties, 353
    filters, 338
    layout of dashboards, 356
    opportunity records, 145–153
    page layouts, 246–247
    personal information, 45–48
    product details in Product catalog, 163–164
    records with inline editing, 59–60
    search layouts, 248
    status of multiple records, 119
    Task view, 32
channel conflict
    defined, 172–173
    reducing with deal registration, 176–177
channel managers
    defined, 172
    roles and responsibilities of, 173–177
channels, managing with Salesforce Partner
        Communities, 177
chart icon, 331
Chat, 198–202
Chatter
    about, 77–78
    configuring feeds, 87
    enabling, 87–92
    following opportunities with, 153–154
    groups, 92–94
    key terms, 80–81
    locating, 83–84
    managing notifications, 94–95
    posts, 85–86
    preparing to use, 78–80
    security, 89
    turning on, 81–83
    updating profile, 84
    using effectively, 95
    using files with, 225
Chatter feed, 25

Salesforce on mobile devices, 48–49
sample dashboards/reports, 349–350
interacting, with customers, 18
Internal Comments field, 185
Internet resources
  AppExchange, 74, 275, 285
  cheat sheet, 3
  Dreamforce, 362
  Salesforce Developers, 324
  Salesforce platform, 314
  Salesforce release notes, 27
  Salesforce Trailblazer Community, 362
  Salesforce Trailhead, 362
  Salesforce Trailhead Academy, 363
  Salesforce.com, 363

## J

joined reports, 344
joining groups in Chatter, 92–93

## K

Kanban, 148
kanban board, 147–149
Kelley, TJ (author)
  *Salesforce Service Cloud For Dummies*, 17, 172
Key Deals - Recent Opportunities, 29
key standard processes, replicating, 238

## L

launching
  Chat, 199
  Chatter, 81–83
  News feature, 263–264
  Price Books, 169
  processes, 258
  schedules, 164–165
  users, 293
  Web-to-Case feature, 197–198
  Web-to-Lead feature, 216
layouts
  assigning to profiles, 247–248
  changing for dashboards, 356

Lead Owner field, 100
Lead queues, 113–114
lead records
  about, 100–102
  duplicate, 114–116
  mass-deleting, 119–120
Lead Source field, 100, 130
Lead Status field, 100
leads
  about, 99
  accepting from queues, 109
  adding new, 102–103
  assigning, 267
  assigning to partners, 175
  choosing default owners, 267–268
  cloning, 103–104
  confirming conversion settings, 268–269
  converting qualified, 111–112
  distribution of, 173
  following up on, 109–112
  identifying with Pardot, 17
  importing, 104–108
  Lead record, 100–102
  maintaining database for, 113–120
  qualifying, 109–110
  setting up, 102–108
  tracking, 99–120
  transferring, 118–119
  updating, 179
  viewing, 179
Leads tab, 34
legacy data, migrating, 314–318
LEX (Lightning Experience)
  about, 27, 276
  App Launcher, 28, 31
  Assistant, 29
  building page layouts, 249–250
  confirming, 371
  defining apps, 31
  finding records with Search, 30–31
  gear icon, 29
  Key Deals - Recent Opportunities, 29
  managing calendar, 31–32
  migration and, 366–367

# N

# P

managing, 55–57

mass-deleting, 321–322

mass-transferring, 320–321

modifying with inline editing, 59–60

navigating in Lightning Experience, 38–39

reassigning ownership, 241–242

recent, 35

restoring from Recycle Bin, 56–57

updating, 243

Recycle Bin, restoring records from, 56–57

related lists, 25, 60, 243–244

Related Lookup Filters, 233–234

Related To field, 72

relationships, building, 282–285

relevance, customization and, 234–235

Remember icon, 3

remote work, 53–54

removing

    account records, 128

    Price Books, 170

reports

    about, 327–328

    adding campaign members from custom, 213

    building custom summary formulas, 341–343

    changing filters, 338

    clearing filters, 338

    creating, 331–335

    creating folders, 339–340

    customizing, 333–335

    determining folder access, 340

    displaying, 330–331

    exporting to Excel, 338–339

    filtering, 335–338

    hiding results, 335–336

    installing sample, 349–350

    maintaining report library, 340–341

    mastering, 341–344

    navigating Reports home page, 328–330

    options for, 344

    organizing, 339–341

    showing results, 335–336

    sorting results, 336–337

    summarizing results, 336–337

Reports home page, 328–330

Reports tab, 34

Reports To field, 130

Re-sort function, 357

resources, Internet

    AppExchange, 74, 275, 285

    cheat sheet, 3

    Dreamforce, 362

    Salesforce Developers, 324

    Salesforce platform, 314

    Salesforce release notes, 27

    Salesforce Trailblazer Community, 362

    Salesforce Trailhead, 362

    Salesforce Trailhead Academy, 363

    Salesforce.com, 363

responses, tracking to marketing campaigns, 215–218

restoring records from Recycle Bin, 56–57

Revenue Scheduling Enabled field, 157

reviewing

    activities, 61–62

    tasks, 33

roles

    about, 294

    contact, 149–151

    hierarchy of, 294, 304–306

Row Counts, 336

# S

Sales Cloud, 14–15

sales groups, improving effectiveness of, 14–15

Sales Path, visualizing deals using, 149

Sales Price option, 158

sales processes, tracking, 265–267

sales productivity, improving, 15

Sales teams Price Books, 166

Salesforce. See also specific topics

    accessing, 25–26

    defined, 24

    editions of, 19–20

    platform (website), 314

    selecting as customer relationship management (CRM) system, 11–12

    sending emails from, 74–75

# About the Author

**Liz Kao:** Liz was an enthusiastic early adopter of the software-as-a-service (SaaS) model and has been using Salesforce for more than twenty years. An early employee of Salesforce, she built Salesforce-centric solutions for both external clients and internal teams, including launching over one-third of the original applications on the AppExchange. Combined with a background in sales and marketing, she blends a hands-on perspective of business needs with using Salesforce (and now, other cloud products) to build solutions that scale. A veteran of the enterprise software industry, Liz lives in San Francisco. When she isn't busy keeping up with the latest enterprise software cloud products and features, she's enjoying all the culinary delights and Internet-signal-free natural surroundings of Northern California.

**Jon Paz:** Jon, a Salesforce consultant, has worked with enterprise clients to deliver world-class solutions to perplexing business challenges. Previously, he worked as an editor for a major international organization. After working with various clients and industries to implement cloud technologies, Jon has witnessed the transformative value of the product. He is an avid globetrotter, can talk to you about your business in five different languages, and is a staunch advocate for the legalization of unpasteurized cheeses!

# Authors' Acknowledgments

Our most sincere thanks go out to family and friends, as well as anyone who has supported us throughout this not-so-insignificant endeavor. Thank you to Ashley Coffey and Christopher Morris, as well as the great Wiley team that helped make this idea a reality. We certainly could not have done any of it without your support, flexibility, and positive attitude. And finally, thanks to the innovators and evangelists at Salesforce.com. You made enterprise software applications fun to write about (we're serious!), and your continuous innovation over the years keeps us eager to spread the good news of your products to the rest of the world.

# Dedication

To friends, family, and former coworkers who have supported me in this journey since the first edition. Thank you for your wisdom, encouragement, insights, patience, and laughter every step of the way.

— Liz Kao

To my family, friends, and those who blur the line between the two. Thanks for putting up with me through the writing process, all the way to the finish line.

— Jon Paz

**Publisher's Acknowledgments**

**Acquisitions Editor:** Ashley Coffey
**Project Editor:** Christopher Morris
**Copy Editor:** Christopher Morris

**Technical Editor:** Michael Wicherski
**Production Editor:** Magesh Elangovan
**Cover Image:** © JuSun/iStock.com

# Leverage the power

*Dummies* is the global leader in the reference category and one of the most trusted and highly regarded brands in the world. No longer just focused on books, customers now have access to the dummies content they need in the format they want. Together we'll craft a solution that engages your customers, stands out from the competition, and helps you meet your goals.

## Advertising & Sponsorships

Connect with an engaged audience on a powerful multimedia site, and position your message alongside expert how-to content. Dummies.com is a one-stop shop for free, online information and know-how curated by a team of experts.

- Targeted ads
- Video
- Email Marketing

- Microsites
- Sweepstakes sponsorship

**20 MILLION** PAGE VIEWS
EVERY SINGLE MONTH

**15 MILLION UNIQUE**
VISITORS PER MONTH

**43%** OF ALL VISITORS ACCESS THE SITE
VIA THEIR MOBILE DEVICES

**700,000** NEWSLETTER SUBSCRIPTIONS

TO THE INBOXES OF

*300,000* UNIQUE INDIVIDUALS EVERY WEEK

# of dummies

## Custom Publishing

Reach a global audience in any language by creating a solution that will differentiate you from competitors, amplify your message, and encourage customers to make a buying decision.

- Apps
- Books
- eBooks
- Video
- Audio
- Webinars

## Brand Licensing & Content

Leverage the strength of the world's most popular reference brand to reach new audiences and channels of distribution.

## For more information, visit dummies.com/biz

# PERSONAL ENRICHMENT

**Staying Sharp** dummies

9781119187790
USA $26.00
CAN $31.99
UK £19.99

**Facebook** dummies
Carolyn Abram

9781119179030
USA $21.99
CAN $25.99
UK £16.99

**Guitar** dummies
Mark Phillips
Jon Chappell

9781119293354
USA $24.99
CAN $29.99
UK £17.99

**Investing** dummies
Eric Tyson, MBA

9781119293347
USA $22.99
CAN $27.99
UK £16.99

**Beekeeping** dummies
Howland Blackiston

9781119310068
USA $22.99
CAN $27.99
UK £16.99

**Digital Photography** dummies
Julie Adair King

9781119235606
USA $24.99
CAN $29.99
UK £17.99

**Meditation** dummies
Stephan Bodian

9781119251163
USA $24.99
CAN $29.99
UK £17.99

**Pregnancy** ALL-IN-ONE dummies
6 Books

9781119235491
USA $26.99
CAN $31.99
UK £19.99

**Samsung Galaxy S 7** dummies
Bill Hughes

9781119279952
USA $24.99
CAN $29.99
UK £17.99

**iPhone** dummies
Edward C. Baig
Bob "Dr. Mac" LeVitus

9781119283133
USA $24.99
CAN $29.99
UK £17.99

**Crocheting** dummies
Karen Manthey
Susan Brittain

9781119287117
USA $24.99
CAN $29.99
UK £16.99

**Nutrition** dummies
Carol Ann Rinzler

9781119130246
USA $22.99
CAN $27.99
UK £16.99

# PROFESSIONAL DEVELOPMENT

**Windows 10** dummies
Andy Rathbone

9781119311041
USA $24.99
CAN $29.99
UK £17.99

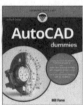
**AutoCAD** dummies
Bill Fane

9781119255796
USA $39.99
CAN $47.99
UK £27.99

**Excel 2016** dummies
Greg Harvey, PhD

9781119293439
USA $26.99
CAN $31.99
UK £19.99

**QuickBooks 2017** dummies
Stephen L. Nelson, MBA, CPA, MS in Taxation

9781119281467
USA $26.99
CAN $31.99
UK £19.99

**macOS Sierra** dummies
Bob "Dr. Mac" LeVitus

9781119280651
USA $29.99
CAN $35.99
UK £21.99

**LinkedIn** dummies
Joel Elad, MBA

9781119251132
USA $24.99
CAN $29.99
UK £17.99

**Windows 10** ALL-IN-ONE dummies
10 Books
Woody Leonhard

9781119310563
USA $34.00
CAN $41.99
UK £24.99

**SharePoint 2016** dummies
Rosemarie Withee
Ken Withee

9781119181705
USA $29.99
CAN $35.99
UK £21.99

**Fundamental Analysis** dummies
Matt Krantz

9781119263593
USA $26.99
CAN $31.99
UK £19.99

**Networking** dummies
Doug Lowe

9781119257769
USA $29.99
CAN $35.99
UK £21.99

**Office 2016** dummies
Wallace Wang

9781119293477
USA $26.99
CAN $31.99
UK £19.99

**Office 365** dummies
Rosemarie Withee
Ken Withee
Jennifer Reed

9781119265313
USA $24.99
CAN $29.99
UK £17.99

**Salesforce.com** dummies
Liz Kao
Jon Paz

9781119239314
USA $29.99
CAN $35.99
UK £21.99

**Coding** dummies
Nikhil Abraham

9781119293323
USA $29.99
CAN $35.99
UK £21.99

# Learning Made Easy

## ACADEMIC

**Algebra I** dummies

Mary Jane Sterling

9781119293576
USA $19.99
CAN $23.99
UK £15.99

**Basic Math & Pre-Algebra** dummies

Mark Zegarelli

9781119293637
USA $19.99
CAN $23.99
UK £15.99

**Calculus** dummies

Mark Ryan

9781119293491
USA $19.99
CAN $23.99
UK £15.99

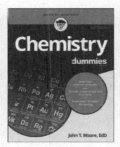

**Chemistry** dummies

John T. Moore, EdD

9781119293460
USA $19.99
CAN $23.99
UK £15.99

**Physics I** dummies

Steven Holzner, PhD

9781119293590
USA $19.99
CAN $23.99
UK £15.99

1,001 Practice Questions
**SAT** dummies

Ron Woldoff

9781119215844
USA $26.99
CAN $31.99
UK £19.99

**Organic Chemistry I** dummies

Arthur Winter

9781119293378
USA $22.99
CAN $27.99
UK £16.99

**Statistics** dummies

Deborah J. Rumsey, PhD

9781119293521
USA $19.99
CAN $23.99
UK £15.99

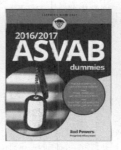

2016/2017
**ASVAB** dummies

Rod Powers

9781119239178
USA $18.99
CAN $22.99
UK £14.99

Includes Online Practice Tests

1,001 Practice Questions
**Praxis Core** dummies

Carla Kirkland
Chan Cleveland

9781119263883
USA $26.99
CAN $31.99
UK £19.99

## Available Everywhere Books Are Sold

**dummies.com**

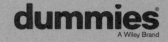